Ruben
Schindler
and
Edward
Allan
Brawley

Social Care at
the Front Line

PARAPROFESSIONALS
WORLDWIDE

Tavistock Publications
NEW YORK AND LONDON

315797

First published in 1987 by
Tavistock Publications
in association with Methuen, Inc.
29 West 35th Street, New York
NY 10001

Published in the UK by
Tavistock Publications Ltd
11 New Fetter Lane, London EC4P 4EE

© 1987 Ruben Schindler and
Edward Allan Brawley

Printed in Great Britain at the
University Press, Cambridge

*Library of Congress Cataloging in
Publication Data*
Schindler, Ruben.
    Social care at the front line.
    Bibliography: p.
    Includes index.
    1. Paraprofessionals in social
    service.   I. Brawley, Edward Allan.
    II. Title.
    HV40.4.S35   1987   361.3
    86–30035
ISBN 0–422–60540–9

*British Library Cataloguing in
Publication Data*
Schindler, Ruben
    Social care at the front line: a
    worldwide study of
    paraprofessionals.
    1. Paraprofessionals in social service
    I. Title   II. Brawley, Edward A.
    361.3   HV10.5
ISBN 0–422–60540–9

Social Care at the Front Line

Contents

Preface

This book is concerned with the training and use of paraprofessional human service personnel around the world, based on data gathered from thirteen developed and developing countries, including four that we studied in depth. The emergence of a variety of kinds of front-line human service workers as important providers of social care and the issues and controversies surrounding their training and employment in different countries are analyzed and compared. For example, the factors that have contributed to the increased use of paraprofessional personnel are examined. How their roles and functions are determined and the ways in which they are used to meet the needs of people and communities are among the questions we address. The relationship between professional and paraprofessional personnel is explored, including areas of strain or conflict. Approaches to training that have been adopted in different countries, including innovative models, are discussed and the opportunities for and barriers to career advancement that exist for the paraprofessional worker are reviewed.

The kinds of front-line workers that are generally regarded as paraprofessionals have always been important participants in human service and social development activities throughout the world. This continues to be the case in all the countries we studied, although the value of their contribution is not uniformly recognized and their potential is not always fully realized. In some instances, their work supplements the work of professionally trained personnel; in other situations, they function independently of professionals;

and in many parts of the world they are the only people available to provide front-line human services to people in need. The latter is particularly the case in less developed countries and in the rural or other underserved areas of more developed countries.

The research on which this book is based was carried out in response to a number of conditions in the human services, including the fact that, in most countries, the bulk of front-line or face-to-face helping activity is carried out by persons who are not professionally trained but by people (often local community residents) who may have had little or no formal preparation for their helping roles, that is, by paraprofessionals. In developing and developed countries alike, there is increasing recognition among government officials, administrators of service organizations, and human service professionals that widespread use of front-line paraprofessional personnel cannot be viewed as a transitional expedient until sufficient professionally trained personnel become available but is likely to be a long-term or even permanent state of affairs. Since paraprofessionals are likely to be the main providers of human services for the foreseeable future, there is a need to clarify the characteristics and functions of this group of personnel, determine how they might best be deployed, and design training and other supportive mechanisms that will maximize their contribution to human service goals. In addition, there is a growing body of opinion within the helping professions in many countries that we need to take a less parochial view of social welfare and social development issues, that greater attention should be devoted to comparative international studies in order to develop a more global perspective on social issues and to identify alternative approaches to promoting human well-being.

As a reflection of these trends, a number of international governmental and voluntary organizations have sponsored activities over the last few years that focus attention on the paraprofessional worker in the human services. The United Nations Department of Economic and Social Affairs, the European Centre for Social Welfare Training and Research, and the International Association of Schools of Social Work are noteworthy among those international bodies that have placed high priority on the development of paraprofessional human service personnel worldwide. All three have convened meetings of experts or set up task forces to address this topic during the past decade. We hope that the information we have gathered and the ideas we discuss here will add to this international effort by helping clarify some important developments and issues involved in the training and employment of front-line paraprofessional human service workers, thereby facilitating more effective and efficient use of these valuable resources and contributing in some small measure to the improvement of human service systems.

As is true of all social workers, our overriding interest is the development of more effective ways of promoting human well-being, with particular concern for the most vulnerable and deprived populations of the world. We recognize that the focus of our study addresses a very limited aspect of the human service or social development task that needs to be undertaken in different countries and on an international scale. For example, it would be absurd to assert that the activities of front-line paraprofessionals can have a major impact on such problems as poverty, malnutrition, poor health, inadequate housing, unemployment, and the like where these exist on a massive scale. We make no such claims. However, based on our research, we do believe that, if they are used properly and given appropriate training and support, front-line paraprofessionals can make a valuable (and sometimes vital) contribution to the welfare of people and communities. In some instances, they may constitute an important element in broader human service or social development strategies.

Our research and the preparation of this book would not have been possible without the cooperation and assistance of many people in different countries. We are particularly indebted to Marguerite Mathieu, former Secretary General of the International Association of Schools of Social Work in Vienna, for the valuable support and assistance she gave us when we undertook the international survey reported in Chapter 2. We are also grateful to those social work colleagues throughout the world who responded to our survey, many of whom took quite extraordinary pains to ensure that we were well-informed about paraprofessionals in their countries and several of whom became regular correspondents and good friends.

Special thanks are due to the following colleagues in India. Chandra Dave, former editor-in-chief of *International Social Work*, is a friend and colleague who opened her home to us and accompanied us to distant villages, often acting as our interpreter in gathering vital research data. Mangala Karandikar, program coordinator of Research and Social Development, was instrumental in arranging for interviews with several prominent social work scholars. We had the privilege of spending much time with one of India's most distinguished social work educators, Dr A. S. Desai, director of the Tata Institute of Social Sciences, who not only enabled us to arrive at new insights into social work and paraprofessional education, but also arranged for us to meet and exchange ideas with her faculty, many of whom were themselves engaged in paraprofessional training. Faculty and teachers from other Indian institutions also served as valuable informants. Thanks are due to Professor K. D. Gangrade, Dean of the Faculty of Social Sciences and School of Social Work, University of New Delhi, Dr J. Siddiqui, Vice President of the National Association of Indian Social Workers, and Dr R. S. Arole, Director of the Rural Health Project in Jamkhed who enabled us to meet with paraprofessionals who spare no time and effort in helping others. Dr P. Chowdhry, Director of the National Institute of Public Cooperation and Child Development, provided us with an important and fascinating picture of paraprofessionals and their role in the field of child care.

In Israel, colleagues from the Bar-Ilan School of Social Work have been supportive of this research over many years. Professor Frank Loewenberg was particularly helpful in reading and commenting on a number of early drafts of this book. Rachel Schindler was involved in the production of this book from its earliest stages and her faith in the project was unwavering.

Hugh Barr and several of his colleagues at the Central Council for Education and Training in Social Work, Anthea Hey at Brunel University's Insititute of Social Studies, Chris Kerr formerly of the Social Work Services Group, Scottish Education Department, Ian Ross at the Central Regional Council's Social Work Department, and Peter Wedge of the School of Economic and Social Studies, University of East Anglia, were all tireless sources of information, insight, and support over the years and provided access to resources that contributed enormously to the research that was undertaken in Britain. In addition, Frank Clemente, Sheldon Gelman, and Emilia Martinez-Brawley, colleagues in the Department of Sociology at the Pennsylvania State University, provided a variety of kinds of support that greatly facilitated the research and writing processes.

Finally, Rita Kline, Amy Miller, and Betsy Will provided valuable

secretarial services during various phases of the project and Debi
Welsby carried the major burden of typing several drafts of this
book, often from illegible hand-written material. We are grateful to
them and hope they will feel that the results justify all their hard
work.

Introduction

1

THE PARAPROFESSIONAL IN THE HUMAN SERVICES: WORLDWIDE TRENDS

In most countries of the world, the great majority of persons involved in front-line social welfare, human service, or social development activities are persons who have received limited or no specific training for the jobs they perform. This is true in developed and developing countries alike. Many reasons are advanced for the widespread use of nonprofessional (or paraprofessional) human service personnel. These include but are not limited to such factors as shortages of professionally trained personnel, a belief that it is neither necessary nor desirable to require that all persons engaged in the provision of human services be highly trained professionals, and a desire to provide job opportunities for groups (women, minorities, the poor) that would otherwise have limited access to the employment market. As well as being more numerous than any other category of human service personnel in most countries, paraprofessionals tend to be more accessible to the people who need services and are more like them in socio-economic and cultural background. As a consequence, it has been suggested that they are in an especially advantageous position to bring about positive change in the lives of the people whom they serve (United Nations 1980: 39).

Paraprofessional human service workers are an extremely diverse group who perform a variety of tasks under a broad range of titles, of which the following are fairly typical: community service worker, social work technician, family planning aide, youth worker, village worker, social welfare assistant, field worker, health auxiliary, community development worker, rural development assistant, family welfare worker, and health education assistant. Strictly speaking, the term paraprofessional refers to persons who work alongside professionally trained workers in an auxiliary role, carrying out tasks and functions that contribute to professional objectives. Usually such workers have less formal education than professionals, they are involved in direct services of a relatively concrete and routine nature, and they are supervised and directed by professionally trained workers. However, in many instances, nonprofessional front-line workers may be found performing vital human services functions in the absence of professional supervision, direction, or even presence, in which case the term paraprofessional is not really appropriate (Pangalangan and de Guzman 1980: 118). For this and other reasons the term is by no means universal. For example, it does not appear to be widely used in Europe (European Centre for Social Welfare Training and Research 1977: 5). However, despite its shortcomings, we use paraprofessional since it is probably the term that is most widely used and understood.

An additional clarification needs to be made in regard to the population considered in this study. Volunteers are used extensively in many countries to supplement the work of professional social workers and paid paraprofessionals (Lauffer and Gorodezky 1980; Darvill and Munday 1984). Some of these volunteers are highly trained and perform very sophisticated functions, such as marriage counseling in Britain (Tyndall 1972). In other countries, for example in Yugoslavia, trained citizen volunteers make up a significant proportion of the social service work force. In fact, the paid "paraprofessional" appears to be unknown in Yugoslavia. Instead, unpaid volunteers play a very significant role in supplementing the roles of professional social workers and, beyond that, in promoting the general well-being of the community (Nedeljkovic 1977). While we regard volunteers as a very important resource in social welfare provision, we view them as distinct from paid paraprofessionals and deserving separate examination. They are, therefore, excluded from our study.

Human services is a term that gained fairly wide currency in the

USA during the 1970s. However, it has many meanings. It is used by some writers as a synonym for social welfare (Morris 1974: 540). Other writers imply a scope of concern and activity that goes beyond what are usually regarded as social welfare services. For example, Alexander (1977: 844) notes that many new people-serving enterprises staffed by groups of personnel with widely divergent backgrounds and training "have permeated the major social institutions of education, health, employment, religion, government, justice, recreation, and the family." In other North American writings, the term human services takes on a normative as well as descriptive tone, implying desirable new patterns of coordinated interdisciplinary services intended to have the maximum impact on human well-being (Chenault and Burnford 1978: 3).

Evidence of a trend toward a broader human service perspective can be found throughout the world. While the factors involved and the patterns that have emerged are distinctive to particular countries, it is clear that "the scope and dimensions of social welfare programs in developing and developed countries alike have significantly increased during the past two decades and all indications are that this trend will continue" (United Nations 1980: 1). For example, throughout the world there has been a significant expansion of organized day care programs, specialized services to women, programs for the aging, youth development programs, family planning services, adult education, nutrition programs, and community development efforts in both urban and rural settings. Many of these expanded human service programs have been integral components of comprehensive national development plans (United Nations 1977: 3–4; 1980: 12–15).

In summary, then, the term human services, as it is used in this study reflects not only the "common purposes served by the extensive and complex array of specialized and technical personnel who comprise the health, social, and educational systems of [a] country," (Palmiere 1978: 143) but also the broader preventive and promotional services performed by diverse categories of organizations and types of personnel engaged in human and social development activities throughout the world.

The rapid expansion of human service programs of ever-increasing diversity over the last two decades has been accompanied by a corresponding realization of the important role played by front-line personnel (mainly paraprofessionals) in the delivery of these services. The activities and accomplishments of China's system of primary health care using "barefoot doctors" (Sidel 1978) has received a great deal of attention but this is only one of a multitude of examples of community-based models of service delivery that rely on paraprofessionals to carry out vital human service functions, especially in rural, remote, or otherwise underserved areas. By way of illustration, village-level workers in Ethiopia provide health and family planning information and supplies, organize women's activities, help communities address local problems, and conduct adult literacy classes. Similarly the government of the Ivory Coast has established a country-wide network of women's centers staffed by local women who have been trained to provide a variety of supportive and developmental services. These indigenous front-line workers not only show village women how to prepare nutritious meals and demonstrate healthy child-rearing practices, but also provide a rudimentary kind of vocational training that prepares women for a variety of public service jobs in post offices, the telephone service, the railways, health centers, and schools (United Nations 1980: 14–15).

These innovative models of service delivery using paraprofessional personnel are not limited to developing countries where professionally trained workers are in short supply. They are also found in developed countries that do not face such stringent resource constraints. For example, in Britain, positive results are reported from the use of mature local women as paraprofessional "patch" workers in community or neighborhood-based social service teams. A major role of these front-line workers is to provide support and practical assistance to frail elderly and handicapped people living at home. Because they live in the neighborhood, are knowledgeable about what is going on, and are readily accessible, they can keep a close eye on vulnerable individuals and make sure they are managing adequately. They can ensure that the persons under their care are eating properly, their houses are well heated, necessary medical attention is received, bills are paid, and help with house cleaning, laundry, shopping, and personal care is provided, if needed (Hadley and McGrath 1980: 1984). Another example from a developed country are the aboriginal health workers who are trained to provide basic front-line medical services to isolated aboriginal communities in Australia. These indigenous paraprofessionals operate clinics, conduct simple medical examinations, carry out routine procedures such as suturing cuts, check water purity and general sanitary conditions in the community, and provide information about health and nutrition (Broome Regional Aboriginal Medical Service 1985).

Available data on the characteristics and activities of paraprofessionals in various countries indicate that, while there are some common themes that appear to transcend national boundaries, there are significant differences among countries. A major purpose in carrying out this comparative international study was to "distinguish the general from the specific, if only to identify what is 'generally true' for all countries and what is unique and 'specifically true' to any situation" (Rodgers, Greve, and Morgan 1968: 11). We felt that examination of the areas of similarity and variation would reveal valuable information and insights for persons interested in identifying optimum mixes of personnel in various types of human service systems and making the most effective and efficient use of the human resources available in a particular country.

The human service professions, including social work, are just beginning to grapple with the problems involved in educating and using an array of different kinds and levels of personnel for activities that have tended to be viewed as the exclusive province of the professionally trained worker. This is so even though many kinds of people have in fact been involved in the provision of human services in the past. Recognition of the fact that there might be a legitimate place in the human service endeavor for persons other than those who have been identified as professionals has led to some effort (primarily in the USA and Britain) to clarify the roles of the different participants and to relate these roles to educational experiences that might constitute appropriate preparation.

The results of this effort have been limited so far, but some promising directions have been identified. The present study seeks to contribute to this overall effort. It looks at the training and utilization of paraprofessional human service personnel from an international perspective using data gathered from thirteen countries (including four which were studied in depth). The emergence of these new human resources and the issues that they raise are examined and compared along several key dimensions, including (1) the factors that have contributed to their use; (2) role definitions and utilization patterns; (3) the relationship between professionals and paraprofessionals; (4) the training and educational approaches that have been developed; and (5) the opportunities that exist for career advancement for the paraprofessional.

FACTORS CONTRIBUTING TO USE
OF PARAPROFESSIONALS

The factors that have contributed to the widespread use of paraprofessional personnel in the human services throughout the world are varied and complex. One of the major purposes of our study is to illuminate unique circumstances and considerations that have been salient in different countries and to identify variables that transcend national boundaries.

As we have already noted, the scope and dimensions of human service programs throughout the world have expanded rapidly during the last two decades, creating new tasks and functions to be performed by a wide array of human service personnel. The need to produce highly trained professional workers to carry a leadership role and perform the most sophisticated functions in the human services has been widely recognized and, to the extent that a particular country's resources would permit it, the pool of professionally trained workers has been increased. However, in most parts of the world (but particularly in developing countries) the supply of trained professionals has not kept pace with the expansion of human service programs. As Pangalangan and de Guzman (1980: 54) note, professional education "can only cater to so many even as the demand for social workers is so great. This is especially so in developing countries where a huge reservoir of manpower is needed to work with the people in the countryside." Not only are professionals in short supply but also those that are available tend to be engaged in administrative or related functions, thereby leaving direct service activities predominantly in the hands of auxiliary or paraprofessional personnel (United Nations 1976: 9; 1979: 34; Kulkarni 1980: 152).

While shortages of professionally trained personnel have been a major contributing factor in the widespread use of paraprofessionals, there are other considerations that appear to have reinforced and legitimized their continued use, even in countries and situations where shortages of professionals may not be as salient. For example, it has been argued that using highly trained and expensive professional personnel to perform relatively unsophisticated human service functions is an inefficient use of available resources. In the human service systems of developing and developed countries alike, "there is a need for a relatively large number of workers qualified to provide fairly simple welfare services for individuals and families and/or provide leadership and assistance in self-help and mutual aid projects and group activities" (United Nations 1969: 78).

In addition to what could be characterized as *logistical* considerations, such as compensating for shortages of professional personnel, making more efficient use of available resources, and extending services to remote areas, Rigby (1978) notes that there have been equally important *substantive* or *qualitative* arguments advanced for using paraprofessional human service personnel. For example, it is asserted that they are socially and culturally closer to the people that are served by human service programs, are more knowledgeable about the communities in which they work, and are more likely to be trusted by members of these communities (Rigby 1978: 5). Although stated differently in different contexts, paraprofessionals are seen as possessing attributes that enable them to make unique and valuable contributions to social development, social welfare, and human service programs that go beyond their value as an ad hoc response to shortages of professional personnel.

In the process of using front-line paraprofessionals for an enormous range of functions, developing countries have found that, "in addition to assisting professional personnel, the efforts of [these] front-line workers have made a unique contribution of extreme value in the effective delivery of social welfare services" (United Nations 1980: 1). This appears to be no less true in the more developed countries. For example, in Europe, it is reported that paraprofessionals perform an important function, "not as substitutes for more qualified personnel, but because they help to maintain a closer contact with the concrete issues in social welfare and with the actual needs and living conditions of the individuals whom social welfare services are intended to benefit" (United Nations 1972: 107). In the USA various social programs of the 1960s and early 1970s supported the training and employment in human service jobs of large members of so-called indigenous paraprofessionals, that is "those who reside in the target area, engage in social, economic and political processes similar to those of program participants, and are matched with them on such characteristics as social class, race, ethnicity, religion, language, culture, and more" (Grosser 1969: 23). These workers were drawn primarily from low-income, minority, and otherwise disadvantaged groups. The range of vital functions performed by paraprofessional personnel and the special contribution they are purported to bring to the human service enterprise (see Sobey 1970; Gartner 1971; Austin 1978; President's Commission on Mental Health 1978; Robin and Wagenfeld 1981) have supported their continued use in the USA long beyond the time when the shortage of professionally trained personnel was an important consideration.

The value of using indigenous paraprofessionals to provide human services at the community or grassroots level (particularly in developing countries) is seen by some observers as a response to the inappropriateness of professional training and service methods that are too heavily influenced by Western industrialized approaches. For example Banerji (1978) states that health care models that emphasize highly sophisticated and expensive equipment, facilities, and personnel are not appropriate for many nations or communities and in particular, have failed to meet the needs of rural populations in developing countries. He points out that more appropriate indigenous approaches to health care have tended to be undervalued (see also World Heath Organisation 1978; Jukanovic and Mach 1975). A similar point is made by Resnick (1980), Midgley (1981), and Brigham (1982) in regard to the inappropriateness of attempting to apply Western social work training and practice models to developing countries rather than using more compatible and potentially more productive indigenous approaches.

In some countries the widespread use of paraprofessionals in the human services has occurred as a more or less ad hoc response to the kinds of factors and considerations described above. In other instances, their recruitment and training has been supported by formal government policy. This was certainly the case in the USA during the 1960s Anti-Poverty Program (Schindler 1977: 1060–061). The governments of Indonesia, Kenya, Senegal, and Tanzania are also reported to have adopted policies that promoted the recruitment, training, and deployment of paraprofessional personnel in the human services (United Nations 1980: 3). For example in Indonesia, the Ministry of Social Affairs (MSA) has adopted a formal policy of using paraprofessionals as a major means of advancing national development objectives. It regards the training and use of paraprofessionals as "a mechanism to promote and improve popular participation in the development process as well as a means to equalize the distribution of the benefits of development among the people" (Pangalangan and de Guzman 1980: 3).

In carrying out this international study, we attempt to identify those factors, including formal government policies, that appear to be most important in contributing to the widespread use of paraprofessional personnel in human service occupations, to identify variations among countries, and finally to draw some theoretical and practical conclusions from our findings.

ROLE DEFINITIONS AND UTILIZATION PATTERNS

As we have already noted, the scope and range of human service activity undertaken by governments throughout the world have increased substantially over the last two decades. These developments have created a wide variety of front-line service delivery roles and tasks which, in most countries, are being performed by paraprofessional personnel.

The functions and activities carried out by paraprofessional human service personnel are extremely diverse but would usually include direct service delivery (information, instruction, counseling, care, leadership, and so on) to individuals, families, groups, and communities; the mobilization of community resources; and serving a mediating, linking, or advocacy role between service providers and needy groups.

In performing their jobs, paraprofessionals may be seen primarily as assistants to professionally trained workers, as in the Philippines, or they may be viewed as the main providers of human services, as is reported to be the case in Sri Lanka (United Nations 1980: 5). The former "profession-centered" approach typically defines the role of paraprofessional personnel in the following terms: "their job, their tasks and activities assist, support, and facilitate the functions of the social worker. They move around with or are beside the professional, thus are called 'paraprofessional', and as such contribute to the attainment of social work objectives" (International Association of Schools of Social Work 1979: 1). The latter, more autonomous model reflects the fact that in many situations there may not be any or enough professionally trained workers around to provide guidance and direction to the paraprofessional who is consequently confronted with the need to carry out whatever tasks need to be done, tasks which on their face may be indistinguishable from those that would be performed by professional workers if they were available. Under these circumstances, it is difficult and may indeed be futile to seek distinctions between professional and paraprofessional tasks and functions.

An intermediate position is taken by Pangalangan and de Guzman (1980: 2) who see paraprofessionals as "partners in development, who work 'around' rather than 'for' professionals, thereby necessitating the identification of the roles, functions, and jobs of these paraprofessionals as they come in different 'forms' and have to be identified in a new context." What is implied here is that those characteristics of paraprofessionals that make them especially valuable in the provision of human services in particular locations or to special populations may provide the most promising approach to defining their roles and activities. In reviewing the literature on the use of the paraprofessional in the human services, one finds abundant examples of role definitions and utilization patterns that fit into one or other of these three basic patterns: assistant, autonomous, and intermediate. When one attempts to go beyond these rather simplistic categories in order to reach a clearer conceptualization of the ways in which paraprofessional roles and tasks are defined and, beyond that, to identify approaches that might hold the greatest promise in terms of the most effective and efficient use of available human resources, the situation becomes much more complicated. However, we believe that it is important to attempt to do so if paraprofessional workers are to make their best contribution to the human services.

The present study seeks to generate as clear a picture as possible of the tasks performed by paraprofessionals in the different countries in our sample, common personnel utilization patterns that have emerged, and promising conceptual approaches to the allocation of professional and paraprofessional tasks and functions. To the extent that we can, we will attempt to identify, analyze, and refine existing conceptual approaches to personnel deployment in the human services in order to clarify and strengthen the contribution of the paraprofessional.

PROFESSIONAL–PARAPROFESSIONAL RELATIONSHIPS

The emergence of the paraprofessional as a significant and enduring element of the human service labor force has elicited mixed reponses from professional social workers in different countries. To the extent that paraprofessionals are viewed as an extension of the professional's reach in situations where professional personnel are in short supply or where professional skills are not necessary, the response has been positive.

For example, in the USA during the 1960s, a major national commitment to improved and expanded social programs was initiated at a time when there had been a long-standing shortage of professionally trained human service workers. This resulted in a radical redefinition of what types of personnel could appropriately be involved in service delivery. The shortage of trained personnel ceased to be defined simply as the need for more professionally trained workers since it was recognized that a wide variety of persons could be recruited and trained to perform valuable roles in the human services without necessarily diminishing the quality of service provided. Large numbers of paraprofessionals (many of them members of low-income and ethnic minority groups) were employed in significant direct service roles in health care, social welfare, education, and related fields. These developments were generally applauded by the social work profession in the USA, since it saw the use of paraprofessionals as a necessary and appropriate way to extend vital services to needy populations.

This affirmation of the need for paraprofessionals to supplement and extend the reach of a limited pool of professionally trained personnel in order to accomplish important human service goals has also been evident in developing areas of the world where professional resources are especially scarce.

"Since an effective reach-out to the very remote areas of each Asian country cannot be done by the professional social workers alone, there should be an increasing partnership with paraprofessionals of different types and categories to promote social development efforts in the rural areas and unserved urban communities in Asian countries."

(Pangalangan 1979: 42)

It seemed clear that professional social workers could make their best contribution to the human service or social development goals of their respective countries if, as Mathieu (1979: 43) suggested, they were to "join forces with members of other professions and with a variety of committed community workers who are all engaged in promoting the welfare of people."

However, Mathieu (1980: v) and others recognized that "the creation of new categories of personnel and the training for various levels of skill may be seen as a threat to the unity of the profession." This seems to be particularly the case where the paraprofessional is viewed as a threat to the status of the professional (for example where distinctions between professional and paraprofessional roles are blurred) or as a competitor for a limited pool of human service jobs.

In North America and Western Europe during the late 1970s and early 1980s, government expenditures for human service programming have generally diminished. Social workers and other human service professionals have become apprehensive about the possibility of having to compete with paraprofessionals for jobs in a shrinking job market. A lack of widely recognized definitions of professional and paraprofessional knowledge and skills has exacerbated the situation. For example, in West Germany, the professional social workers' association sees the employment of paraprofessionals or "social assistants" as a serious threat to the job security and status of its members (European Centre for Social Welfare Training and Research 1977: 7–8). Similarly in the USA the early enthusiasm of the social work profession for the contribution of the paraprofessional appears to have diminished significantly in recent years, in the face of the same factors evident in West Germany (see Brawley 1980). In both countries, resistance to the perceived encroachment of paraprofessionals into what is considered to be the exclusive domain of professionals is argued in terms of maintaining standards of service and protecting the recipients of service from unqualified workers (Nouvertne 1977; Pecora and Austin 1983).

While these tensions between professionals and paraprofessionals may not exist to the same degree in other parts of the world where the supply of professionally trained personnel is still quite limited, the potential for conflict does seem to exist. In most developing countries, the social work profession is of fairly recent origin (United Nations 1980: 25) and consequently is neither well established nor very secure. This makes it quite vulnerable to threats of encroachment by paraprofessional personnel, particularly since the overlap of professional and paraprofessional social work activities appears to be especially prevalent in developing countries (Pangalangan and de Guzman 1980: 24).

In carrying out this international study of the paraprofessional in the human services, we seek to illuminate the nature of the relationshp between professional and paraprofessional personnel in different countries. We examine the sources and nature of the tensions that exist in some instances in order that these may be better understood and perhaps resolved. In particular, we have sought examples of positive resolution of conflict, tension, or strain between professional and paraprofessional personnel since we agree with Almanzor (1979: 37) that it is the responsibility of social workers and other human service professionals to "harness and maximize the participation and contribution of all individuals in the community, including the paraprofessionals, as members of a free and dynamic society."

Because both authors of this book are social workers and are particularly interested in illuminating the roles and functions of paraprofessionals in relation to their own profession, the present study has a distinctly social work orientation. We recognize, of course, that "Frontline workers, especially those doing community work, do not belong exclusively to the social work profession. They are also paraprofessionals for other professions" (Ranade 1979: 39). Taking account of the complex relationships between paraprofessionals and the many professions engaged in human service activity throughout the world was beyond our resources. We had to simplify and, at the same time, capitalize on our particular strengths which meant that we had to approach the topic from our own professional perspective.

TRAINING AND EDUCATIONAL APPROACHES

During the past few years, there has been increasing recognition that educating personnel at the highest levels of expertise must be supplemented by training policies and programs geared to the mass of direct service workers at the grassroots level. In developing and developed countries alike, it is suggested, "the rational use of scarce personnel resources calls for particular attention being given to the

training of staff at the auxiliary level" (United Nations 1980: 2).
Particularly in those countries with large underdeveloped rural
areas, the training of front-line paraprofessionals is deemed to be a
priority concern, not only on account of chronic shortages of
professional personnel but also because of the types of cultural gaps
mentioned earlier that may exist between professionally trained
personnel and certain population groups.

Because paraprofessionals constitute the bulk of the direct service
social welfare work force in many countries, national governments
and international bodies alike have begun to focus greater attention
on the training of these front-line personnel so that their contribution to social welfare and social development goals can be
maximized. It is recognized that "for the effective discharge of their
assigned functions, field-level workers in social welfare need the
supports and stimulation provided through appropriate training
programs" (United Nations 1980: 7).

Since those paraprofessional training programs that have been
developed have emerged in response to very specific local needs,
there is great diversity in the examples that can be found
worldwide. Depending on the particular setting, training can be
short or long term, formal or informal, provided prior to
employment or on an in-service basis. It can have an academic or
practical emphasis or some combination of these and it can be
offered by institutions of higher education, specialized training
institutes, government agencies, or employers. While much of the
paraprofessional training that has been carried out has been
developed on an ad hoc basis to respond to immediate local needs,
there also appear to be some broad trends or approaches that
reflect the preferences or policies of national governments or expert
opinion about the most appropriate strategy to adopt.

Among the purposes of the present study is the examination of
the form, content, and auspices of paraprofessional training in
various countries. We were interested in identifying the range of
alternative approaches that have been developed to meet the needs
of the enormously diverse paraprofessional human service work force,
including examples of innovative educational models and those
that appeared to be most promising and worthy of consideration
beyond their location of origin. For example we were interested in
the type of training provided for front-line workers who function in
some parts of India as multipurpose community health workers as

well as family planning motivators and counselors (United Nations 1979: 15); the "home helps" who provide important front-line care to the frail, the elderly, and to vulnerable families in Britain (Local Government Training Board undated b: 27–8); and the *ovdim schunotim* (indigenous community aides) who play a vital role in community and neighborhood development efforts in Israel (Schindler 1980; 1985).

We were particularly interested in contrasting and comparing the training approaches that have been developed to meet a population that ranges in formal educational background from village-level workers in some developing countries who may be illiterate (Srinivasan 1978: 18) to paraprofessionals in some developed countries who may be college or university graduates (Brawley 1981b; 1982). Or course, models that work well in one situation can rarely be translated to other settings without substantial modification, if at all. However, we were sure that, among the rich array of innovation and experimentation that was taking place in paraprofessional training throughout the world, there were likely to be ideas and approaches that would be illuminating and worthy of wider consideration.

OPPORTUNITIES FOR CAREER ADVANCEMENT

Related to the provision of appropriate training for paraprofessional human service workers is the question of how best to provide opportunities for promotion or career advancement. Many paraprofessional human service workers, particularly those who are most effective in their work, will expect to take on more responsibility and be accorded higher status and greater rewards as their experience and competence increase. Indeed, many of the personal characteristics that contribute to effective job performance by paraprofessional personnel (for example motivation, initiative, intelligence) are likely to be the same qualities associated with high expectations and ambition (Rigby 1978: 16). A question then arises about the types of opportunities for promotion and career advancement that exist or should be provided for talented and motivated paraprofessional human service workers, since it is likely that the absence of such opportunities will have a negative impact on the contribution of paraprofessionals or even cause the most able ones to leave the human service field for more rewarding pursuits (United Nations 1979: 26–7).

Based on our earlier research in the USA (Brawley and Schindler 1972; Brawley 1975; Schindler 1977; Brawley 1980; 1982), we were aware that it had been important to develop realistic avenues for career advancement for the large groups of paraprofessionals who had been brought into the human services during the 1960s "War on Poverty". Pearl and Riessman (1965: 2), the architects of the "new careers" movement that was such an important part of the anti-poverty program, advocated that paraprofessional jobs in the human services be "permanent and provide opportunity for life-long careers" and that there should be the "opportunity for the motivated and talented poor to advance from low-skill entry jobs to any station available to the more favored members of society."

It appears that in most developed countries, opportunities for career advancement are closely tied to the acquisition of formal academic qualifications. This may or may not be true throughout the world and we were eager to identify alternative mechanisms that might exist in the countries that we studied. There are, of course, enormous difficulties in providing realistic career ladders for certain kinds of paraprofessionals involved in grassroots community work in the less developed regions of the world. Pangalangan and de Guzman (1980: 8) see this as one of the greatest challenges facing social work education in Asia. It is recognized that employer or government-provided in-service training can provide knowledge and skill for immediate use but is limited in terms of the career mobility that it provides. If the social development goals of a country's or a region's human service efforts are to be realized in their fullest sense, it is felt by some authorities that it is important and should be possible to "devise an educational system which would provide some means for the para-professional to change his [or her] life situation positively in job and salary" (International Association of Schools of Social Work 1979: 35–6). The fact that women constitute the bulk of the paraprofessional human service work force in large segments of the human services in most countries and that disadvantaged racial and other minority groups are involved in many instances adds other significant elements and dynamics to the examination of both the need for and barriers to the establishment of opportunities for career advancement.

In summary, in carrying out our study of paraprofessional human service personnel in different parts of the world, we have sought (1) to determine the degree to which career opportunities have been created for these workers, (2) to examine the barriers that may exist to the development of realistic career advancement mechanisms, and (3) to identify examples of positive action.

OVERVIEW OF THE PRESENT STUDY

In carrying out our research on paraprofessional human service personnel, we have attempted to produce information that would give a broad general picture of these front-line workers from a global perspective and, at the same time, provide detailed information that would clarify or illuminate broad trends and permit more rigorous discussion of the major issues surrounding the training and deployment of paraprofessionals. The organization of this book reflects this dual approach. By moving from a broad treatment of paraprofessionals from a worldwide perspective to detailed examination of the training and use of these workers in four selected countries, we have sought to capitalize on the complementary strengths of the "macro" and "micro" approaches to comparative social policy analysis: "The macro approach offers broader perspectives and provides context for micro studies, while the micro approach provides facts, information and precision without which the macro approach would be hollow and abstract" (Higgins 1981: 160).

In Chapter 2 we report the results of a worldwide survey of the use and training of paraprofessional human service personnel that we carried out in 1983 (Brawley and Schindler 1985; 1986; Schindler and Brawley 1986). This survey produced sufficient data to allow us to present a picture of the paraprofessional in thirteen countries: Australia, Britain, Canada, Denmark, India, Indonesia, Israel, Japan, the Philippines, South Africa, Uganda, the USA, and West Germany. While we cannot claim that these thirteen countries are fully representative of all regions of the world, we feel that they are diverse enough to form a fairly accurate impression of the paraprofessional human service worker as this person operates in widely divergent situations throughout the world. As is the case throughout this book, the data presented and the issues discussed

18   SOCIAL CARE AT THE FRONT LINE

on the paraprofessional in different parts of the world are organized under five major headings: (1) the factors contributing to the use of paraprofessionals; (2) role definitions and utilization patterns; (3) professional–paraprofessional relationships; (4) training and educational approaches; and (5) opportunities for career advancement. Based on a comparative analysis of the data we were able to generate, areas of similarity among countries and examples of distinctive developments are identified and discussed.

In Chapters 4–8 we present the results of our detailed research on the paraprofessional in four countries: Britain, India, Israel, and the USA. Our in-depth studies of the paraprofessional in each of these countries permitted a much closer attention to detail, and a more thorough treatment of the practical and theoretical issues involved in making the best use of this important personnel resource in national human service systems.

The final chapter of the book is devoted to a comprehensive cross-national analysis of the paraprofessional in the human services, drawing upon both the broad-gauge and detailed material presented and discussed earlier. The most salient themes and issues emerging from our study are identified and the theoretical implications of these are considered in detail.

There is growing recognition by social workers and other human service professionals of the interconnectedness of social systems and human well-being across national boundaries. Noting our increasing realization that "we don't live alone, that we are part of the main, . . . we are involved not only on moral grounds but also because our own well-being, social, economic and political is at stake," Boehm (1978: 44) sees, among his more perceptive colleagues, "an emerging sense of commitment to human well-being on a global scale." It is our hope that this comparative study of paraprofessional human service personnel, will, in some small way, contribute to an increased understanding of human service issues and policies from an international perspective, facilitate more rational approaches to human resource development and utilization, and perhaps indirectly lead to improved systems for meeting people's needs.

2

The paraprofessional in thirteen countries: results of an international survey

In this chapter we present a summary of the results of an international survey of paraprofessional human service personnel that we carried out in 1983 (Brawley and Schindler 1985; 1986; Schindler and Brawley 1986). The purpose of the survey was to identify the characteristics and significance of the paraprofessional human service worker in different parts of the world, similarities and differences among countries, and emerging trends and issues in the training and use of paraprofessionals. We hoped to produce valuable new information on what appeared to be a significant segment of the human service work force in many countries, adding to the work already done on this topic by such organizations as the International Association of Schools of Social Work (IASSW 1979; Pangalangan and de Guzman 1980; Rigby 1978), the United Nations (1969; 1972; 1976; 1977; 1979; 1980), and other international bodies concerned with social welfare and social development issues (European Centre for Social Welfare Training and Research 1977).

The information generated by our survey of the employment and training of paraprofessional human service workers in thirteen developed and developing countries (Australia, Britain, Canada, Denmark, India, Indonesia, Israel, Japan, the Philippines, South Africa, Uganda, the USA, and West Germany) illustrates and clarifies some of the major trends and issues identified in Chapter 1.

Examples of paraprofessionals in action in different parts of the world are provided, including categories of front-line personnel that are unique to certain countries. Distinctive training approaches are also identified. The data and issues reported in this chapter set the scene for the more detailed examination of paraprofessionals in Britain, India, Israel, and the USA that follow.

METHODS OF THE STUDY

A thirty-three-item survey questionnaire and explanatory letter that had been pre-tested with social work educators from Israel, India, the USA, and Austria were mailed in 1983 to all member colleges, universities, and associations of the International Association of Schools of Social Work, and to a list of individuals who had been identified as experts on paraprofessional social welfare personnel in their own countries or internationally. Respondents were asked to identify additional persons who were knowledgeable about the paraprofessional in their country. Many did so and follow-up questionnaires were mailed to these individuals and organizations. Although we received responses from forty-five countries, we wanted to be sure that our data would be as reliable as possible. We decided, therefore, to report only on those countries from which we had received at least three responses that were complete and among which there was a high level of agreement. This narrowed our sample to the thirteen countries listed above. Data from these thirteen countries were tabulated, summarized, and then compared along the five key dimensions that constitute the major organizational themes of this book.

Respondents to our survey included social work educators at the graduate, undergraduate, and paraprofessional levels. As well as administrators and faculty of college and university-based social work education programs, several were associated with government-operated training centers and institutes. Many respondents were senior-level representatives of national government agencies responsible for social welfare services, including ministers, research directors, and training officers. In addition, we had responses from senior officials of national voluntary welfare boards, professional social work organizations, and national accrediting or standard-setting bodies for social work education programs. The mix of types of respondents varied from country to country. However, we are fairly satisfied that the respondents provided us with an informed and accurate picture of the paraprofessional human service worker in the thirteen countries in our sample.

The results of our research are less comprehensive (that is less global) than we would have preferred. It had been our intention to attempt to present a picture of the paraprofessional in the human services throughout the world. Unfortunately, we were not able to gather sufficient data from enough countries to accomplish that goal. However, we feel that the findings reported from the thirteen countries included here permit a useful international comparison of the characteristics and significance of the paraprofessional in different parts of the world, reveal interesting similarities and differences among countries, and illuminate current trends and issues.

FACTORS CONTRIBUTING TO THE USE OF PARAPROFESSIONALS

Paraprofessionals have always played an important role in the provision of human services and our study indicated that this continues to be the case in the countries we studied. A number of historical and other factors have contributed to the past and continuing use of paraprofessionals in the human services, among which the following appear to be the most significant.

Respondents from all countries in our sample cited current or historical shortages of professionally trained workers as a major factor contributing to the widespread use of paraprofessionals in the provision of social welfare services. These shortages of professionally trained workers are particularly acute in rural areas or remote provinces.

Several respondents noted that, in their countries, the professionalization of the social work labor force is of relatively recent origin and that there is a long history of use of untrained personnel in the social services. Even in a relatively highly developed country like Britain where social work has a fairly long history, it is reported that the emergence of professionally trained social workers as the core of the social services did not occur until the 1970s, in practical terms. Prior to this, most social workers were untrained or paraprofessional as we are using that term. Although most "social work" positions are now occupied by professionally qualified workers, there are reported to be many jobs in the social services (an estimated 75 per cent) that do not require professional social work training.

Among the reasons given for the widespread use of paraprofessionals in Japan were the rapid expansion of social welfare services and the underdevelopment of the social work profession. Professionalism has not occurred as rapidly as other changes in Japanese society; therefore the paraprofessional represents the rule rather than the exception. The paraprofessional is relatively well-established while the movement toward professionalism is still quite new and not very strong.

The issue of differential tasks or functions was mentioned by respondents from several countries (for example, Britain, South Africa, and the USA). Although stated differently by various respondents, the point was the same. Recognition that people other than professionally trained social workers could make worthwhile contributions to the social welfare services and that different roles or functions could be specified for different kinds of personnel had contributed to the widespread use of paraprofessionals. Paradoxically some respondents noted that the *absence* of clear distinctions between professional and paraprofessional roles had supported the continued or expanded use of the latter.

Many respondents note that there had been recent expansion of social welfare services in their countries in order to address a broader range of social problems or to meet the special needs of particular populations. For example, Israeli respondents mentioned the growth in the older segment of the populations and the development of services to meet their needs. Philippine respondents cited government social programs designed to reach the "most needy" segments of the population.

Cost was cited as an important factor determining the wide use of paraprofessionals. This was stated differently by respondents from different countries. Some observed that paraprofessionals were a cheaper alternative to professionally trained workers and implied that this was an undesirable situation. Others felt that the appropriate use of the former reflected a desire for greater efficiency in the use of the range of available human resources and applauded this trend.

The need for indigenous front-line workers to bridge social, economic, cultural, and ethnic gaps between professional workers and certain needy populations was mentioned by respondents from several countries. In Uganda the need is to relate to people at the village or community level; in Canada and Australia, to reach out efectively to ethnic minorities; and in India, to bridge the gap between the "haves" and "have-nots." Indian respondents also expressed the opinion that there is an "operational incompatibility" between the clinical approach of many professional social workers and the needs of certain needy populations. A Ugandan respondent suggested that, with grassroots experience and some training, paraprofessionals could do front-line tasks that "colonial professionals could not handle." Related to these points, respondents from Britain, Israel, and the USA felt that movements in their countries toward greater citizen participation or community involvement in the identification and solution of community problems had contributed to increased recruitment of paraprofessionals into human service employment.

Several countries in our sample are reported to have explicit national government policies supporting the use of paraprofessionals in the provision of social welfare services. For example Indonesia has specific legislation requiring the employment of low-income and other disadvantaged persons in certain kinds of social service jobs. The Japanese central government strongly supports a system of in-service training for paraprofessional social welfare personnel. Responsibility for actual implementation of this national policy is usually delegated to local governments and to voluntary organizations such as the National Council of Social Welfare but the national government establishes qualifications for various categories of personnel, such as social welfare officers and child-care workers, and supports training that will qualify people for these positions. The national policy in Uganda is to involve indigenous leadership as much as possible in the delivery of services at the grassroots level and to use rural training centers to identify and train these local resources. An important element of this policy is to provide training to paraprofessionals in order to improve their performance in direct services to people as part of the national "Recovery Program."

There was a difference of opinion among respondents from the USA about government policy regarding the use of paraprofessionals. The majority agreed that the national policy, initiated during the

1960s "War on Poverty," of employing low-income and otherwise disadvantaged community residents in social service roles has largely disappeared. However, there was some feeling that vestiges of that policy remain in some isolated programs, such as "Head Start," an early childhood education program for the children of poor families. Several US respondents noted that, at the subnational level, many state civil service systems include job classifications for paraprofessional social service personnel. This was related by one respondent to the recent "declassification" movement whereby a number of states have lowered the educational qualifications for various categories of jobs as a result of court rulings that have found that, in some instances, education requirements are unrelated to actual job demands and may be descriminatory in effect.

Respondents from the majority of the countries in our sample reported that their national governments had no explicit policy regarding the use of paraprofessionals in the provision of social welfare services, although (as in the USA) subnational units may recognize and support paraprofessional employment and training. However, many reported that specific national government agencies actively support and encourage the training and use of paraprofessionals, either on a widespread basis (the Philippines), on an ad hoc basis in relation to specific needs and programs (India, Israel), or implicitly, by supporting training for persons who, by definition, are paraprofessionals (Britain, Canada, Denmark, West Germany).

In summary, even though only a minority of the countries in our sample can be said to have explicit government policies supporting the training and use of the paraprofessional, it is clear that, in different ways and to varying degrees, national or subnational government units in all the countries surveyed recognize and implicitly support the paraprofessional human service worker, especially in regard to training.

ROLE DEFINITIONS AND UTILIZATION PATTERNS

Our respondents reported that paraprofessionals are widely used in the provision of social welfare services in all thirteen countries included in our sample. For example in India paraprofessionals represent the mainstream of human service provision and in Japan, where professional social work is not well developed, as one respondent put it, paraprofessionals are the rule rather than the exception. Even in countries like Britain and the USA which have large cadres of professionally trained social workers, persons without professional social work training are reported to constitute the majority of the social service work force.

The fields of service in which paraprofessionals are engaged and their typical job titles are very extensive – so extensive that, as one British respondent put it, a complete listing would take several pages. An Australian informant noted that paraprofessionals are found virtually everywhere that social workers are employed. The areas listed in *Table 1* give a sense of the range mentioned.

TABLE 1   *Some areas or fields of paraprofessional activity*

adoption	day care	mental health
aging	drug abuse	mental retardation
alcohol abuse	education – adult	neighborhood work
big brother programs	education – early	nutrition
block-level work	childhood	physical handicap
child protection	education – elemen-	rural development
child welfare	tary and secondary	probation/parole
children's institutions	education – special	urban renewal
community develop-	family planning	village-level work
ment	family welfare	vocational rehabilita-
community health	foster care	tion
services	home health care	youth work
corrections	juvenile delinquency	

Among the most common fields of service mentioned by all countries were child care, family welfare, youth work, and services to the aging. In addition to these commonly mentioned fields, countries like India, Indonesia, the Philippines, and Uganda stressed the importance of community development, rural development, adult education, and health care, including family planning. Respondents from countries like Canada, Denmark, and the USA included drug and alcohol abuse services among the common areas of paraprofessional activity, while these services tended not to be mentioned by respondents from less developed countries.

In a number of countries, there are reported to be paraprofessionals who are engaged in activities that are somewhat unique to those particular countries. "Agricultural overseers" in South Africa and persons who work with refugee groups in Denmark are examples of paraprofessionals who were not mentioned by respondents from other countries in our sample. Other more common functions (child care, services to the aging, community work, and so on) seem to have unique aspects in certain countries. For example, in Japan, the *hobo* or child-care worker in children's homes and the *ryobo* or caregiver in services for the aging are long established and widely recognized occupations in their own right.

Paraprofessionals in several countries are engaged in outreach activities to cultural and ethnic minorities and to poor and otherwise disadvantaged urban or rural communities. However, there appear to be unique aspects of these activities in certain countries. In addition to Australia's ethnic health workers and aboriginal health and legal workers and Uganda's village improvement programs, Israel has its community aides or *ovdim schunotim* and India has a variety of somewhat unique paraprofessionals – village level workers, block development workers, community workers in urban slums, and family planning and women's welfare officers – that are noteworthy. Space limitations allow us to provide only brief descriptions in this chapter of some of these unique paraprofessionals. They are described more fully in subsequent chapters.

Since 1978 a special group of community workers or community aides (*ovdim schunotim*) have been involved in Project Renewal in Israel. This is a comprehensive program to rehabilitate 160 neighborhood communities encompassing over 70,000 families or 300,000 people, at a cost of approximately 100 million dollars. The *ovdim schunotim* are recruited from the primarily indigenous communities involved in Project Renewal and are trained to provide a wide range of services to their communities (Schindler 1980).

Because four-fifths of India's population live in approximately 560,000 villages, 60 per cent of which have fewer than 500 people (Indian Council of Social Welfare 1982), indigenous paraprofessionals known as "village-level workers" are very important social welfare service providers in India. Village-level workers enjoy a position of trust, authority, and influence. They are knowledgeable about local customs, religion, and culture and they are aware of existing or impending problems. They are the front-line social workers in rural

THE PARAPROFESSIONAL IN THIRTEEN COUNTRIES 27

India. Above the village level, India has developed a decentralized form of grassroots planning and development based on "blocks" of approximately 100 villages with total populations of 100,000 to 150,000 people. A block is usually comprised of territories that are homogeneous in terms of socio-ethnic and other demographic characteristics. Block development officers in India perform a broad range of planning and development functions related to agriculture, animal husbandry, social education, and family welfare, making them a unique kind of paraprofessional (Singh 1980).

Among our respondents, those from Australia and Denmark tended to see the least difference between professional and paraprofessional roles. In the case of Denmark, any difference was considered to be insignificant. Most other respondents noted the overlap between professional and paraprofessional roles and activities but added that there were important distinctions that could be made. The majority observed that paraprofessionals were likely to be engaged in direct face-to-face work with clients (individuals, families, groups, and communities) in relation to relatively concrete, practical, routine services, such as information-giving, resource-identification, case-finding, and access-provision.

What is clear is that paraprofessionals in many countries carry roles and functions that are critical to the survival of individuals, families, and communities. Examples of these "life-line" functions include the work that is done by paraprofessionals in India on irrigation and agricultural projects in flood-ravaged villages in order to increase food production and reduce malnutrition or starvation, the basic medical services provided by Australia's aboriginal health workers, and the "home help" and "meals-on-wheels" programs for the sick and frail elderly that are delivered by paraprofessionals in Britain, the USA, and several other countries.

Some respondents included clerical and data-gathering functions among the typical paraprofessional tasks (Canada and the Philippines). Others referred to the paraprofessionals' "caring" or "tending" role (Britain, Japan, and South Africa), "grassroots" (India) or "front-line" (Indonesia) service functions, their auxiliary position in relation to professionals (Israel, the Philippines, South Africa), and the "bridging" function they serve between professionals and clients (Israel). It was noted by several respondents that many of these functions are unique to the paraprofessional. It was also observed that the degree of interchange between professional and paraprofessional roles was likely to be greatest in those situations where professionals were least accessible, for example in remote areas of a country (Philippines).

In all countries it is reported that paraprofessionals are likely to have the most frequent and direct contact with clients. On the other hand, professionals were seen by the great majority of respondents as being more likely to be engaged in administration, supervision, training, planning, research, analysis, diagnosis, and the provision of those direct services of a relatively complex nature, that is those that need more knowledge, skill, and judgment than paraprofessionals typically possess, including "clinical" or "therapeutic" intervention.

PROFESSIONAL–PARAPROFESSIONAL RELATIONSHIPS

The degree of acceptance of the paraprofessional by the social work profession varies greatly among the countries in our sample. Respondents from West Germany, Indonesia, Japan, and the Philippines reported that paraprofessionals have been readily accepted by social workers and their professional associations. This is attributed to the fact that the social work profession is relatively weak in West Germany and Japan and the recognition by social workers in Indonesia and the Philippines that a fully professionalized social service work force is not attainable and that paraprofessionals are needed to carry out vital service functions. In the latter two countries, the social work profession actively supports the work of paraprofessionals through such activities as supervision, training, and educating their own members about the appropriate roles of paraprofessionals.

Most respondents reported some degree of ambivalence on the part of their countries' social work profession to the use of paraprofessionals. This ranged from relatively mild reservations in some quarters of the profession (Australia, Britain, Canada, Denmark, South Africa, Uganda), to a situation reflecting some degree of strain between professionals and paraprofessionals (India and Israel) and, in the case of the USA, general acceptance but strong resistance or rejection by some influential segments of the organized social work profession. Despite the reported ambivalence of the social work profession in many countries, there was a strong

THE PARAPROFESSIONAL IN THIRTEEN COUNTRIES 29

belief on the part of respondents from all countries that the widespread use of paraprofessionals would continue and probably grow, even in countries with strong social work professional organizations that exercise a powerful gatekeeping function (Israel) or where professionalism is revered (India).

In all countries in our sample, it is expected that paraprofessionals will receive supervision in their work, although the nature, quality, and frequency varies, depending on such factors as the agency or organizational setting, the services being provided, and whether the location is urban or rural. The majority of respondents from all countries reported that paraprofessionals usually work directly with clients over fairly extended periods of time without a professional worker present. Therefore, while professional or other appropriate supervision is expected to ensure accountability for proper job performance, paraprofessionals appear to enjoy a fairly high degree of autonomy in their day-to-day service activities.

TRAINING AND EDUCATIONAL APPROACHES

Respondents reported a wide range of training practices and opportunities for paraprofessionals in the countries in our sample. These include pre-service and in-service training provided by employers, by public and voluntary welfare organizations, in government-run or supported training institutes or training centers, and in high schools, vocational schools, technical institutes, community colleges, colleges of advanced education, four-year colleges, and universities. The length of this training ranges from a few days for some types of training provided by employers to programs of up to four years' duration for the more formal education provided by colleges and universities. While short-term in-service training is likely to be practical in nature, the more formal programs tend to include some mix of theoretical and practical instruction, the exact mix depending on the nature and auspices of the training.

Some of the countries in our sample are reported to have examples of most of the above training options available (for example, the USA). However, most have developed only a few of these alternatives (beyond basic in-service training or induction by employers) and place special emphasis on a particular training approach. In West Germany, for example, a variety of programs offered by vocational schools are very important training resources for paraprofessional human service personnel. These include one-year training programs for persons who work with the aging (*Altenfleger*), two-year programs in youth work (*Jugendleiter*), and three-year programs in teaching and institutional work (*Erzcher*).

As we noted earlier, in Japan, the national priority has been placed on the expansion of a wide range of in-service training programs for various categories of social welfare personnel. This training is provided by different government and voluntary social welfare agencies. In addition, some well-established pre-service training programs exist for certain categories of paraprofessional social welfare workers, such as the *hobo* (child-care worker) mentioned earlier in this chapter.

Community colleges (or comparable educational institutions) seem to be especially important training resources for the parapro-fessional in countries like Australia, Britain, Canada, and the USA. For example, within the rich mixture of formal training programs that is available in the USA, two-year community college programs leading to an associate degree in a variety of human service areas (for example, mental heatlh, child welfare, social service) seem to have established a central role in paraprofessional training. In Britain colleges of further education (not unlike the US community colleges) serve an important function in nationally recognized training programs for paraprofessionals, such as the In-Service Course in Social Care (ICSC) and the Certificate in Social Service (CSS).

Government-run training centers constitute the major training resources for paraprofessionals in Indonesia. These centers offer a variety of training courses in such areas as rural welfare development, population education, and child and family welfare, ranging in length from three weeks to twelve months. Training centers such as these are also important in India, Israel, South Africa, and Uganda. For example, Uganda's Nzamizi (National) Training Institute for Social Development offers a variety of short-term training courses as well as a one-year certificate program and a two-year diploma program in social development.

Somewhat unusual types of paraprofessional training that were reported by our respondents include high school courses in social welfare topics in Indonesia, and correspondence courses for paraprofessional social service personnel in Britain, Japan, and South Africa. Also noteworthy are some university-based training programs for paraprofessionals in Denmark, India, and the USA. The existence of the above-mentioned rich array of training approaches does not mean that all (or even most) paraprofessional human service workers are being appropriately trained. Respondents to our survey noted that it is impossible to know what proportion of the paraprofessional work force in a particular country receives any training beyond a very rudimentary form of in-service orientation to their jobs. What seems fairly clear from the responses we received is that in most countries only a small percentage of paraprofessionals receives formal training that leads to a recognized credential. This appears to be the case even in countries that have a relatively well-developed range of formal training programs for paraprofessionals. What also appear to be widely lacking are systematic linkages between paraprofessional training and professional social work education programs.

OPPORTUNITIES FOR CAREER ADVANCEMENT

In most of the countries in our sample it is clear that the avenue to career advancement for the paraprofessional is through post-secondary education. The most notable exception is Japan where there is reported to be no clear demarcation between professionals and paraprofessionals in the human services. Promotion and career advancement are based on evaluation of job performance rather than academic credentials. According to one of our Japanese respondents, it is not common for people who are employed to return to academic settings for further education.

In several countries there are opportunities for paraprofessionals to advance professionally by taking the types of training mentioned earlier. They may not attain professional status but can improve their skills and may qualify for higher level paraprofessional positions. At least in principle, the most gifted and highly motivated can pursue professional studies and it is reported by our respondents in several countries that this is done in some instances. For example, in the Philippines gifted paraprofessionals can receive scholarships for professional study from the Ministry of Social Services and Development or can be given time off from work to attend classes on a part-time basis. In some cases, they may be granted paid leaves to pursue full-time professional education. These opportunities are available to a very small number of paraprofessionals and are contingent upon the person's ability to satisfy college or university entrance requirements. The latter is a serious barrier to career advancement for many paraprofessionals, especially in less developed countries and regions.

In general, opportunities for career advancement for most paraprofessionals in the countries in our sample appear to be quite limited, despite the exceptions noted by some of our respondents. Our findings suggest that, in most countries of the world, there is some way to go before the following observations and recommendations of an earlier United Nations (1980: 41) study are close to reality: "training programmes for front line social welfare personnel should be developed in close relationship with career development programs, so that participation in training leads to better service to people and this in turn contributes to the career advancement and job satisfaction of front line personnel."

SUMMARY AND CONCLUSIONS

A shortage of professionally trained social welfare personnel, particularly in developing countries and in rural areas, the unique role of the paraprofessional, and rising social welfare costs are universal factors contributing to the widespread employment of paraprofessionals in the countries we studied. These variables transcend geographic boundaries and seem likely to ensure that paraprofessionals will continue to be in the mainstream of human service activity for the foreseeable future, providing important and vital services to those in need. However, in spite of this situation, we have found only limited commitment to comprehensive human resource planning and development in the majority of the countries studied.

The significance of the paraprofessional to human service provision is reflected in the diverse tasks and heterogeneous fields in which they are engaged. We identified over thirty fields and there are certainly more than that. Greater proximity to grassroots problems and special skills in dealing with them account, at least in part, for the widespread use of the paraprofessional.

The importance of the paraprofessional's contribution is also reflected in the nature of the functions that they perform. While these are determined largely by local conditions and needs, what we have called "life-line" functions permeate geographic boundaries. In all countries, examples of paraprofessional activities that are vital to the health and well-being of individuals, families, groups, and communities were reported.

While both men and women are engaged in paraprofessional social service activity in all of the countries in our sample, women predominate in most countries. The exceptions are India and Uganda where there is reported to be an equal proportion of males and females. Undoubtedly a variety of social, cultural, and economic factors account for the male/female distribution in paraprofessional employment in different countries, including the nature of national investments in human capital, cultural attitudes, the relative status of human service employment, and salary levels. For example in Israel low pay and low status may be dominant factors in the very low percentage of males in paraprofessional human service employment. These factors have implications for policy planners, especially in those countries where investment in human capital (including the employment of deprived populations in human service roles) is adopted as a major anti-poverty or social development strategy.

Our study attempted to identify some dominant patterns in the allocation of functions between professional and paraprofessional personnel. While there is some overlap between the two, a general trend indicates that paraprofessionals carry the more concrete, routine, and resource-related functions at the grassroots level. Professional workers, on the other hand, tend to perform the more complicated treatment functions and have greater responsibility for supervision, administration, planning, research, and training. The development of educational and practice models that recognize these distinctions and that integrate the activities of the two groups would be a valuable contribution to more rational and systematic human service personnel systems.

Unfortunately we found limited uniformity or commitment to integrated educational systems among the countries studied. A variety of dominant training patterns were identified, with some evidence of increased involvement by community colleges and other institutions of higher education. An important step toward greater clarity of goals and functions would be the development of closer and more explicit linkages between university, community college, and the host of in-service and other educational programs that exist in most countries.

Another interesting aspect of the professional–paraprofessional relationship is the fact that, in most of the countries we studied, the professional social work associations have accepted the contributions of paraprofessionals with serious reservations and, in some cases, have resisted them. Respondents from several countries (for example, Britain, South Africa, Uganda, and the USA) report an ambivalent posture on the part of the social work profession. In the USA there is great concern about perceived paraprofessional infringement into the domain of the professional. On the other hand, human service employers and government agencies have accepted paraprofessionals quite readily – with enthusiasm in many cases. This acceptance, which permeates national boundaries, is not surprising, given the personnel resource and cost considerations mentioned earlier. Several of our respondents stressed that the pursuit of professional excellence and service effectiveness need not be threatened by supporting the helping actions performed by non-professionals. The resistance of professionals to the perceived infringement by paraprofessionals may account for some of the barriers to career advancement that the latter face. The problems that these barriers create in terms of locking people into dead-end jobs, reduced job satisfaction, worker burn-out, and high turnover are serious not only for paraprofessionals but also for the recipients of human services.

In essence our findings suggest that paraprofessionals are likely to be the main front-line providers of human services in most countries for the foreseeable future. This being so, there is a need to clarify the characteristics and functions of this important group of workers, determine how they might best be deployed, and design training and other supportive mechanisms that will maximize their contribution to human service goals.

3

Four countries in detail: an introduction

This chapter provides a brief introduction to the heart of the book – detailed study of the paraprofessional human service worker in Britain, India, Israel, and the USA along the five major dimensions that emerged from the review of the literature in Chapter 1 and the findings of our international survey of paraprofessional human service personnel summarized in Chapter 2. As a result of the information produced by our international survey, some of our original questions became more focused or took on new aspects. In some instances, new questions or issues emerged, exemplifying "the reflexive nature of the research process" (Black *et al.* 1983: vi).

While we tend to agree with Feldman's (1978: 293–94) observation that "few scholars know enough about more than one country to venture into detailed examination of public policy beyond one country's borders," we felt that it was important to attempt to understand as fully as possible the paraprofessional in countries other than the two with which we were most familiar – Israel and the USA. We had previously devoted a considerable amount of study to the paraprofessional human service worker in these two countries (see, for example, Brawley and Schindler 1972; Brawley 1975; 1978; 1980; 1981a; 1981b; 1982; Schindler 1977; 1980; 1982; 1985) and, therefore, were relatively well informed about the most salient issues being addressed there. However, we felt that we needed to look at the front-line paraprofessional in depth in at least two other countries if we were to move beyond our own country-bound views and develop a truly international perspective on our topic. We were particularly eager to include both developed and developing countries among those that we studied in detail since we were aware that paraprofessional personnel are an especially valuable resource in the human service systems of the less developed countries.

Among the most important considerations in selecting Britain and India for detailed study was the fact that in both of those countries the use of front-line paraprofessionals was fairly well established, we were able to spend time in each country studying the paraprofessional at first hand, and we had access to a large number of well-informed local sources of information on this topic. In addition, there was a substantial and growing body of literature on the paraprofessional human service worker in Britain and India that would serve to verify or challenge our own observations and the information provided by our informants.

A number of issues emerged from our preliminary work, including our international survey, that we wanted to explore in detail. For example, it was clear that front-line paraprofessionals were performing a multiplicity of service roles and functions in relation to a wide variety of client groups in all kinds of human service and social development programs throughout the world. Based on our initial findings, we found ourselves in agreement with the following observations about paraprofessional human service workers:

"perhaps their few commonly shared characteristics are that they are extremely diverse, function at the lower echelons of the service structures and consequently are of low status, receive low remuneration and are perhaps the last to have any significant claim on developmental resources. On the other hand, they are perhaps more numerous than any other category of personnel, are closest to the people who are recipients of services, are most similar in the socio-cultural and economic make-up to the vast majority of people and potentially are capable of sparking significant attitudinal and behavioural changes among people with whom they are in close and constant contact."

(United Nations 1980: 39)

However, while these kinds of general observations about the paraprofessional are useful, they leave some important questions unanswered.

Much of the literature and many of our respondents in different countries ascribed to front-line paraprofessionals knowledge, skills, and other attributes that make them particularly valuable providers of human services, especially to certain client populations or communities. On the other hand, many professionals appear to believe or operate on the assumption that, in the best of all possible worlds, people who need help should receive it only from professionals and that paraprofessionals perform functions that could be performed better by professionals if sufficient numbers of the latter were available. They see the use of paraprofessionals as an interim measure until the supply of professionally trained personnel expands or as a cheap substitute for the employment of professionals in situations where governments or human service agencies do not have the resources or the will to provide more professionalized services. From this perspective, arguments in support of the valuable qualities of the paraprofessional are viewed as mere rationalizations of existing arrangements or flowing from anti-professionalism or misguided egalitarianism.

In essence, there appear to be two opposing views on the place of the paraprofessional human service worker which, at their extreme, can be characterized as, on the one hand, idealizing paraprofessionals with perhaps an exaggeration of their capabilities or contributions and, on the other hand, the assertion that they are merely a cheap and less desirable substitute for professionally trained personnel. We believe that continuing efforts to determine the nature of the paraprofessional's contribution to the human services and to define appropriate roles and functions for this category of personnel are necessary in order to move beyond such overly simplistic assumptions, reduce the polemic that surrounds this issue in some circumstances, and lead to more rational and efficient use of available resources.

In our introductory chapter we noted the great expansion in human service activity that had occurred worldwide during the 1950s, 1960s, and 1970s. However, we were aware that these increased efforts by national governments to address a wider range of human needs had left large groups of people unserved (Romanyshyn 1971). The use of paraprofessional personnel has been advanced as one mechanism for reaching out to underserved groups and as a means of engaging local citizens and communities, particularly disadvantaged and minority groups, in social development or social change efforts. We were interested in examining the paraprofessional's role in these kinds of efforts in both developed and developing countries. We were particularly interested in seeing the degree to which the paraprofessional movement in different countries might have contributed to the embodiment of policies that reflected Mumford's (1970) view that people should be the subject rather than the object of development.

The four countries that we chose to study in detail had all (in varying ways, with different emphases, and at different times) espoused the idea that social policies, programs, and services are likely to be most effective when the people affected are participants in defining their own needs and determining how these might best be met. Paraprofessional personnel, particularly if drawn from local communities, were frequently an important element in putting this idea into operation. We wanted to explore the question of how paraprofessionals in both developed and developing countries might improve the relationship between people at the grassroots and those social institutions, arrangements, and initiatives designed to promote their well-being.

Related to this issue were questions about the precise qualities that make indigenous helpers particularly effective with certain populations and how helping methods in general might be made more appropriate to local needs. As we have already noted, there was considerable evidence in the literature (supported by responses to our survey) which suggested that paraprofessionals not only were used as substitutes for professionals where these were not available or were in short supply, but also were used in many cases because they possess knowledge, skills, or attributes that professionals did not have. This might be membership or special knowledge of a particular community or client group (the indigenous factor) or it might be that professional skills were not particularly useful in dealing with certain kinds of problems – what one of our Indian respondents called the "operational incompatibility" between the clinical approach of many social workers and the pressing social problems of many needy populations. There was some suggestion that professional social workers had become somewhat removed from the most needy populations in many countries (especially in the less developed parts of the world) and we were interested in exploring the two related issues of determining the special value of the indigenous helper and the need for helping methods to be appropriate to specific local needs and populations.

To illustrate this point, the suggestion has been made that social work in the USA, in its efforts to gain recognition by emulating the higher-status professions, most notably the medical specialty of psychiatry, and its concentration on the refinement of practice skills of the therapeutic variety, became somewhat removed from certain major client groups – the poor, the disadvantaged, and minorities (Bisno 1956). While US social workers did not necessarily deliberately adopt practices that created barriers to serving certain client groups (often the most deprived), nevertheless, as Reynolds (1951: 3–4) has observed, it is "easy to refine one's techniques to the point where only relatively refined people can make use of them."

This issue appears to be especially critical in developing countries where professional social work methods not only may be inappropriate to the pressing survival needs of the majority of the population but also, it has been suggested, are alien to the culture and values of these countries.

> "Western social workers exerted a powerful influence over their Third World colleagues and, claiming that social work had a universally relevant methodology and an international professional identity, they imposed alien theories and techniques on developing countries, which were unsuited to their cultures and development needs."
>
> (Midgley 1981: xiii)

We were eager to explore these issues in some depth in order to clarify the nature of the problems being confronted and to see what solutions might be possible.

Based on our own observations in Israel and the USA and the responses we received to our international survey, we were aware of the mixed reaction of professionally trained social workers to the paraprofessional. For example, it was clear that the paraprofessional enjoyed more acceptance and support by social workers in some countries than in others. We were interested in clarifying why social workers who are committed to meeting people's needs would be antagonistic to a group of workers who (according to all available evidence) are an important human service personnel resource. We wanted to determine under what circumstances the relationship between the two groups was likely to be most productive. While we recognized that social workers might have legitimate concerns about the quality of service provided by front-line paraprofessionals with limited or no training, among our operating assumptions were (1) that paraprofessionals are a valuable (in some instances, vital) human service resource; and (2) that professionals should support and, where possible, strengthen the contribution that paraprofessionals can make to human well-being.

We were fully aware that paraprofessionals throughout the world work alongside many professionals besides social workers and that focusing on their relationship to this one professional group would illuminate only one aspect of a much larger and more complex picture. However, we felt justified in limiting our attention to this particular relationship, not only because of our own identity as social workers and our limited knowledge of the values and priorities of other professions, but also because we believe that social work is probably the most generic of the human service professions, having an important role in most of the human service systems in the countries we studied. Social workers are committed to promoting the well-being of individuals, families, groups, and communities and are expected to identify, develop, and integrate available societal resources in order to meet people's needs and help them function at their best possible level. Since paraprofessional human service personnel are an important resource for meeting people's needs, we assumed that social workers would view them in this light and would do what they could to support and develop this resource. However, we were aware that, in some instances, this was not happening, either because social work education programs were not adequately preparing social workers for this role or because social workers were perceiving themselves to be in a conflictual or competitive rather than a collaborative or supportive relationship with paraprofessionals. We wanted to explore these issues in some depth in different countries.

Our international survey revealed great variation in the types of training provided for paraprofessionals among countries and even within some countries. The overwhelming impression was that very little systematic planning was taking place in relation to any country's human service personnel resources, with most paraprofessional training occurring on an ad hoc basis. Furthermore, it appeared that most paraprofessionals received no formal training, even in countries with substantial training resources. We were interested, therefore, in determining what could be done to bridge the enormous gulf between the completely untrained paraprofessional who, in most instances, was providing the bulk of a country's front-line human service and the highly trained professional who was likely to be providing direct services to a very small proportion of the people who needed help. In particular, we were looking for training strategies that held promise of upgrading the knowledge and skills of significant numbers of front-line paraprofessionals so that this group of workers might make their fullest possible contribution to their country's social welfare and social development goals. It was our assumption that something more than basic in-service training offered by employers was needed while, at the same time, attempting to professionalize the entire front-line human service work force was neither practical nor necessary. In addition, we wanted to see if professional social work education programs had responded positively to the exhortations of various authorities (for example, International Association of Schools of Social Work 1979; United Nations 1980; Pangalangan and de Guzman 1980) that they play a more active role in the training of front-line paraprofessionals.

Another area of special interest was the manner and degree to which opportunities for promotion and career advancement were being provided for paraprofessionals in different countries. It was our assumption that the provision of such opportunities would be important if the paraprofessionals' job satisfaction and their contributions to human service goals were to be maximized. Our international survey had sensitized us to the barriers to career advancement that confront paraprofessionals in most countries and we were concerned about the consequences of the severely limited opportunities that are available. Since most paraprofessionals are women and many are drawn from the most disadvantaged population groups, communities, or ethnic minorities, we were aware of both the promise and the problems of employment in front-line paraprofessional human service jobs. These employment opportunities could be an important first step out of poverty and disadvantage for members of deprived or excluded groups. However, they could also be a cruel trap – locking people into low-paying, low-status, dead-end jobs unless steps were taken to open up realistic avenues to personal development, job enrichment, appropriate training, and career advancement for the incumbents. Therefore, we especially wanted to identify promising efforts to create appropriate opportunities for career advancement for front-line paraprofessionals.

In the chapters that follow we have adopted a comparative analytic approach to understanding some of the issues that surround the training and employment of front-line paraprofessional human service workers. In doing so, we have sought to capitalize on the strengths of this approach while keeping in mind its limitations. A major advantage of looking at the way in which other countries have addressed certain social policy issues is that it may "help us to reformulate or redefine our concepts and improve our analysis, and so our understanding of the inter-relationships of complex social phenomena" (Rodgers 1979: xi). Of course, one of the dangers of drawing lessons from the experience of other countries is that "the lessons may be inadequately learned so that one country is lured into imitating the policies of another without regard for differences in national contexts" (Higgins 1981: 14). Certainly no social policy or program "is so simple or so isolated from its national context as to commend itself for direct importation into another country" (Finer Report 1974: 16). However, we believe that "nations can learn from the experience of others, and even where lessons are ambiguous, different approaches can suggest a broader range of policy options than might appear in isolation" (Finer Report 1974: 16). We categorically reject what Marmor and Bridges have referred to as the "law of comparative difference" which states that:

> "if nations differ in any respect then they cannot learn from one another. Whenever a comparative finding is presented the criticism from this perspective is automatic. Lists of factors which differentiate the countries in question are supplied. The inference is that such differences render transplantation of lessons locally impossible." (Marmor and Bridges 1977: 6–7)

While our analysis of a number of important issues emerging from the use of paraprofessionals in different countries is not likely to result in any absolutely "right" answers to the difficult choices that face decision-makers (Heidenheimer, Heclo, and Adams 1976: 281), we hope that our efforts will serve to illuminate the nature of the choices that have to be made and how different courses of action might be evaluated (Higgins 1981: 163).

4

Factors contributing
to the use of
paraprofessionals

The varied and complex social, economic, political, and cultural factors that have led to widespread use of paraprofessional personnel in Britain, India, Israel, and the USA are considered in this chapter. What could be characterized as quantitative or logistical considerations, such as compensating for shortages of professionals, making more efficient use of available human resources, and extending services to remote rural areas, as well as qualitative or substantive factors such as the need for social, cultural, and ethnic closeness between helpers and clients are analyzed. Common themes that transcend national boundaries (for example, historical or current shortages of professionally trained personnel) and factors or circumstances that are unique to particular countries (for example, the unique value of indigenous village-level workers in remote areas of India and the limited utility of Western, industrialized models of professional helping in such settings) are discussed.

BRITAIN

While the term "paraprofessional" is not commonly used in relation to social service personnel in Britain, there are several categories of personnel engaged in social service provision who do fit well into the paraprofessional category as we are using the term. For example, many local authority social services departments employ social work assistants (sometimes called welfare assistants) who perform tasks that are closely related to the functions of social workers. In principle they handle cases that are less complex and demanding than those assigned to professionally trained workers.

In addition to social work assistants, a wide range of paraprofessional personnel are used in the provision of social services and, in fact, paraprofessionals constitute the majority of the social service work force (Billis et al. 1980: 59). A recent government-initiated study of the roles and tasks of social workers in Britain recognized the important roles of paraprofessional personnel whom it referred to as "social services workers."

"*Social services workers* is the term we use for a range of staff employed in local authority social services departments or voluntary agencies to help people in their own homes or in day centers or residential homes. They carry various designations including 'home help organizer', 'care assistant', 'home help', and 'family aide'. They undoubtedly carry out social work in the informal sense . . . and many will also undertake formal social work . . . when the circumstances demand it, whether or not under the supervision of a social worker. . . . They are distinguished from social workers in that they provide a specific service, often undertaken following a social worker's assessment."

(Barclay Report 1982: xv)

Although they are found in a variety of public and voluntary social service agencies and also in a small but growing number of proprietary organizations, most professional social workers and paraprofessional social service personnel are employed by the large general social services departments (called social work departments in Scotland) that are operated by local authorities (country, metropolitan, or regional government bodies) in Britain. Those factors that have been significant in making paraprofessional personnel an important element of the social service work force can best be understood in the context of the functions of local authority social services departments.

Until 1969 in Scotland and 1970 in England and Wales, the personal social services in Britain were provided by local authority (usually county, city, or borough) departments that separately addressed the needs of children, the elderly, and handicapped people. In addition, the local authority departments of education, housing, and health and, under separate auspices, hospitals and probation departments also provided social services. When voluntary social agencies were added to the above array, the multiple nature and consequent fragmentation of social service delivery became evident (Butterworth and Holman 1975: 235–36). The consequences of these fragmented services for families who needed help became a matter of public concern in the mid-1960s and the government appointed a committee under the chairmanship of Sir Frederick (later Lord) Seebohm to "review the organization and responsibilities of the local authority personal social services in England and Wales, and to consider what changes are desirable to secure an effective family service" (Seebohm Report 1968). A corresponding process had been initiated for Scotland a little earlier (Kilbrandon Report 1964).

While the Seebohm Report ranged far and wide in its examination of the social services and its recommendations for reform, the central thrust of the proposals which emerged was the consolidation of all local authority social work functions in one department. The justification for such an arrangement was based on the following types of considerations.

"Firstly, it would help to overcome the problem of co-ordination. Secondly, a family with multiple needs would be saved a multiplicity of workers and instead could be helped by one worker able to see the family as a whole unit. Thirdly, a single department would serve to lessen confusion as to which department clients should approach. By having to go through fewer doors access would be simplified. Fourthly, a single department would result in a larger staff and a better staff career structure. In turn, this would lead to a greater ability to increase the recruitment and training of appropriate staff and to deploy them better. Fifthly, a larger, all embracing department would be better fitted to collect information, to fix objectives, to make plans to achieve them, and to evaluate progress."
(Butterworth and Holman 1975: 239)

The approach advocated by the Seebohm Committee was for a single social services department "outgoing in character to the extent of encouraging people to use its services, and strengthened by community support and participation" (Butterworth and Holman 1975: 239). The problems of individuals were seen as occurring in the context of the family and the community and it was within these contexts that problems were to be addressed and controlled.

All social services departments have within them an extensive array of domiciliary and day treatment services that are designed to support the elderly, handicapped, ill, mentally ill, and mentally retarded people living in the community. These services, which are more extensive than those offered by single comparable organizations in other parts of the world, include home helps, home visitors, a variety of types of day care programs, sheltered workshops, home-delivered and congregate meals, transportation, occupational therapy, and necessary equipment and adaptations to people's homes to enable them to live independently. Departments also have a range of residential accommodation in institutions, group homes, hostels, and foster homes for children, the elderly, and handicapped people. The Seebohm Report recommended that social service departments, in order to be accessible to and oriented to local communities, should have area offices, each serving about 50,000 to 100,000 people. The local offices would be staffed by an area team of ten to twelve social workers along with ancillary staff. This arrangement was adopted by most social services departments (Glennerster 1975: 78) although the size and composition of area teams shows wide variation from place to place (Stevenson and Parsloe 1978; Payne 1982; Black et al. 1983).

Given the wide range of services provided by the new social service departments and the area teams within them, it is not surprising that many of these services are of a type that does not require the skills of professionally trained social workers.

"As the new Seebohm departments settled down it became clear that something like three-quarters of the work pressure on area teams consisted of demands for help which could as easily be provided by [nonprofessionals] as by professionally qualified staff. Moreover, because of the practical nature of the tasks it could be argued that it was more appropriate for them to be done by ordinary people. The spin-off in terms of shared experience and mutual aid which could result from professional and non-professional working together could be a valuable addition to community well-being."

(Cooper 1980: 29)

From the inception of the new departments in the early 1970s, then, paraprofessional personnel have had a recognized and significant place within them. Despite the emergence of increasing numbers of professionaly trained social workers during the last fifteen years, the importance of the paraprofessional's role has in no way diminished. If anything, the contribution that this category of social service personnel can make to the helping process has been increasingly recognized.

Other factors contributing to the use of paraprofessionals

In Britain, as in other countries, paraprofessionals often bring an indigenous dimension to social service departments and area teams, since they are "more likely to share and respond to the interests, accents, and priorities of local people than an outside professional" and "relate better and more quickly to clients, especially where differences are considerable (e.g., ethnic differences)" (Payne 1982: 94). This indigenous factor is stressed by some proponents of "patch" systems of social service delivery which involve organizing social service staff in such a way that individual workers or small teams are responsible for responding to all service demands within a relatively small community or neighborhood (patch) of 5,000–10,000 people. Hadley and McGrath (1980: 97) emphasize the advantages that accrue to patch teams that recruit local people in service delivery roles since they believe that, "when this is done, it is more likely that local interests will be understood in the department and reflected in the way services are organized." In one such patch system, in the coal-mining community of Normanton in the north of England, it is noted that "wherever possible, the ancillary workers are recruited from local people. Common experience of living in the same area, personal contacts through relatives, friends, neighbours, and membership of local organizations, all tend to reduce the gap between workers and clients and to make access to the team easier" (Hadley and McGrath 1980: 97). Cooper (1980: 35) notes that the Normanton patch workers, who are locally recruited women in the 28–50 age range, "have had a broad life

experience and possess a level of maturity enabling them to cope
with the varied demands expected of them." He adds that, in
carrying out their work, they "have shown a high level of
competence, commitment and devoted altruism."

The recruitment of local community residents into paraprofessional
roles in the social services has some job creation potential for low-
skilled and low-income people in areas of high unemployment but
this is seldom stressed in Britain. The use of paraprofessionals in the
British social services has, therefore, little in common with the
"new careers" movement of the 1960s in the USA or with
comparable social development efforts in other countries. Examples
can be found of projects that had explicit job creation purposes for
the chronically unemployed, for ex-offenders, and for recovered
alcoholics and drug addicts. For instance, in the Strathclyde region
in Scotland, an area with large pockets of chronically high
unemployment, a project was developed a few years ago by the
regional social work department to recruit, train, and offer
permanent social service jobs to unemployed people (*Community
Care* 1980). Specific projects like this and others developed by the
Manpower Services Commission and various voluntary organizations are noteworthy (Bishop 1984; Councils for Voluntary Service
1984). However, these do not reflect a national policy to use human
service employment as a major job creation or anti-poverty
strategy.

A number of demographic, social, and economic trends have led
to new demands on the British social service system and many of
these demands are of a type that can appropriately be met by
paraprofessional personnel, as well as informal helpers. As is the
case in many other Western industrialized societies, Britain's
population is aging rapidly. Already more than 15 per cent of the
population is at least 65 years of age and the number of elderly
persons is continuing to grow. Not only is the over-65 age group
growing but the average age of this group is increasing. The fastest
growing segment of the elderly population between now and the
end of the century will be those over 85 years old (Local
Government Training Board undated a: 3). These population
trends have created needs for expanded systems of social care
within which paraprofessional personnel have a crucial role.

"ordinary, mainly unskilled, people both in the informal network
and in formal social service institutions constitute the majority of

those involved in tending and caring for those who are becoming increasingly dependent. These are the growing proportion of the very frail elderly, the growing number of survivors suffering from severe physical or mental handicap, and possibly also an increasing number of children among the rising number of one-parent and reconstituted families."

(Goldberg 1981:80)

Parker (1981) notes that the expansion of the elderly population has occurred at a time when increasing proportions of women (the traditional informal care-takers of the elderly and other dependent groups) are engaged in paid employment and thus less likely to be available for the care of dependent kin. This has resulted in enormous growth in the numbers of people employed in "tending" or "caring" roles in the social services in recent years.

Examples of paraprofessional activity

Among those paraprofessionals who can be expected to be involved in the provision of expanded "tending" or "caring" services to vulnerable or dependent populations are *care assistants* in homes for the elderly, *wardens* of sheltered housing for the elderly, *home helps* who provide in-home services to elderly and handicapped people and to families, and *family aides*, a category of personnel (often former home helps) who provide important supportive service to vulnerable individuals and families.

Care assistants are the front-line providers of care in homes for the elderly in Britain. Their job is to respond directly to the physical, social, and emotional needs of the residents and to help them maintain their optimum level of functioning. In the past, care assistants have typically been married women, many of them working on a part-time basis. However, this is changing as a result of persistent unemployment of younger workers in Britain, larger numbers of whom are seeking employment as care assistants (Local Government Training Board undated a: 3).

In addition to homes for the most frail and dependent elderly, Britain (like many other countries) has developed a variety of services that are intended to make it possible for older persons to remain within the community for as long as possible. One example of these services is the expanding range of sheltered housing operated for elderly people and other vulnerable individuals by local authority housing departments (social work departments in Scotland), housing associations, voluntary organizations, and a growing number of commercial enterprises in Britain. The purpose is to provide tenants with a sheltered and supportive living environment where help is readily available from staff (usually called wardens) but where tenants are allowed and encouraged to maintain as high a level of independence as is possible for them. A recent study suggests that there are more than 6,000 sheltered housing programs in Britain, employing at least 12,000 wardens. These are of varying size and kind, ranging from those that provide only minimal on-call support for a tenant group that is able to maintain a relatively high level of independent functioning to programs that serve a more dependent tenant population through more direct monitoring and support and a variety of communal services – catering, recreational, social, and so on. Wardens of these varied types of sheltered housing arrangements for elderly people constitute another important and growing category of para-professional social service personnel in Britain (Local Government Training Board undated c).

Several of our informants made special mention of the role of home helps in the British social services. It is estimated that there are over 100,000 home helps employed by the 115 local authority social services departments in England and Wales (Local Government Training Board undated b: 3). Therefore, although most of them work only on a part-time basis, they constitute a significant segment of the typical social service department's work force. Theoretically the persons functioning in this capacity are involved simply in providing domestic help to needy individuals and families. However, many play a broader supportive role with the frail elderly, enabling them to remain in their own homes rather than be admitted to residential care; with physically and mentally handicapped people living in the community; with vulnerable families; and with people in crisis situations. It is being recognized that, with appropriate in-service training, home helps have the potential for providing a broad range of valuable supportive services to needy individuals and families and, in many instances, are vital front-line members of social service teams since they have the most frequent and regular contacts with many vulnerable clients (Dexter and Harbert 1983).

An interesting category of personnel is emerging from among the ranks of the home helps. These workers, often referred to as "family aides," provide more intensive and skilled services to the most vulnerable individuals and families. The emergence of the family aide has occurred in recognition of the important front-line supportive work that can be performed by some home helps and by other paraprofessional personnel if they are given training designed to upgrade their level of functioning.

A government-sponsored study of social service teams found that family aides were performing quite demanding functions in a number of area teams in Scotland.

"The family aides were usually allocated the 'worst' cases and the nature of the work and the type of families involved made the turnover of cases very slow. Most of the families they dealt with were described as 'inadequate', typically with many children, father unemployed, poor housing and perhaps with the parents borderline mentally handicapped. They usually had arrears of rent and various other debts."

(Hallett 1978: 161)

It can be seen, therefore, that there are several categories of paraprofessional social service personnel (in addition to the social work assistants mentioned earlier) who are providing vital front-line services to vulnerable individuals and families in Britain. The need for their contribution to the social services is expected to continue to grow and the importance of the functions they perform is being increasingly recognized.

Current trends

The changes that occurred in the organization of the social services in Britain in the early 1970s were quite dramatic and were perceived by British social workers as a major milestone in the evolution of the "welfare state." Social workers and their paraprofessional colleagues in the new unified social services departments expected to be able to "tackle a wider universe of needs with a more comprehensive range of services in a more positive, promotional manner" (Algie 1980: 181; see also Rowbottom, Hey, and Billis 1974: 213).

The present British government clearly takes a more residual view of what is an appropriate role for social services departments, expressing through a former secretary of state for social services the belief that social services departments "should seek to meet directly only those needs which others cannot or will not meet" and "their task is to act as a safety net, the final protection for people for whom there is no other, not as a first port of call" (Jenkin 1981). Recent government cuts in social service spending (Algie 1980), a movement towards "privatization" of some types of care (Department of Health and Social Security 1981a; 1981b; Marley and Wulff-Cochrane 1985), and a renewed emphasis on voluntarism and self-sufficiency (Department of Health and Social Security 1983) could be viewed as tending to encourage the use of cheaper nonprofessional helpers. However, there is no tangible evidence that this is so. What seems clear is that a variety of groups of paraprofessional personnel carry important functions in the provision of the social services in Britain, that these functions (which are distinct from those performed by professional social workers) are well established, and that a number of demographic, social, and economic trends are likely to result in these functions taking on greater significance in the years ahead.

INDIA

Social welfare services in India

With a population of over 700 million people, India is the second most populous country in the world. The population is expected to be around the 1 billion mark by the year 2000 and it has been observed that India's annual increase of 12 million persons exceeds the total population of more than one hundred member nations of the UN (Indian Council Of Social Welfare 1982: 1). These annual increases in population not only drain national resources but also make it extremely difficult to undertake effective planning and action in the social welfare sphere (Desai 1985). At least 80 per cent of India's population live in rural areas and over 70 per cent live below the poverty line (Nagpaul 1971; *Social Work Today* 1982). The factors that contribute to persistent poverty in countries like India are many and complex and solutions are elusive. While industrialization has been viewed as a key to India's economic progress and social development, the number of persons employed in industry in India comprises only about 10 per cent of the labor force (Moore and Eldridge 1970: 286–90). Over 70 per cent are engaged in the agricultural sector and this population group is largely unorganized, exploited, and poorly paid. These problems are compounded by the fact that "for centuries India has been based on a traditional social structure of caste, delimited social loyalties, and inequalities. Change is being sought both in economic and social development" (Desai 1975: 16–17).

While many factors leading to poverty and disadvantage can be enumerated, a major problem is one of bringing the lowest social and economic groups into the mainstream of national life. Economic inequality is frequently compounded by social inequality. Vestiges of the caste system oppress those who are in the bottom caste, comprising 15 per cent of the population (Government of India 1982: 1). In addition, basic infrastructural problems (for example, access to a potable water supply) and a variety of serious health problems, such as tuberculosis and leprosy, persists (Government of India: Chapters 8 and 9, pages 94–111 in particular). Since social policy and social welfare planning are tied to a country's particular social conditions, one must keep these demographic characteristics in mind when comparing India with other countries in our study.

Before the nineteenth century little organized effort was made to provide welfare services for the people of India. Certain features of Indian society, such as the joint family and the caste system, were suited to the care of the aged, the ill, and the infirm. However, these institutions weakened over time and became less reliable in terms of their informal caring functions.

Mahatma Gandhi, the founding father of modern India, not only advocated nonviolent resistance to colonial rule but also was active in the realm of social justice and social welfare. In 1920 Gandhi had a profound impact on welfare services by attacking the evil of "untouchability" and establishing several institutions for untouchables and lepers. In this, as in other social welfare measures that he and his followers initiated (for example, donations for redistribution among the landless) emphasis was placed on voluntary rather than governmental action (Moore and Eldridge 1970: 161–80).

During British rule, voluntary organizations rather than the State had been the main providers of welfare services. Following independence in 1947, responsibility for social welfare was placed

on the central government and the states. According to the Indian
Constitution, the State "shall strive to promote the welfare of the
people by securing and protecting as effectively as it may a social
order in which justice, social, economic and political, shall form all
the institutions of the national life" (Ministry of Social Welfare
1982: 2).

The central government is responsible for formulating the
nation's policy for social welfare services and for coordinating,
guiding, and promoting the implementation of human services by
the states. However, the bulk of these services is still operated by
the voluntary sector. The Central Social Welfare Board (CSWB)
was created in 1953 to guide and promote voluntary action
throughout the country. In general, it assesses the needs for
services, provides consultation to voluntary human service organizations, and provides financial support for the programs they operate.
The board also promotes the development of voluntary human
service organizations in underserved areas. The grant-in-aid programs
that the CSWB administers support a broad range of human
services, including hostels for working women, welfare extension
programs in rural areas, and adult education courses for women.
Paraprofessional personnel perform important functions and, in
fact, are the main providers of services in most of the programs.

Major factors in use of paraprofessionals

Interviews with social work educators and practitioners (Chowdhry
1985; Desai 1985; Gangrade 1985) confirm the findings of our
international survey which indicate that paraprofessionals have
always been and will almost certainly continue to be the primary
group of front-line workers in the human services in India.
Professionally trained workers are in short supply in urban and
rural areas alike. A recent study by Pathah (1983: 99–100)
revealed that only 10 per cent of social service personnel in Uttar
Pradesh and 20 per cent in Delhi were professionally trained social
workers. The same is probably true in similar relatively developed
or urbanized areas. However, the proportion of professionally
trained workers is even smaller in the more remote rural areas. For
example, in a rural health project that one of the authors visited in
the remote Ahmednagar district of Maharashtra state, less than a
dozen of the more than 700 front-line health workers were
professionally trained (Arole 1985). Professional workers are

reluctant to work in such isolated rural areas which means that the provision of human services is left almost exclusively to paraprofessional personnel.

An additional factor that is said to contribute to the widespread use of paraprofessional personnel in India is the gulf between the "haves" and "have-nots" in an underdeveloped society like this. Social, cultural, and economic differences make it difficult for the professional social worker to work effectively with the rural poor or with urban slum-dwellers. These difficulties are compounded by traditional and clinically oriented social work education that emphasizes individual problems of pathology rather than problems in the context of social development. As we noted in Chapter 2, respondents from India expressed the opinion that there is an "operational incompatibility" between the clinical approach of many professional social workers and the needs of the majority of the people.

Schools of social work and other training centers have not been able to produce enough of the right kind of front-line workers to meet even the partial needs for India's social development. An autonomous educational review committee set up by the government of India to study the social work curriculum has called for substantial change in the focus of social work education (University Grants Commission 1980). Noting that, by concentrating on "assisting people in their adjustment to an industrial urban metropolis dominated social milieu rather than identifying the causes of poverty and working for its removal" (12), the social work profession and the training its practitioners receive do not reflect the country's major problems or the actual needs for which personnel should be trained, the committee concluded that social work schools are not training at the level at which the bulk of the workers should actively be functioning. The need for greater concentration on the training of paraprofessionals is made clear by the committee and it challenged the social work profession in India to take up this task in the years ahead. In the meantime, the paraprofessional (usually indigenous to the community or client population being served) is performing the bulk of front-line human service functions in India.

Child welfare and development

Child welfare and development is a prime example of a human

service field in which indigenous paraprofessional workers play a key role. Children form a large proportion of India's 700 million people: 270 million (40 per cent of the population) are under 14 years old and 109 million (16 per cent) are under 6 (Ministry of Social Welfare 1984: 5). Consequently child welfare and development has been accorded high priority by the government of India. In 1974 a national policy was adopted that created the framework for a comprehensive approach to child development. This resulted in an integrated system of early childhood services that include health check-ups, immunization, supplementary nutrition, referral services, informal pre-school education, and nutrition and health education. By 1984 over 600 of these programs were in operation throughout the country (Chowdhry 1985).

The key participants in the delivery of these integrated child development services are the *anganwadi* workers who are recruited from the local village or community. These workers are familiar with the local traditions and customs and, therefore, are viewed as having advantages over professionals. As one social worker commented: "At first we thought the answer was to employ professionally trained social workers, but many of the professionals were useless. They didn't know how to talk to the poor and expected too much too quickly" (*Social Work Today* 1982: 14). In contrast, the indigenous paraprofessional child-care workers understood the problems faced by local people and could communicate effectively with them about their children's health and development.

In order to ensure that these front-line child development workers are properly prepared for the important work they do the states and the central government, in cooperation with the integrated child development services, operate a number of paraprofessional training centers. By 1985 there were fifty centers throughout India in which both short-term and long-term (up to eleven months) training was provided, including such subjects as pre-school education, recreation, health, nutrition, and neighborhood work.

Paraprofessionals in rural areas

As we have already noted, India is still predominantly a rural society. The rural areas include about 560,000 villages of which nearly 60 per cent have a population of fewer than 500 (Indian

Council of Social Welfare 1982: 1). In the vast rural hinterland, village-level workers perform critical front-line human service functions where the focus is often upon providing a minimum base for community survival. These persons are not professionals but are reported to be effective in dealing with the complexity and diversity of village problems. They enjoy a position of authority in the community, are considered influential by the villagers, and are usually among the first to be aware of "impending crises, such as near starvation, communal tensions and natural calamities" (Singh 1980: 160). They are frequently the first line of defense against serious health problems.

"The majority of health problems in rural areas can be treated but these problems can become worse and even cause death if not identified and treated early. What is needed is a health agent who will conscientiously reach the local people and will prevent serious diseases by bringing about positive change in the habits and attitudes towards illness."

(Arole 1985)

Front-line paraprofessionals perform these vital functions in the villages of India, as well as in urban slums. They provide a wide range of specific medical services. For example in one village visited, they are engaged in the management of leprosy, the prevention of malnutrition, controlling the spread of malaria, and the conservation of safe drinking water (Village Committee 1985).

Unlike the problems encountered in the more developed countries in our study, the difficulties faced in India, particularly in meeting the basic needs of its people, are enormous. For example, over 50 per cent of the rural population is made up of marginal farmers and landless laborers (Prakash 1979: 391). The problem is exacerbated by the limited employment opportunities available to the rural poor. It is also suggested that economic and social development have primarily benefited the less needy segments of society. According to Nanavatty (1981: 266) "the process of development has benefited the middle class and well off farmers against the interest of the landless laborers and marginal farmers." Though social planners have tried to reverse this trend, the obstacles are often formidable. These include a lack of organization at the grassroots level and a tendency to impose solutions from the top down, with little opportunity for people to participate in problem-solving and planning at the village or community level (Prakash 1979: 393).

Nanavatty (1981: 270) acknowledges that in recent years "change has to take place in favor of distribution of ownership of production including land and industries on a wider scale among people". He concludes, however, that in order for this to have much impact on the mass of people the system of distribution requires to be universalized with the help of people's organizations, such as consumer groups, women's organizations, and youth organizations (265–67).

In spite of these obstacles we found examples of positive action at the community level in which paraprofessionals perform vital functions. For example, in a settlement such as Akbarpur, consisting of 101 households with 610 people living in poverty, the most significant contribution by the front-line worker was helping develop an irrigation system that enables farmers to cultivate two crops instead of one (Indian Council of Social Welfare 1982: 1–4). Nanavatty (1981: 272) suggests that supporting the work of such front-line workers is the most valuable role that social workers and other human service professionals could play in India if they are to make any significant contribution to social development, particularly in rural areas.

A similar point is made by D'Souza in relation to community development efforts in deprived urban areas.

"It is essential to train indigenous community personnel if we believe in the philosophical conviction that the community must be helped to work on its own problems through its own local leadership. . . .

Given adequate knowledge, skills and attitudes, local persons belonging to a similar cultural milieu can turn out to be effective change agents in slums . . . playing a front line leadership role."

(D'Souza 1982: 6)

Block development

Some attempts have been made to promote community participation in social development through such initiatives as the block-level planning program. Blocks are geographic entities that are comprised of approximately 100 villages, with a total population of 100,000 and 150,000 persons. The block usually encompasses territories that are homogenous in respect to the socio-ethnic characteristics of the population. This decentralized form of social action is "a successsor of various attempts in the country in the last 30 years to develop an optimal system of grass-roots participatory planning" (Singh 1980: 133; see also Gangrade 1985). The concept was introduced to encourage popular participation in and responsibility for the economic, social, and political development of local communities. The model calls for decentralized planning with specific expectations for community participation. As the Working Group on Block Level Planning (1977–78: 12–13) put it, "The planning team must not only consult the people – which does not mean only their elected representatives – in regard to their felt needs and aspirations but also regarding their resources and potential."

The block planning program is carried out by block officers who are in contact with the rural population through extension workers. The latter include a variety of paraprofessionals such as family welfare officers, welfare inspectors, agricultural officers, village-level workers, child-care workers, and health workers, many of whom perform the critical "life-line" functions described earlier. In addition, many of them play active roles in the organization of the rural poor, women's groups, occupational groups such as bangle-makers and fishermen, and informal caste groupings that provide important information about community problems and crises. The challenges facing those responsible for implementing block level planning are enormous. They must recruit personnel to carry out grassroots functions and, through these front-line workers, achieve block level development goals. This is no easy task for the goals include (1) achieving an increase in income and employment on the block level; (2) obtaining access to adequate health care and medical facilities, drinking water, housing, and essential commodities; (3) developing a social and economic infrastructure to achieve the above objectives; and (4) organizing the poor, especially to protect them from exploitation, and the promotion of a progressively more egalitarian structure of ownership of assets. Addressing goals such as these not only has required a rethinking in the area of social policy and its potential for redistribution but also goes to the very roots of economic policy and social development.

Paraprofessionals and the aged

This brief section focuses on the aging in India. We are including this population group because its accelerating growth has implications for the human services in India and for the personnel who staff them. For example the proportion of people in India aged 65 and above was only 1.5 per cent in 1963. Less than a decade later, the percentage had increased to 3.36 (Ministry of Social Welfare 1982: 23). By the year 2000 the elderly are expected to constitute between 15 and 20 per cent of India's population (Pathasarathy 1980; Dave 1985).

It should be mentioned that the attitude toward the aged in India is somewhat different from that found in Western cultures. India is a society which is not youth oriented. Interdependency among family members and between generations is encouraged from childhood. These supportive functions have to a large extent helped reduce the social and emotional problems of the aging. Dependency on the younger generation is accepted and often cherished, but change is occurring. While the caring functions of the joint family are still strong in India, they are losing some of their efficacy as a result of modernization. There are already many elderly persons who lack adequate shelter and care and are living in poverty (Sengupta 1976). Nagpaul (1971: 12–14) notes that while the traditional joint family continues to take care of its elderly, frail, and sick members, there are situations where this does not occur. "Where family incomes are inadequate or there is no family or where the family has failed to accept the responsibility for the aged and the infirm . . . and this is likely to increase if traditional social institutions are seriously affected by the processes of urbanization and industrialization." In the face of these developments, India is likely to have to expand its formal systems of care for its growing elderly population, just as other countries that we studied are having to do. These expanded systems of social care can be expected to increase the need for front-line paraprofessional human service personnel.

We are aware that the complex problems mentioned in this introductory section on India cannot be solved by front-line parapro-fessionals. Broad programs of economic and social development will be required if the life situation of the mass of people in a country like India is going to be improved (Conyers 1982;

Roxborough 1982). However, we believe that front-line paraprofessionals are providing vital human services to urban and rural
communities and that they have an important place in the social
development of India.

ISRAEL

Historical background

Myrdal (1963: 62) observed that "the welfare state is nowhere as
yet an accomplishment; it is continuously in the process of coming
into being." The nature of the modern welfare state is, in Myrdal's
view, constantly evolving. Its planners and architects are continuously
engaged in the process of refining it in order to improve its
effectiveness and efficiency. Israel has seen continuous evolution in
the welfare arena. From the first large influx of European
immigrants at the beginning of the century, through the creation of
the state in 1948, up until the present day, new social welfare
policies and programs have been designed and a variety of social
legislation enacted. Over this period, new thinking about society's
role and its relationship to its needy citizens emerged.

A major influence on welfare thinking at the turn of the twentieth
century were the 40,000 Jewish immigrants who came to Palestine
in 1904 to escape growing oppression in several Eastern European
countries. Pogroms and repression that followed the assassination
of Alexander II of Russia, limitations on Jewish autonomy in
Poland, and restrictions of Jewish trade in Romania, were among the
events that caused Theodor Herzel to advocate a homeland for the
Jewish people. The young men and women who arrived in 1904
were primarily committed to building the land and spoke of
kibbush-ha-avodah – conquest through labor. This meant the
establishment of a national economy with an all-embracing
productive and organizational framework. It implied that the
individual was not only to advocate national revival but also to
settle in the land as a pioneer. He or she should be prepared to
do any kind of work, no matter how arduous and dangerous.
Furthermore, it was a matter of principle that only those who lived
by their own labor and did not exploit the work of others were to
be considered legitimate members of the new community. This deep

commitment to labor became the sacred inheritance of all ensuing pioneers who came to build the land.

The ideology of labor as a spiritual end was advocated by A. D. Gordon, a secular mystic, born in Russia, who came to Palestine in 1904. He conveyed the essence of the labor ethic in the following terms:

> "The Jewish people have been completely cut off from nature and imprisoned within city walls these two thousand years. We have become accustomed to every form of life except to a life of labor. . . . We lack the habit of labor – not labor performed out of external compulsion but labor to which one is attached in a natural and organic way."
>
> (Gordon 1960: 374)

Ideologies, however, are transformed by the realities of everyday life (Mannheim 1968) and, in the long struggle for statehood from 1904 to 1948, the pioneer groups recognized the need for pragmatic responses to emerging situations as they worked toward achievement of their goals (Schindler 1981). In the social welfare sphere this meant developing an array of services and institutions to meet the needs of persons who could not stand up to the demands of building a new society through labor. These institutions included health clinics, consumer cooperatives, funds for disabled and unemployed people, support for the elderly, and disability assistance.

Although these services were generally selective, they included features of modern human welfare organizations. For example, the health services that were introduced in 1912 operated on the insurance principle, with members having rights to benefits. Accountability and the absence of a profit motive were two important features of the program. Detailed financial accounts were forwarded by the local health clinics to the central office (Kupat Holim 1913). It should be noted, however, that these health and other services organized by the labor groups were not universal. Persons who qualified as members of the pioneering group were entitled to benefits, others were not. About 70 per cent of the Jewish community in Palestine were non-labor affiliated (Kanev 1951; 1975). This necessitated the development of alternative public services and it was through these that the non-affiliated received benefits and help in times of need.

Many of the day-to-day activities in the health clinics and

hospitals (both labor-affiliated and public) were carried out by paraprofessionals (Ben Ahron 1976). Professional nursing services were in their infancy and social work would not emerge as a profession until the mid-1950s, with schools of social work being planned and established at that time. Aides (as volunteers or paid employees) not only assisted nurses and doctors but also served as an important link with patients' families.

Growth of the public services and the emergence of human service workers

The person responsible for the initiative and development of public welfare services was Henrietta Szold. Szold was born in the USA and at the age of 60 settled in Palestine. She was a humanitarian, a reformer, and an advocate for the poor and indigent. Szold was determined to improve the quality of life for all citizens.

In 1930 through Szold's leadership, the *Vaad Leumi* – the National Executive Council of the Jewish Community in Palestine – was instrumental in the establishment of a Department of Social Services. Within this department were created social welfare bureaus that had the following mandate:

> "Not only to devise and dispense constructive relief, but actually to be pension master to the old, the blind, the maimed, the paralysed, the chronically sick, the invalid that cannot be trained even to the lightest form of productive work, and especially to widows and children."
>
> (Department of Social Services 1932: 5)

Three years after the Department of Social Services was founded, over 30,000 people (nearly 12 per cent of the population) were being served by welfare bureaus (Social Services in Knesset Israel 1946).

With the growth of the local bureaus a policy of some significance relating to the treatment of welfare recipients began to emerge. From the early development of local bureaus, the provision of cash benefits was accompanied by some form of counseling. The question of who precisely was to help people solve their problems became an issue of some significance. Szold had her own perspective on this question:

> "It is one of the most interesting questions in modern social

service – the relation of the volunteer to the professional and
vice versa. Social service has sometimes been in danger of
becoming mechanized . . . it can be averted if the volunteer is
retained and if he brings to the task an instructed mind as well as
natural feeling."

(Szold 1931)

One can understand the positive view expounded by Szold in
relation to voluntarism, since she was the architect and founder
of *Hadassah*, the largest Jewish women's voluntary organization
in the USA. A strong voluntary sector was advocated in view of
the magnitude and persistence of the social problems facing the
Jewish community. It was believed that the best results could be
achieved if volunteers worked side by side with professionals. In
time paid non-professional persons were engaged to join the fight
against human suffering. Many of these nonprofessionals worked
together with the volunteers in *gescholssenc Fuersarge*, residential
welfare services. Child placement services and youth villages,
homes for elderly people, and treatment centers for juvenile delinquents were other typical agencies that employed non-professional
staff.

Nonprofessionals also played a role within the local welfare
bureaus which were developing dramatically in the 1930s and
1940s. In these and other settings, professional and nonprofessional
functions were not well delineated and there was a great deal of
overlap between the tasks they performed. A number of reasons
account for this. As we have already noted, social work as a
profession was beginning to develop only in the 1930s. An institute
for the training of social workers was established by the Department
of Social Services in 1934 but a theoretical base in social work was
only in its formative stages. In addition, the nature and dimensions
of emerging social problems, particularly in relation to the plight
of immigrants fleeing Nazi Germany, required every helping hand,
both professional and nonprofessional.

With the creation of the State in 1948, social work began to gain
increasing recognition as a profession. Paraprofessionals continued
to be employed in the social services but without much support
from social workers. It was not until the 1970s that the place, role,
and function of paraprofessional personnel became an important
issue in the delivery of human services in Israel.

Contemporary period

As is the case in many other countries, paraprofessionals in Israel work in a host of social service agencies, from public welfare bureaus to rehabilitation centers; from child-care clinics to clubs for the elderly. Their use has recently increased (and in a sense has been legitimized) as a result of their involvement in Project Renewal, the major rural and urban rehabilitation program initiated by the government in 1977 that we have already mentioned. An interdisciplinary effort among architects, planners, and social workers, Project Renewal has sought to rehabilitate a number of poor neighborhoods and communities. At the time of writing, about ninety urban and rural communities are undergoing improvement (International Committee for the Evaluation of Project Renewal 1983).

It is important to consider the factors that prompted the use of paraprofessionals in Project Renewal. Shortages of professional social workers was an important element, as a former executive secretary of the Israeli Association of Social Workers has noted:

"In our opinion there is a grave shortage of manpower in this country. These shortages include all fields of practice. There has not been a significant increase of social workers in relation to the growth of the population. Nor will there be sufficient personnel to meet the growing social problems and expanding social services of this country."

(Kadmon 1981: 2–3)

Thirty per cent of the Project Renewal budget is earmarked for social and other enrichment programs. These activities cover a broad spectrum of individual, group, and community services. Many of the services have had to be staffed by paraprofessionals since there are insufficient numbers of professionally trained social workers available. This situation is reflected throughout the human services in Israel and it is likely that paraprofessionals will play an increasingly important role in dealing with the growing social problems that Israel is facing. These problems have been exacerbated by decreases in the number of established positions for social workers in the welfare sector. For example in 1977 2,860 social work positions were designated for local, municipal, and national welfare services; this number was increased to 3,100 in 1979, and then cut back to 2,200 in 1985 because of government austerity measures (Silverstein 1985).

A working paper of the Israeli Association of Social Workers (1981) has recognized the significance of the personnel shortages and, in a sense, has sanctioned the employment of paraprofessionals. It acknowledges the necessity of recruiting "block workers, club leaders, aides for the elderly, big brother and sister personnel to be employed in Project Renewal" (1–2).

The use of paraprofessionals, however, has not been an outcome of personnel shortages alone. There is growing recognition that if Project Renewal is to succeed there must be an integration of physical and social service planning. At present most agencies in Israel have not coordinated their planning with that of other government agencies. Project Renewal requires that each local community submit an integrated plan within which physical renovation and building must be accompanied by appropriate social and community services. Physical change without corresponding social services, it is suggested, will only bring about a renewal of the poverty cycle (Jaffe 1981).

Integrated planning has also stressed local citizen participation, recognizing that community residents must become part of the decision-making process. A recent report by the International Committee for the Evaluation of Project Renewal (1983) places particular emphasis on this vital dimension. The committee states that "Rehabilitation should be accomplished with and by (rather than for) neighborhood residents. The residents should be involved in planning and implementation" (4). Particular emphasis is placed upon the use of the indigenous paraprofessional, that is recruiting persons with socio-economic or cultural backgrounds similar to the client population. It is believed that community residents have a basic right to take part in the planning and operation of programs relevant to their lives. This principle has become well established in the human services by now. As Magill and Clark (1975: 43) have noted, "sub-sectors of a community may be defined as benefiting to the degree that programs are consistent with their preferences." Therefore programs "should be formulated in terms desirable to the major sub-groups within the community." Communities themselves have begun to expect to be involved. For example, persons living in Ofakim, a development town in the northern Negev region of Israel, have asserted that "effective community development and viable community life depend on the active involvement of community members and on their self functioning" (Ben Gurion University of the Negev 1981: 2; also Minasheri 1981; 1982).

The increasing use of paraprofessionals in Israel is also an outcome of the characteristic social and cultural differences that exist between professional social workers and their clients. A study by Sali and Harel (1978) indicates that professional social workers in this country are predominantly of European and US backgrounds while their clients are primarily from Asian and African countries. In a similar vein, it has been suggested that the middle-class orientation of professionals may make it difficult for them to communicate effectively with and understand fully their lower-class clients (Etgar 1980). An additional barrier to effective service is the difference in values and expectations between service providers and service recipients. For example the Ministry of Social Welfare has a clear policy that clients must show indications of change if they are to continue to receive help. A perceived lack of progress can disqualify them from further service. However, many lower-class and ethnic minority families subscribe to values and follow life styles that are in conflict with official expectations, thereby jeopardizing their rights to such benefits as income maintenance, health care, and housing. Consequently many welfare families are trapped in poverty and cannot easily break the cycle. It is felt that some of these problems can be overcome by employing skilled paraprofessionals on the local level who share class, cultural, and ethnic backgrounds with the clients in question.

Paraprofessionals in the human services

In Israel today one can find paraprofessionals working with a wide spectrum of client groups in a variety of human service settings, including neighborhood services (such as Project Renewal), social welfare bureaus, mental health centers, informal settings for early childhood education, community centers, homes and centers for the aged, correctional institutions, rehabilitation centers, counseling and family service agencies, and residential and community centers for retarded people.

The role of paraprofessionals in services to multi-problem families is especially noteworthy. Multi-problem families have been helped by paraprofessionals since the establishment of the social services in this country and they continue to be important in this area. They are referred to as *Somhot*, literally someone to lean on or family aides, they operate out of social welfare agencies, and are generally recruited from similar social and cultural backgrounds as their clients. Family aides are expected to support the family in its daily activities within the home and facilitate access to other services in the community. In addition, multi-problem families are helped in urban and rural renewal projects by paraprofessionals who serve as neighborhood or block workers and operate out of local community centers under the auspices of public housing organizations.

There is increased recognition in Israel of the need to provide educational enrichment programs for children from early infancy up to the age of 6. Paraprofessional personnel are trained to assist parents to enrich their children's cognitive and motor skills and facilitate their integration into primary school. There are two major programs of this type in Israel today which are referred to as *Hatav*, that is guidance in the development of toddlers aged 1 to 3 years, and *Etgar*, guiding mothers in early childhood education aged 4 to 6 years. These programs are discussed in some detail in later chapters.

Paraprofessionals are also important in those personal social services that are designed to help individuals who are coping with special physical and psychological problems. For example, they help mentally retarded people, ex-prisoners, and alcoholics. Paraprofessionals outnumber professionals in these services by a considerable margin.

In addition to the above examples of paraprofessional acitivity, an area of human service employment that is becoming increasingly important is in programs needed to support Israel's expanding elderly population. This has grown from 3.9 per cent in 1948 to 6.7 per cent in 1967 and reached 8 per cent in 1973 (Doron 1976). By 1982 the population aged 65 and over was approximately 10 per cent, with the group over 75 years of age growing fastest (Central Bureau of Statistics 1984).

A national survey of this population published a decade ago indicated that many elderly persons are isolated, physically and psychologically. The survey found that 73.7 per cent of the elderly lived by themselves while only 26.5 per cent lived with other people. Among the single aged, 50 per cent lived alone (Ministry of Social Welfare 1975). Though efforts have been made to extend social activities to this group, a stark absence of community facilities is noted. For example, a survey of two major cities in Israel, Beersheba in the south and Petah Tikvah near Tel Aviv, indicated that over 90 per cent of the elderly did not use or visit any community clubs. Of these, 55 per cent indicated they had no social club in their neighborhood and 70 per cent reported that they had no access to a social service center (S. Cohen and Morgenstein 1974).

In recent years clubs for the aged have become recognized as valuable forms of community support for elderly people. The first such club was founded in 1950 and, by 1974, 137 were in operation in 66 localities, with a permanent membership of close to 12,000 (Ministry of Social Welfare 1974–75). It is estimated, however, that only about 7 per cent of the entire aged population uses these facilities. A major problem has been finding personnel to direct and staff these centers. A survey of social clubs in 1971 showed that only thirteen out of a hundred clubs were open for the entire day, while the rest were open only in the afternoon or evening. The majority of the personnel who operated these programs were paraprofessionals and there was reported to be an urgent need for additional staff (Tarmovski 1971). Among the broad range of supportive services that will be needed for Israel's expanding aging population, social service centers or clubs are but one area where demand for paraprofessional personnel is likely to be high.

Finally, it is important to note that in Israel today thousands of families are facing economic strain. The Central Bureau of Statistics (1984) projects that by April 1986 the number of unemployed will reach 8.3 per cent or 115,000 members of the work force. Other projections are even more pessimistic, suggesting that 150,000 persons representing approximately 10 per cent of the working population will be unemployed. Furthermore, increasing numbers of wage-earners are requesting supplementary income from the National Insurance Institute, on account of economic hardship. These developments suggest that accelerating social problems and challenges will confront the human services system in the years ahead, all of which will require substantial numbers of additional personnel, both professional and paraprofessional.

United States of America

A number of factors have been important in contributing to the widespread use of paraprofessional personnel in the human services in the USA. These include the emergence during the 1960s of the human services as a major source of employment in the US economy, a shortage of professionally trained human service personnel, the New Careers movement that was part of the Federal Government's War on Poverty, and substantial evidence that paraprofessionals could play valuable front-line roles in the human services.

EMPLOYMENT IN THE HUMAN SERVICES

The need to provide sources of employment for the worker who was rapidly being displaced by automation and for minority and other disadvantaged groups who were not being absorbed by the existing labor market was under close scrutiny in the 1960s. Studies of the labor market began to focus on the creation of new types of jobs that would no longer rely on private industry as the principal source of employment, but on the helping services as the sector with the greatest potential for absorbing growing numbers of workers (David 1965). As one observer put it, "if more jobs are a major anti-poverty tool, the service fields must become for the minorities and the disadvantaged of our day what the railroads were to the Irish or the needletrades were to the Jews in the past" (Feldstein 1968: 2).

Many studies pointed out that the human services were among the areas of employment least likely to be susceptible to automation. The human services had the virtue of being very broad in scope, encompassing as they did the large and expanding fields of social welfare, education, and health care. All areas of human service activity were experiencing a critical shortage of trained personnel and population projections indicated that the demand for services would continue to grow. In addition, there was perceived to be a pressing need to improve the quality of welfare, education, and health services. This was expected to result in a need for many more people if services were to be provided more effectively. In short, the human services were viewed as a rapidly expanding field with enormous employment potential (US Department of Labor 1967).

Shortages of trained human service personnel

Among the studies of the human service labor force that were influential in establishing the need for expanded use of paraprofessionals was *Closing The Gap . . . in Social Work Manpower* (US Department of Health, Education, and Welfare 1965). Considered a landmark document on social welfare personnel at the time, this report subsequently proved to be overly optimistic in its projections of future growth in the human services and corresponding demands for personnel. However, it did provide an accurate picture of current needs for trained staff, estimated future shortages that would exist if current and projected service needs were to be adequately met, and helped legitimize the place of the paraprofessional in the human services.

The mental health services provide one example of many human service fields that began to absorb increasing numbers of paraprofessional personnel in the 1960s. While a 1959 report that had been prepared for the Joint Commission on Mental Illness and Health dealing with the shortages of personnel in the field of mental health was concerned primarily with the inadequate supply of psychiatrists, psychologists, psychiatric nurses, and social workers needed to staff the existing mental health facilities and with the future implications of such shortages as mental health services were expanded to meet projected needs, its author, Albee (1959) made it clear that the manpower gap in the mental health field was not going to be filled by the traditional professionals.

In its final report to the United States Congress, the Joint Commission concurred with Albee's conclusions that new kinds of mental health personnel would have to be found, especially in light of its major recommendation that a new comprehensive system of community-based mental health services be established (Joint Commission on Mental Illness and Health 1961).

Although the Joint Commission recognized that certain forms of therapeutic activities should be performed only by persons with the highest levels of professional preparation, it recommended strongly that a broad range of people with different kinds of training should be recruited to the mental health field. The recommendations of the Joint Commission and the subsequent legislation creating community mental health centers throughout the nation revolutionized the way mental health services were organized and staffed. New personnel resources began to be tapped, including the recruitment and training of large numbers of paraprofessionals (many of whom were local community residents) to provide a wide range of mental health services.

The new careers movement

As part of the US government's "War on Poverty," a 1966 amendment to the Economic Opportunity Act of 1964 instituted what came to be known as the New Careers program in an effort to engage the poor and other disadvantaged groups in meaningful employment, primarily in the human services. According to its proponents, the "New Careers" movement had the following goals:

"1 A sufficient number of jobs for all persons without work.
 2 The jobs to be so defined and distributed that placements exist for the unskilled and uneducated.
 3 The jobs to be permanent and provide opportunity for life-long careers.
 4 An opportunity for the motivated and talented poor to advance from low-skill entry jobs to any station available to the more favored members of society.
 5 The work to contribute to the well-being of society."

(Pearl and Riessman 1965: 2)

Not only were the persons who were recruited into human service jobs given in-service training but adult education opportunities leading to the attainment of high school equivalency were provided for those persons who, after they had obtained employment, wanted to upgrade their educational status. This was carried further to support the efforts of many participants to pursue further education by taking college courses.

"if New Careers are to be meaningful channels for employment, educational advancement has to be created. The non-professional aide must easily be able to become the sub-professional technical assistant and to move from there into full professional status, if he has capabilities and desire."

(MacLennan 1965: 110)

The emergence during the 1960s of the community colleges as a major force in US higher education (Gleazer 1968) provided a readily available means for the "new careerists" to move beyond the aide or entry level into more demanding positions in the human services. In the mid-1960s the interest of the National Institute of Mental Health (NIMH) in finding ways to increase the supply of trained mental health workers led to community colleges being given an important role in mental health training. The close ties that community colleges had with their community was seen as having much in common with the community mental health movement. Partially as a result of the financial support provided for a number of pilot programs by NIMH, two-year associate degree programs in community colleges emerged as a significant training resource for paraprofessional personnel not only in the mental health field but also in the broader human services (Feldstein 1968; Brawley and Schindler 1972; Brawley 1975).

The community college programs provided a critical point of entry into or continuation of careers in the human services for large numbers of "new careerists" during the late 1960s and early 1970s. They continue to serve this function for significant numbers of minority-group and low-income students. In general, they provide an important step in the educational career ladder for the paraprofessional group as a whole (Brawley 1981a).

The unique role of the paraprofessional

Primarily as a result of the New Careers movement, there was a radical redefinition of who could and who should be involved in the provision of human services. For the first time, large numbers of low-income and minority group members were enabled to carry significant direct service roles in health care, mental health, social welfare, and education. These new kinds of staff often shared ethnic, cultural, socio-economic, and other characteristics with the clients of human service agencies and frequently lived in the same neighborhoods. The unique contribution that these indigenous paraprofessionals could make to the human services was seen as being particularly valuable. Social workers and other professionals recognized that not only could they fill gaps left by shortages of professional staff but also they could "bridge gaps with clients and provide service organizations with skills congenial to client populations" (Grosser, Henry, and Kelly 1969: 5). The long-

standing shortage of trained personnel in the human services ceased
to be viewed solely as a need for more holders of professional
qualifications. For example the social work profession resolved a
long-standing internal debate and decided that it was possible to
prepare workers for the social services with less than graduate
education and that this need not lead to a lowering of the standards
of service offered. In fact it was suggested, though not necessarily
widely believed, that, given the proper preparation of the new
workers and the development of appropriate ways of deploying
them, a qualitative as well as quantitative improvement in service
might result (Briggs 1973b: 11). At any rate, the place of
paraprofessionals was given formal recognition by the National
Association of Social Workers (NASW) in a six-level personnel
classification system that included two paraprofessional and four
professional levels:

1 *Social Service Aide* – no specific educational preparation
  required.
2 *Social Service Technician* – usually requiring a two-year
  associate degree in a social services area or a bachelor's degree
  in some other field.
3 *Social Worker* – requiring a bachelor's degree from an
  accredited social work program (BSW)
4 *Graduate Social Worker* – requiring a master's degree from
  an accredited social work program (MSW).
5 *Certified Social Worker* – requiring membership in the Academy
  of Certified Social Workers (ACSW).
6 *Social Work Fellow* – usually requiring a doctorate in social
  work (DSW) or extensive experience beyond the ACSW level.
        (National Association of Social Workers 1974: 5)

The purpose of this system was "to help bring order and uniformity
to the personnel classification systems of social agencies, enable
more appropriate utilization of personnel, and provide more
effective service," on the assumption that "the optimum effectiveness in the provision of most social services requires the use of
various levels of competence" (Alexander 1975: 5).

By the middle of the 1960s a great many articles had begun to
appear in the social work and related literature on the subject of
paraprofessionals in the human services. These articles either
reported examples of the use of paraprofessionals or advocated

their increased use on various grounds, usually the continuing shortage of professional workers or the unique contribution that the paraprofessional could make. Barker and Briggs (1966) reviewed almost 200 publications reporting the use of non-professionals in social welfare settings and found that most of these indicated that certain tasks, traditionally carried out by professionals, could be delegated to others without professional training or that professional services could be supplemented by the additional work that paraprofessionals could do. By the beginning of the 1970s substantial research evidence was accumulating on the valuable contribution that paraprofessionals could make to the human services. Gartner (1971) reported the results of studies of parapro-fessionals' work performance in a variety of human service fields to support his thesis that the introduction and innovative use of these new kinds of personnel led to qualitative as well as quantitative benefits for the clients of human services.

Similarly, in a study of the roles of over 100,000 paraprofessionals working in 185 mental health settings, Sobey (1970: 174) found that paraprofessional workers were contributing to mental health service provision in two ways: "(1) filling new roles based on patient needs which were previously unfulfilled by any staff; and (2) performing parts of tasks previously performed by professionals, but tailoring the task to the non-professionals' abilities." The combination of the two roles was seen as resulting in a "task gestalt" unique to the paraprofessional. Specifically paraprofessionals were providing such services as "individual counseling, group counseling, activity group therapy, milieu therapy, and case finding; playing screening roles of a non-clerical nature; helping people adjust to community life; providing tutoring services; and promoting client self-help activity" (Sobey 1970: vi). Subsequent studies have confirmed that paraprofessionals were being used effectively in a wide range of roles in a variety of human service fields (Hirayama 1975; Austin 1978; Alley et al. 1978; Robin and Wagenfeld 1981).

Current status of the paraprofessional

Despite the positive results achieved by paraprofessional human service personnel in the USA, a number of factors that contributed to their introduction into human service employment in large numbers during the 1960s are less salient in the more conservative climate of the 1980s. These developments have tended to diminish professional and organizational support of paraprofessionals and undermine their status and security. For example, recent US government policy has been to limit the scope of the human services rather than to expand them in order to address unmet needs or to create jobs for the unemployed. At the same time that growth in the human service sector has been curtailed, the supply of professionally trained personnel has expanded. This has resulted in a tighter job market for social workers and other human service professionals, leading them to see less need for paraprofessional personnel and to be less supportive of them (Brawley 1980).

In his study of paraprofessionals in community mental health and neighborhood health centers, Hirayama (1975: 126) found that, while professional workers gave high ratings to the job performance of paraprofessionals, "the predominant attitudes of professionals [were] superiority and indifference toward the non-professional" and he raised questions about "the centers' commitment to the continuing and best use of these workers." Citing such factors as federal funding cutbacks, a more conservative mood in US society, and a diminished commitment to racial equality (88 per cent of the paraprofessionals in this study were Black or Hispanic), Hirayama concluded that the paraprofessionals' status, jobs, and career prospects were not as secure as one would expect based on the quality of their reported performance (126–27).

The lack of long-range commitment to the paraprofessional that Hirayama found in community mental health centers and neighborhood health centers appears to apply in other settings also. In their study of the impact of federal anti-poverty funds on voluntary social agencies, Lambert and Lambert (1970) found that traditional social work agencies had tended not to incorporate paraprofessionals into their regular service and budget operations, even though they had had extensive positive experience using them. A similar theme emerged from Austin's (1978) study of professionals and paraprofessionals employed in family, neighborhood, and community health services in six US cities. Again, the performance of the paraprofessionals was rated highly by the professional workers in the agencies studied. However, the paraprofessionals had not been integrated into the agencies' personnel systems with appropriately defined functions, permanent positions, and opportunities for career advancement and Austin was at a loss to understand "why it is taking agencies so long to adapt administrative practices to this new personnel thrust" (237–38). In the absence of the necessary systemic changes, and faced with decreased support from social workers and other human service professionals, the status of the paraprofessionals remains somewhat precarious.

Nevertheless, few authorities expect paraprofessionals to disappear from the human services in the USA. For example, the President's Commission on Mental Health (1978) sees them as having performed a very valuable function in the delivery of mental health services and expects them to continue to do so. Noting that "more than half of the personnel in mental health are paraprofessionals," Gartner (1981: 53–4) states that they are "no longer exceptional." Paraprofessionals have become an integral part of the human services in the USA. What remains to be done is to formalize their presence, define clearly the roles and functions that they should carry, ensure that they have appropriate training and career advancement opportunities, and integrate them properly into human service personnel systems.

DISCUSSION

The international survey that we conducted in 1983 revealed that a variety of factors had contributed to widespread use of paraprofessional personnel in the human services throughout the world. These included historical or current shortages of professionally trained personnel, the unique contribution that paraprofessionals (especially those who share common characteristics with client groups) were purported to make to human service provision, recognition that not all human service tasks required professionally trained workers to carry them out, and the need to create employment opportunities for groups that had not or could not be absorbed in the employment market. The importance of these different factors varied among the countries included in our international survey. Some factors (for example shortages of professionally trained personnel) were fairly widespread and were critical issues in some countries, particularly the less developed nations. Other factors (for example the need to create new and expanded job opportunities for significant portions of a nation's work force) were less commonly cited as important and, where cited, tended to be particularly salient in the more developed parts of the world. It also appeared that certain factors were important at certain times and not important at others. In looking at four countries in detail, we hoped to be able to clarify which factors were the most enduring and the most universal.

In all four countries that we studied in depth a shortage of professionally trained social work personnel has been an important factor contributing to the use of paraprofessionals. This has been less important (relatively speaking) in Britain and Israel than in the USA and India. In India it continues to be an overriding reality, particularly in remote rural areas. This situation is not likely to change much in the foreseeable future. In the USA this was a major argument advanced during the 1960s for greater use of paraprofessional personnel. With a greatly expanded pool of professionally trained personnel, a seriously curtailed commitment to human service provision, and a corresponding contraction of the human service job market during the 1970s and 1980s, this factor has become less salient.

If this were the only factor determining the use of paraprofessional personnel, then their use could simply be viewed as a temporary phenomenon, a transitory expedient until sufficient professionally trained personnel become available or as an unfortunate but unavoidable compromise dictated by a country's limited resources that prevent it from making professional help available to all persons who need it. Some observers, particularly in the USA, would put this construction on the paraprofessional movement and would conclude that while they may continue to be an important factor in human service delivery in countries like India, they are no longer needed, or indeed desirable, in the USA. Under this interpretation, other arguments for the use of paraprofessional personnel (the unique contribution of the paraprofessional, identification of tasks that do not need professional-level skills, and so on) are viewed as a natural tendency to make virtue out of necessity or thinly veiled excuses for cutting costs.

However, when we look at the use of paraprofessional personnel in different countries, it becomes clear that they are no mere expedient. There appear to be characteristics intrinsic to (1) the nature of much of the work that is done in the human service field, and (2) the nature of a large proportion of paraprofessional workers that makes it both appropriate and desirable that the latter form a significant and permanent element of the human service work force in all countries.

First, in all four countries we studied in detail, it is clear that there are many human service tasks and functions that can be adequately performed by persons who do not have professional training and skills. For example, in Britain, where most jobs that call for professionally trained social workers are now filled by professionally qualified personnel, the bulk of the work of local authority social services departments (the core of the human service delivery system) is performed by persons we would define as paraprofessionals. While there has been a national commitment (largely fulfilled) to produce enough trained social workers to meet the need for this level of worker, there has also been recognition that there is a wide range of tasks that can be performed by other kinds of personnel. This decision does not appear to have been based on expediency or on cost considerations but on an analysis of the range of tasks and functions that have to be performed. Clearly in Britain the use of paraprofessional personnel is not viewed as a temporary stop-gap until sufficient professionally trained workers are available or as a way of reducing the costs of providing services. Paraprofessionals are seen as an integral part of the human service work force because there are many tasks and functions that they are perfectly capable of performing. Research on human service staff differentiation carried out in the USA in the 1960s (mentioned briefly in this chapter and discussed more fully in the next) supports this view.

Many of the tasks and functions that are viewed as appropriate for paraprofessionals in Britain are those that primarily involve the provision of concrete assistance to particularly vulnerable populations or tending and caring for the very young, the very old, or disabled people in institutions, in day treatment centers, or in their own homes. Demographic trends in all four countries examined here are expected to increase the need for these kinds of services. Especially in Britain and the USA, but also to a significant degree in India and Israel, there have been and will continue to be increases in the number and proportion of elderly and frail persons at a time when changes in family roles, including the increased participation of women (the traditional care-givers) in the employment market, are reducing the availability of informal care. New systems of care are having to be developed to meet the needs of these populations. These developments are creating jobs for people who can perform tending and caring functions, for example, home helps, care assistants, staff of senior citizen centers, family aides, and day care workers. The nature of the work to be performed in these expanded systems of care, major growth areas of the human services, are appropriate for the paraprofessional.

When we turn to the characteristics of paraprofessional personnel that make them particularly valuable in human service provision, we find that in all four countries the indigenous factor is recognized as being important. A major impetus behind the paraprofessional movement in the USA in the 1960s was a desire to reach disadvantaged minority groups that the traditional professionals had not been able to serve. This is also a major factor in the use of paraprofessional personnel in India and Israel. It is less true in Britain, although it is beginning to be mentioned as the new "patch" or neighborhood-based systems of social service delivery are developed and it may become more important as the needs of Britain's racial minority groups receive more attention.

In all of these countries, it is noted that paraprofessional helpers are more likely than professionals to share class, cultural, ethnic, racial, and other characteristics with their clients. Whether it is class and accent in Britain, language and religious affiliation in India, racial and cultural characteristics in the USA, or ethnic and socio-economic background in Israel, it is reported that the gaps or barriers between paraprofessional workers and their clients are not as great as those that exist between professional workers and certain client populations, often the most needy. When the paraprofessional is a member of the community that is being served, when he or she speaks the language and shares the experience and outlook of the person who is to be helped, it is assumed that the help offered will be more appropriate, more readily accepted, and more effective.

Another aspect of the indigenous dimension is the belief in both India and Israel that there is a need to involve people at the grassroots in any effort to transform deprived communities into viable entities. If poor rural communities and urban slums are to be helped effectively, one important aspect of the process is to provide local persons with the skills needed to become agents of change. In other words, community residents can play an effective front-line leadership role in community development efforts.

Finally, it is important to reaffirm the developmental potential of employing large numbers of paraprofessional workers in human service occupations. As we have noted earlier in this chapter, the paraprofessional human service jobs that were created in the USA in the 1960s for persons who were not being absorbed by the labor market as a result of major changes in the structure of the economy, the training that these workers received and the services that they were able to provide were part of a policy that reflected a major commitment to social, economic, and human development. While the national commitment to this job development strategy of expanded human service employment has largely disappeared, the need for such a policy has not, in the light of continuing failures of national economies on a global scale to make the best use of human capital.

5

Role definitions and utilization patterns

An attempt is made in this chapter to develop a clear picture of the tasks performed by different kinds of paraprofessional workers in each country, to examine common personnel utilization patterns that have emerged, and to identify promising conceptual approaches to the division of labor between professional and paraprofessional human service personnel. One of our primary purposes is to identify and analyze existing theoretical approaches to personnel deployment in the human services (particularly in Britain and the USA) in order to clarify and strengthen the contribution that the paraprofessional can make to any country's human service system.

BRITAIN

A government-sponsored study of the activities of area teams in local authority social services departments in Britain (Stevenson and Parsloe 1978) noted that, in addition to social workers, a variety of paraprofessional personnel are involved in the provision of social services at the local level. The composition of the teams that were studied typically included "not just social workers but family aides, social work assistants, unqualified social workers and staff who may have had a different training, such as community workers or . . . occupational therapists" (Parsloe 1978: 352). Typical roles of paraprofessional social service personnel in Britain are examined here, building upon the preliminary descriptions of social services departments, area teams, patch teams, and types of paraprofessional personnel that were provided earlier. Particular attention is given to ways in which functions, tasks, or activities are allocated among different categories of social service personnel, in both theoretical and practical terms.

Paraprofessional roles

One respondent to our international survey noted that there are so many specific job titles for paraprofessional social service workers in Britain that a comprehensive listing would fill several pages. The more common job titles include residential child-care worker, residential care assistant (for elderly people), home help, day centre worker (with physically and mentally handicapped people), youth worker, community worker, welfare assistant, social work assistant, social services officer, ancillary worker, family aide, and hostel warden. The types of roles and functions which they typically perform include residential care of children and the elderly, day center services for physically and mentally handicapped people, domiciliary care for elderly and disabled people, youth work, probation and after-care of offenders, general community work, and social casework.

In all service areas, paraprofessionals work directly with clients. In some instances their roles and tasks are quite distinct from those of professional social workers; in other cases, the differences are not as obvious. For example, many are engaged in direct "care-giving" or "tending" roles with children, handicapped people, and the frail elderly. Their direct service activities are usually practical and focused on a client's physical needs, although they also involve attention to the client's emotional well-being. This is the case with the home helps, care assistants, and wardens whose activities were mentioned in the last chapter. The importance of "tending" and "caring-for" functions for certain kinds of clients is being increasingly recognized in Britain, as reflected in the national training initiatives (described in Chapter 7) that have been mounted in relation to home helps, care assistants in homes for the elderly, wardens of sheltered housing for elderly and handicapped people, and the staff of homes for children and young people. As Parker (1981: 29) notes, while tending and caring may involve basically simple activities, they often also "entail complicated and demanding relationships that have to be nurtured with considerable sensitivity and skill."

While it is relatively easy to distinguish the tasks and activities of home helps, care assistants, wardens of sheltered housing, and residential child-care staff from the tasks and functions of professional social workers, the distinctions are less obvious in the case of social work assistants and "patch" workers who frequently function as the primary front-line providers of social services in area or patch teams. Apparently, despite what their title implies, social work assistants rarely function as assistants to social workers (Hallett 1978: 150). They more often carry responsibility for individual cases that come to the attention of the area team that are considered appropriate for allocation to social work assistants. Decisions about the allocation of cases to them are "usually made with reference to broad and undifferentiated client group labels rather than to the skills and/or knowledge required to deal with the range of problems present in a particular case" (144). Frequently, social work assistants function as *the* social workers with elderly and handicapped people (140; see also Rowlings 1978; Hey 1978; Black *et al.* 1983).

Another category of paraprofessional social service personnel who constitute the primary front-line providers of service are the patch workers who are an integral part of some community- or neighborhood-based systems of social service delivery that have received a great deal of attention in recent years (Hadley and McGrath 1980; 1984; Bayley *et al.* 1981). Typically these patch workers are the members of the neighborhood social service team who are in most direct and continuing contact with clients. As is the case with social work assistants in more conventional social service teams, much of their attention is devoted to elderly and handicapped people (Cooper 1980: 35). At the same time there is often considerable overlap of professional and paraprofessional activities since "the patch team holds the work of the patch in common and any one member may be involved in the work of any other" (34).

Team approaches to social service staff deployment

As noted in an earlier chapter, with the creation of the new large consolidated local authority social services departments (SSDs) in 1971, area social service teams serving populations of 50,000 to

100,000 people emerged as the front-line organizational units in the provision of social services in Britain. Area teams made up of professionally trained social workers and a variety of paraprofessional personnel were expected to bring their joint resources to bear on the range of service needs that come to their attention. At least in principle, the opportunity exists in area teams to develop a model of social service delivery based on the differentiation and allocation of tasks and functions among diverse staff and the coordination of the work of these different staff members in a unified team response to client and community needs. However, area social service teams in Britain have not tended to function in a way that brings their joint and coordinated resources to bear on the problems and needs of their clients or communities. Rather, the "one worker/one case" approach to work allocation seems to have been the norm. As Parsloe (1978: 347) noted after studying the work of social service teams in Britain: "Our findings make clear that work was seen in terms of caseloads and allocation of work took the form of handing cases to individual workers. The possibility of managing work in terms of task rather than case, or by group action rather than by individual action, seemed scarcely ever to be recognized." In general, there seems to be little understanding of "the potential of the team for *team work*" (347).

Even in teams in which paraprofessionals function in a more or less auxiliary role to social workers, there is very little sharing of work among staff with different levels of training (Hallett 1978: 151). Goldberg and Fruin (1976: 10) have noted "the reluctance of social workers to involve other, possibly less trained colleagues, volunteers or other community resources in situations which appear to be fairly stabilized and not to require the special skills of a trained social worker." Hallett (1978: 154) attributed this reluctance to engage in shared team work to the fact that the case remains the dominant unit of work in area social service teams and she sees "a need for considerable changes in the organization of work and, crucially, in thinking and attitudes if there is to be a shift from the one worker/one case model towards more sharing of tasks, or the implementation of team models of service delivery" (167).

The Barclay Report (1982) on the role and tasks of social workers apparently recognized the limitations of the prevailing "one case/one worker" approach to social service provision and felt there was some merit in an alternative community/team approach based on the "patch" model to which we have already made some reference. A neighborhood or community-based model of practice, using teams of diverse personnel, is what is envisaged.

> "The team leader in a community social work team may be responsible for a mixed group of workers which includes, perhaps, home help organizers, occupational therapists, ancillaries, street wardens and family aides, and their development will be partly his responsibility. He will also have to allocate work between different kinds of workers and may have to coordinate the resources of the department – including day and residential as well as field work services – in a locality or for a client group."   (Barclay Report 1982: 211)

The Barclay Committee acknowledged the problems involved in determining the levels of difficulty and complexity in the work that has to be carried out in the social services and the barriers that exist to sharing this work among different kinds of personnel but concluded that, "nevertheless, some distinction in work levels is possible and necessary in our view, and this is most practicable where there is close teamwork and an emphasis on 'team responsibility' for cases" (137–38).

The committee urged social services departments to free themselves from the "tyranny of the case" (92) and stressed the advantages of teams of social service staff of different kinds over the current model of practice. In such a team, work would be allocated to staff "in such a way that the collective resources of the group are available when needed, to all clients" (133).

Payne (1982: 24) notes that the value of teamwork has been realized in both the USA and Britain as the contribution of paraprofessional personnel to social service provision has grown. Based on the positive results achieved on both sides of the Atlantic, he asserts that teams of professional and paraprofessional personnel, such as those operating in patch systems, have the potential for more effective work than other service delivery approaches. They can make better use of available personnel and can lead to increased clarity about the tasks that are performed (26–7). Payne acknowledges that there are barriers to the achievement of the potential benefits of team work but he believes there is sufficient evidence to suggest that these can be overcome (27).

Theoretical perspectives on staff differentiation

Proponents of more sophisticated team models of social service delivery and more refined approaches to differentiating the tasks and functions to be performed by the diverse participants in the social service system in Britain make frequent reference to the research that has been carried out on these topics in the USA (for example Barker and Briggs 1968; 1969; Teare and McPheeters 1970; Brieland, Briggs, and Leuenberger 1973; Brill 1976). However, some important work has been done in this area by British researchers that offers a useful perspective on appropriate distinctions between the functions of professional and paraprofessional social service personnel.

Members of the Brunel Institute of Organization and Social Studies have been engaged in a systematic program of research on the organization and management of local authority social services departments since 1969. This work has included efforts to identify the nature of the work carried out in SSDs and to define the levels of responsibility carried by different grades of social service staff. For example Rowbottom, Hey, and Billis (1974) found that social services departments are engaged in a range of direct service activities that go beyond what is usually regarded as social work. They identified three broad categories of functions performed by SSDs that they characterized as (1) social work, (2) services, and (3) supplementary services. Hey (1975) describes these three functions as follows:

"*Social Work* as we see it is concerned with developing and maintaining the social functioning capacities of individual families, community groups and the social institutions with which they are involved."

"*Services* are concerned to secure the basic necessities of life for those who are unable to secure such for themselves – food, money and goods, accommodation, help with person and property care, transport, [and] recreational, cultural and social opportunity."

"*Supplementary Services* . . . [are] concerned with improving the physical (and thereby the psychological and social) communication and mobility skills of the physically and mentally handicapped.

Specifically, the supply of relevant aids and adaptations, and training and sheltered employment . . . aimed at the same clientele."

(Hey 1975: 2–3)

In a later work (Hey 1978), these three functions are called (1)
social work with individuals and families, (2) basic services, and (3)
special services, and a fourth function is added – work at the
community level.

Within each of these broad categories of functions performed by
social services departments, the Brunel group identified a series of
distinct levels or "strata" of work, each of which requires the
exercise of increased responsibility or discretion as one moves from
the lower to the higher levels (Rowbottom and Billis 1977: 55; Hey
1978: Appendix 2). They suggest that, in social services departments,
at least five of these strata can be identified and these have been
designated by the following labels that describe the essential
characteristics of the work performed, starting at the lowest level:
(1) prescribed output; (2) situational response; (3) systematic
service provision; (4) comprehensive service provision; and (5)
comprehensive field coverage (Rowbottom and Billis 1977: 56). At
least initially, the Brunel group paid greater attention to those
strata of work at or above the professional level (2 through 5) since
they were particularly interested in types and gradations of
professional, supervisory, and managerial responsibility in social
services departments. However, their general theory included what
we are calling paraprofessional human service personnel and it is
worth looking at how they distinguished the nature of the work
performed by these workers from that performed by professional
personnel.

It was expected that personnel in stratum 1 (the lowest level and
that described as having "prescribed output") would be "working
toward objectives which can be completely specified (as far as is
significant) beforehand, according to defined circumstances which
may present themselves" (Rowbottom and Billis 1977: 57).

"At the lowest stratum of work the output required of the
worker is completely prescribed or prescribable, as are the
specific circumstances in which this or that task should be
pursued. . . . Work consists of such things as rendering given
services, collecting given information, making prescribed checks

or tests, [etc]. . . . What is to be done, in terms of the kind or form of results to be achieved does not have to be decided."
(Rowbottom and Billis 1977: 58)

Rowbottom and Billis (1977: 58) stress that work at this level is not totally prescribed since there is some discretion in *how* the work is to be carried out. However, there is no discretion in *what* is to be done and they include within this stratum the typical work of such social service personnel as social work assistants and care assistants. Hey (1978: Appendix 2) includes among the common tasks of persons working at this level – "checking on the well-being of an isolated person."

In contrast to the prescribed tasks performed by persons in the first stratum, those workers functioning in the second (situational response) stratum would be "carrying out work where the precise objectives to be pursued have to be judged according to the needs of each specific concrete situation which presents itself" (Rowbottom and Billis 1977: 57). "Within this stratum 'demands' can never be taken at their face value; there is always an implicit requirement to explore and assess what the 'real' needs of the situation are" (59). According to Rowbottom and Billis, it is the ability to go beyond the surface reality of certain situations, drawing upon a body of theoretical knowledge, that distinguishes the second stratum from the first stratum worker or the professional from the paraprofessional. They stress that this does not mean that only members of the recognized professions can function at or above the second stratum, "since the ability is the thing in question, not any body of explicit theory" (59–60). However, Hey (1978: Appendix 2) states that "all true 'professionals' are expected to work at this level (or higher even)" and she gives as typical example of the work performed by social service personnel in the second stratum – "assessing the needs of a problem family."

At least in principle, Hey (1975) sees social work assistants as performing clearly prescribed tasks within the Brunel group's stratum 1 category of social service functions. However, she acknowledges that, in practice, the distinction between the work of social workers and social work assistants may not be entirely clear-cut. She feels that the confusion may have arisen from past shortages of professional social workers that resulted in inappropriate tasks being allocated to untrained assistants and may also be due to the tendency of professional workers to take on basic service functions inappropriately. She concedes that, whatever the reason, "social work assistants are allocated tasks which requisitely need a situational response" and she gives as a typical example – "assessing the need for reception into care of the elderly" (7). This anomalous situation in regard to the functions of social work assistants is yet to be resolved satisfactorily.

Applying the Brunel model of social service staff differentiation is less problematic in the case of those broad categories of personnel who function primarily in tending and caring roles. Relatively speaking, the work of such domiciliary, day, and residential care staff as home helps and care assistants can be fairly clearly prescribed. This is probably also true in the case of family aides since, as Hey (1980: 91–2) notes, they usually perform tasks that have been formulated by social workers with the purpose of bringing about specific changes in client functioning. The need for situational responses in their work is likely to be less common than seems to be the case with many social work assistants.

Despite the apparent contradictions that exist in regard to social work assistants, the efforts of the Brunel Institute to grapple with the issue of social service staff differentiation have produced some promising results. These efforts should be continued since it is clear in Britain, as in the human services throughout the world, that there is a need "to articulate more clearly those welfare functions which do not need social work skills and to find ways to rationalize these so as to avoid expensive overlap" (Goldberg 1981: 85).

In summary, we believe that current trends in Britain towards greater use of community-based teams of mixed professional and paraprofessional personnel are encouraging. If these teams are organized in such a way that service is provided jointly by a diverse group of staff whose functions are clearly differentiated and whose work on behalf of clients is properly coordinated, the contribution of each member and of the team as a whole is likely to be strengthened.

INDIA

As we noted earlier, paraprofessionals constitute the majority of persons employed in social welfare programs in India. They come from all walks of life and can be found operating in both rural and urban areas, in all geographic regions, from the Punjab in the north to Madras in the south. Their titles vary according to the jobs they perform and many of these jobs and their titles are unique to India, for example, the *anganwadi* (child health care) worker, *balwadi* (pre-school) worker, village-level worker, and block development worker. In this section we will examine the roles and functions that some of these paraprofessionals carry in child welfare, rural and village development, block planning, and community or slum neighborhood work.

Child development services

Despite the progress achieved since India's independence, the quality of life of most children remains below acceptable standards. A majority of India's 270 million children (representing about 40 per cent of the population) live in impoverished economic, social, and environmental conditions which impede both their physical and social development. This is reflected by key indicators such as high infant mortality rates and a high incidence of malnutrition. Almost half (47 per cent) of all deaths in India occur among children under 4 years; about one-third occur in the first year of life; nearly a fifth occur in the first month of life; and about a tenth occur in the first week (United Nations 1984: 23). In light of these problems, child welfare has become an important field of service in India. As we have already noted, in 1974 the government of India adopted a national policy resolution for children, designed to provide the framework for an integrated approach to child development. The following objectives were set forth for this Integrated Child Development Services (ICDS) Program:

"1 To lay the foundation for the proper psychological, physical and social development of the child.
 2 To improve the nutritional and health status of children below 6 years of age.
 3 To reduce the incidence of mortality.
 4 To enhance the capability of the mother to look after the normal health and nutritional needs of the child through proper nutrition and health care."

(Ministry of Social Welfare 1982: 10)

Under this program children receive annual health checkups, immunization, supplementary nutrition, and pre-school education. The program was originally directed to children below the age of 3 years in backward tribal and rural areas and in the slums of the larger cities but it was later extended to children up to 6 years of age. By 1985 the program was serving some 10 million children (Chowdhry 1985).

The front-line child development worker in this program has two major functions, one educational and the other medical. In regard to the former, the objectives include the provision of socialization skills and preparing children for entry into primary school. Basic reading and writing skills are introduced and emphasis is placed on the value of learning and study. In India early childhood education has taken on special importance since the school dropout rate after grades four and five is very high and is a cause for serious concern. Consequently the concept of *anganwadi* has been introduced. In the Gujaroti language *angan* means courtyard and *wadi* is garden. The idea was the use of courtyards as early childhood learning centers in backward and tribal areas where children can be brought together for growth and development. The *anganwadi* also provides an important service for working mothers who are able to leave their young children (1 month to 6 years of age) in the center under supervision. In addition to her child care and child development functions, the *anganwadi* worker also performs an important health care role.

It has long been recognized in India that nonphysicians and non-professionals can play valuable roles in primary health care, particularly in rural areas. Historically, paraprofessionals were used to meet the most pressing health needs of the moment (for example vaccinations) and were trained to perform this one task. Gradually the types of auxiliaries and the range of functions they carried out were expanded to correspond to many of the activities carried out by traditional professional and paramedical staff such as nurses, midwives, and laboratory technicians. The rationale for using auxiliaries in the health care field in India is similar to that advanced in other developing countries.

"Auxiliaries seem to be the best answer given the conditions in our country. We have a large population spread out mostly in rural areas. The number of physicians required is very great . . .

many of them are not only unwilling but also have a limited capacity for work outside cities. The people by and large retain their traditional outlook and do not share the scientific perspective of professionals. Communication and establishment of trust is not easy for an outsider. A person who retains the prevailing values can function more effectively. A large proportion of the population is comprised of infants and children. . . . There is a predominance of children's diseases and high infant and child mortality. . . . We can train a sufficient number of auxiliaries to allow a much larger proportion of people to benefit from medical care."

(Sethi 1984: 35)

Typically those front-line auxiliaries (*anganwadi* workers) who function in rural areas in India have responsibility for the health needs of about 1,000 people. Their principal functions include the identification of cases of malaria, tuberculosis, and leprosy; motivating people to use family planning and immunization services and helping to provide these services; identifying mothers and children who need nutritional supplements; providing prenatal care, including attendance at normal deliveries; and engaging in health education activities.

There are several projects in India where medical auxiliaries selected from the village are trained to handle the majority of the community's basic health needs. Probably the most widely known is the Comprehensive Rural Health Project at Jamkhed which one of the authors (Schindler) visited. The director of this project credited the introduction of village health workers with a significant reduction in infant mortality (Arole 1985). These village health workers weigh children, keep medical records, and provide health education and nutritional services. They attend to expectant and nursing mothers and perform deliveries. They are trained to recognize mature cataracts and refer people with these problems to a mobile medical team. They also follow through with leprosy and tuberculosis patients to make sure they receive regular care. Treatment of minor ailments at an early stage is also one of the responsibilities of these auxiliary health workers. They make a general check on the health of the children and visit those who are sick at home. They also make regular family rounds, systematically covering the whole village once a week. In addition, they spend much of their time in broader preventive work with the community, educating them about environmental health matters, such as the importance of a safe water supply, adequate sewage disposal, and the control of disease-carrying insects.

In carrying out functions and tasks described above, the *anganwadi* worker is critical to the success of the comprehensive child health and development services envisaged by the Integrated Child Development Services (ICDS) program. Without indigenous front-line paraprofessionals as members of primary health care teams, it would be impossible to implement rural and village health programs in general and, without the contributions of the *anganwadi* worker, the specific child health and development goals of the ICDS could not be achieved.

> "The anganwadi worker assumes a pivotal role in the I.C.D.S. due to her close and continuous contact with the community. As the crucial link between the village population and the government administration, she became a central figure in ascertaining and meeting the needs of the community she lives in."
>
> (Sadka 1984: 20)

The blending of early childhood educational and health care functions in one indigenous front-line paraprofessional may be unique to India's *anganwadi* worker.

Other rural and village level workers

An example was given in the last chapter of the activities of a village-level worker in the poverty-stricken and drought-ravaged rural settlement of Akbarpur where the most significant achievement was the development of better irrigation facilities for the village so that food production could be increased. The village worker also organized the small community and worked with the village council to solve other community problems. Some of the effects and achievements reported from community work carried out by village-level workers include:

> "1 More efficient utilization of land, water and human resources.
> 2 Nutrition improvement where starvation is no longer evident.
> 3 Persons no longer take up forced labour in caste villages.

4 The village [Akbarpur] has become more self sufficient, and is depending less on money lenders and big landlords.
5 Gradual [improvements in] status and dignity have been achieved through economic betterment."

(Indian Council of Social Welfare 1982: 5)

Recently special programs have been developed to address the needs of women in villages and rural areas. The purpose of these services is to redress the inequitable treatment (in terms of resources and services) that women have received. With the Indian population increasing at a rate of 12 million persons a year, unemployment has been growing and this has had a particularly serious impact on women. In order to address these economic problems, local women have been recruited to play key roles in organizing a variety of rural projects. The women serve as front-line women workers and carry out a broad range of valuable functions at the village level, including:

"1 Getting to know women of their village on a personal basis in order to encourage them to participate in income generating and other economic activities.
2 Helping women understand their socioeconomic situation and find solutions to their problems.
3 Formation of women's groups for collective strength and action. The front line worker has to help women see the commonality of their problems, and develop a sense of confidence in themselves as a group."

(Apte 1985)

Income-producing activities include exploring markets for traditional skills and trades such as home-based bead or match-making. The paraprofessional helps women secure bank loans to support their business activities, facilitates access to technical, financial, and marketing cooperatives. These sources of support, together with district and village industry centers are important resources for income-producing activities in rural areas. One of the most important functions performed by front-line women workers in rural areas is providing access to services. They make village residents aware of government financial assistance for horticulture, goatkeeping, beekeeping, and modest irrigation projects. They also guide persons to classes in reading and writing. These activities are often difficult, of course, because of the household burdens carried by these women but there are strong efforts today to encourage women to participate in these programs (Apte 1985).

In discussing grassroots participation in social development, one must take note of the *Panchayadi Raj* or village councils in Indian society. Article 40 of the Indian Constitution states that "the state shall take steps to organize village Panchayadi and endow them with such power and authority as may be necessary to enable them to function as units of self government" (Indian Council of Social Welfare 1982: 3). The rationale for the creation of the *Panchayadi Raj* was to ensure the continual participation of all citizens in India's democratic process (Dubey and Murida 1972); that is to involve the rural population in decision-making in order to obtain a realistic picture of the problems and progress of the community. The idea was that the villagers themselves would be in the best position to define their own needs. Indigenous personnel were seen as playing an important role in whatever social development efforts were needed. Critics of the *Panchayadi Raj* have argued that it has not been effective in addressing the needs of people at the grassroots level (that is, the most needy) because of limited financial resources, lack of trained workers, and vested interests (Myrdal 1969; Hesbur 1979; Nanavatty 1981). Recent modifications in the program, for example, the introduction of the Integrated Rural Development Plan may overcome some of these shortcomings. In any case, indigenous workers have an important place in these grassroots community development efforts.

Block level and neighborhood workers

As we noted in the last chapter, above the village structure in India, there is a decentralized form of social and community planning known as block level planning. Its philosophy reflects a commitment to popular participation in the planning process (Singh 1980: 133). Locating problems at the block level, which is relatively small in terms of area and population, promotes closer communication and understanding between the planners and the populace. In the last chapter we focused on block planning in rural areas. However, the block planning process operates in urban areas also. Within some block areas, there are projects involving community work in slum areas. In India about 40 per cent of the people live below the poverty line (United Nations 1984). In urban areas most of the poor are congregated in slums. D'Souza (1982: 3) has described the plight of the slum dwellers as one of untold misery. "They have been rejected by their villages which offered them no employment. Struggling to make ends meet, they succumbed to the lure of potential employment in the city. Now, the slum dwellers are rejected by the city as causing a menace to the welfare of the public."

It is important to recognize, when speaking of slum areas in India, that comparisons with slum areas in the Western world are misleading. While some aspects of the slum culture may be similar, the infrastructure is not. In many urban slums in India such basic facilities as sewage disposal, electricity, and piped water are non-existent (Parikah 1985; Pacione 1981). Housing is a major problem. In the slum area of Bombay (Lokmamya Nagar Compound) which one of the authors (Schindler) visited, a population of over 3,000 persons live in 400 huts. Such gross overcrowding is common and slums continue to grow at an accelerating rate, adding to the already widespread urban blight. This situation is exacerbated by the fact that many slums are situated on private land and thus are not eligible for government amenities. Although Bombay has a relatively large supply of water from different sources, this is not enough to meet the city's needs and consequently the supply of water in slum areas is a critical issue. In addition to housing, sewage, and water problems, amenities such as hospitals, primary and secondary schools, play grounds, and health facilities are in extremely short supply.

The role of the paraprofessional worker in intervention in these situations is critical. As D'Souza (1982: 5) suggests, "she is most suited to function as a grass roots level worker which is indispensable for community work." Furthermore, "she fills the lacuna left by professional social workers because of their lack of involvement in community work." There are many programs in urban centers which have involved front-line workers. For example, *Apnalya*, an organization that operates fifteen urban slum projects, exemplifies the approach to urban community development that relies on the use of indigenous paraprofessionals. One of the founders of this program gives the philosophy behind the approach: "The involvement of paraprofessionals grew out of our firm belief in the ability of slum dwellers to work toward solving their own problems and improving their living conditions" (Panwalkar 1985).

The activities of front-line paraprofessionals in slum areas include educational, mediating, and advocacy tasks. They typically provide information to local citizens about their rights and organize them to express their demands in relation to water distribution, housing needs, and sewage disposal. They also become involved in the recruitment of *balwadi* (pre-school) teachers, organizing classes for youth at work, securing monetary help for community improvement schemes, and organizing bread distribution schemes for needy families.

In discussions with paraprofessionals and professionals in India it is becoming clear that a stronger advocacy role was being sought, particularly in the urban areas. The need for activism was frequently stressed, although the precise meaning of that term varied. Some human service personnel suggested greater involvement of the poor in seeking change and others called for a more aggressive approach, extending to civil disobedience. At any rate, the general theme was that some sort of social or community action was necessary on behalf of poor urban residents.

Team approaches to personnel deployment

There is increasing recognition among human service personnel in India that teamwork, particularly in multidisciplinary teams, can result in greater effectiveness in service delivery. The village-level health workers mentioned earlier often work alone and, therefore, there is a need for some mechanism that will support them in their work and make them a more integral part of the health care system. The concept of the health care team as an organizational alternative to the individual practitioner is not yet widely accepted in the Indian human services. However, there is some promising experimentation taking place (for example, the Jamkhed Comprehensive Rural Health Project mentioned earlier) that can serve as a model of effective team work (Arole and Arole 1984; Arole 1985). In the Jamkhed model, service delivery is based on a three-tier system. The first tier consists of a village health worker, resident in each village.

> "The key to health programs has been the selection and training of village health workers. Village participation starts from the very beginning with each village choosing a local woman to be

trained as its own health worker. She is expected to give primary health care to each and every person of the village irrespective of caste or financial ability."

(Arole and Arole 1984: 8)

The village-based health worker is helped to carry out her functions by a mobile team (the second tier of the system) which consists of the team leader, who is generally a nurse, a paramedical worker, or sometimes a physician or social worker. The team is based at a district center or subcenter and visits each village in its area on a weekly or bi-weekly schedule. The role of the health team is to support the village health worker in her activities by providing consultation, treatment that is beyond the skill of the village worker, and referral of patients who cannot be treated in the village to the main health center (the third tier) in Jamkhed which has facilities for diagnosis, acute care, in-patient treatment, and training. All members of this three-tier system are trained as a team.

Among the specific tasks of the village health worker is to follow up on leprosy and tuberculosis patients, making sure they receive regular treatments. In addition, she screens leprosy patients for deformities, carries out skin smears for them, and collects sputum samples from those suspected of having tuberculosis. The mobile team provides her with consultation on the most effective means of rehabilitating leprosy or tuberculosis patients.

The value of the kind of team approach which operates in Jamkhed is beginning to be recognized in other rural areas in India. However, it is difficult to operationalize such a program on a widespread basis since its success is very much dependent on the availability of physicians who have a community health orientation and the skills to train and lead a decentralized and multidisciplinary team of the kind described above (Taylor 1972).

Future trends

Desai (1975) has observed that at present there is no comprehensive manpower plan for human service personnel in India and questions whether there will be such a program in the near future. However, she believes that it is possible to undertake human resource planning on a more limited scale and suggests that schools of social work take leadership in this area. She proposes that schools of

social work need to shift their emphasis from the doctoral and
master's levels of education to the training of undergraduate social
work practitioners and paraprofessional personnel, if priority needs
are to be met.

There is a particular need for trained paraprofessionals to work
with children under 5 in *balwadis* (pre-primary schools) providing
educational and supplementary nutrition services. Desai stresses the
importance of this area since *balwadis* play a crucial role in later
school success and continued attendance. Of equal importance is
the training of auxiliary personnel for work with school-aged
children, including school dropouts, in rural areas. Desai (1975:
19) suggests that, unless we have policies and programs specifically
addressed to the needs of the bottom 40 per cent of the rural and
tribal population, "our scarce resources will not be able to
percolate to the bottom layers of society as the most advantaged
rural population is most likely to utilize the services." In urban
areas paraprofessionals are needed to work in large housing
projects, especially those for lower income groups, to develop an
infrastructure of social services, including *balwadis*, day care
centers for working mothers, and programs designed to prevent
delinquency. In summary Desai suggests that:

"The future prospects of solving problems of poverty due to the
inability of populations to use their inherent capacities, societal
opportunities and resistance against exploitation will remain
limited unless technically trained social workers at different
levels of training are fully associated with improving the quality
of life of that population."

(Desai 1975: 21)

ISRAEL

In Israel one can identify ten major types of human service
organization or setting serving distinct client populations where
paraprofessionals are employed. These include neighborhood
services, social welfare agencies, mental health settings, early
childhood education programs, community centers, homes and
centers for the aged, correctional institutions, rehabilitation centers

for alcoholics, counseling and family agencies, and residential and community centers for the retarded (Gidron and Katan 1985; Goldstein 1985; Sadan 1985; Kestenbaum and Shebar 1984; Kestenbaum and Bar-On 1982; Schindler 1982; Itzhaki 1981). In this section we will examine the tasks, functions, and roles of paraprofessionals in these major human service settings.

In Israel, as is true in other countries, the people we are calling paraprofessionals are referred to by a variety of titles. Persons without professional social work qualifications are frequently called semi-professionals, nonprofessionals, subprofessionals, case aides, care assistants, and community or neighborhood aides. Because of the diversity of paraprofessional functions and areas of activity, arriving at a widely accepted title for this level of worker has been difficult. If a role is defined as a description of social behavior that is situationally appropriate for a person in terms of his or her cultural context, then diversity of title may be appropriate. If it is seen as the expectation of an individual occupying a given status, then a more universal title may be more desirable. In Israel paraprofessional titles are generally related to the client population served and the auspices of the service. For example, a person working with elderly people is given the name *matasit*, literally, caring for the elderly, and a person working with citizens in community-based programs is referred to as *oved schunot*, literally, neighborhood worker.

Paraprofessional tasks and functions

In *Table 2* we describe in more detail the tasks and functions carried out by paraprofessionals in the main human service organizations in Israel, including the target populations they serve. As *Table 2* shows, there are many paraprofessional tasks and functions that are unique to a particular field of practice or to the client population served. However, within this wide range of specific tasks, we have identified some broad roles that cut across different fields of practice and can be considered to be common to the paraprofessional in Israel. These include advocacy, caring, counseling, mediation, service catalyst, social policy formulation, teaching, and outreach.

TABLE 2   *Human service organizations, client populations served, and primary tasks and functions performed by paraprofessionals*

human service organization	target population	paraprofessional tasks and functions
1 neighborhood services	multi-problem families	*oved schunot (neighborhood or community worker):* (a) problem identification regarding income maintenance, housing, and health; (b) teaching skills, such as budgeting; (c) giving advice about relevant services; (d) emotional support for people facing crises; (e) organization of block and tenant committees, clubs for women and children, and programs for neighborhood cleanliness; and (f) outreach.
2 social welfare agencies	multi-problem families	*somchot (support aide):* (a) serves as a listening board for clients and information base for professionals; (b) offers direct help such as budgeting; (c) accompanying to services, etc.
3 mental health centers	individuals and families	*mental health aide:* (a) welcoming clients at intake; (b) group counseling; (c) emotional support as part of interdisciplinary team; (d) link to employment, housing, half-way houses upon discharge; (e) advocate for integration into community; (f) mediates between agency and other relevant services that are related to rehabilitation; (g) referrals and follow-up, particularly home visits after discharge.
4 informal settings for early childhood education	mothers and children	*assistant to social worker or teacher:* (a) enriching the language of children and mothers; (b) developing

human service organization	target population	paraprofessional tasks and functions
		mother's awareness of child's developmental needs; (c) teaching mother how to use games and toys for child's physical and emotional growth; (d) working with groups of mothers and children to enrich their common growth experiences.
5 community centers	individuals, groups, and families	*game room leader and leader of enrichment program*: (a) home visitation to families and instruction in the use of educational toys; (b) teaching families how toys can be used to supplement formal learning; (c) using games as a tool for sharing individual and family problems; (d) dealing with problems in both a supportive and concrete way; (e) encouraging families to utilize the community center and other community services; (f) referring clients to professionals when problems become too complex.
6 clubs, community centers, and homes for the aged	the elderly	*social work assistant in work with the aged*: (a) outreach to the elderly population; (b) advice and support to the elderly; (c) connecting the elderly with other age groups; (d) advocating for the rights of the elderly; (e) referring the elderly to services in the community; (f) services in the home; (g) all aspects of care in residential settings.

human service organization	target population	paraprofessional tasks and functions
7 correctional institutions and half-way houses	ex-prisoners	*corrections aide:* (a) assisting prisoner upon discharge, such as finding employment and housing; (b) advocating for the ex-prisoner in regard to benefits; (c) link to the family in helping them cope with problems of the prisoner; (d) providing support and encouragement to the prisoner upon discharge; (e) performing the role of big brother.
8 rehabilitation centers	alcoholics	*social work assistant in work with alcoholics:* (a) intake work, including routine administrative functions; (b) identifying potential problem drinkers in the community and referring them to appropriate services; (c) accompanying clients to group sessions such as AA; (d) support and individual treatment of alcoholics; (e) heading groups of ex-alcoholics in continued rehabilitation; (f) involving ex-alcoholics in organizing educational programs in the community.
9 counseling and family agencies	couples and families in crises	*case aide:* (a) intake; (b) looking after children while couples are in therapy; (c) gathering information for court orders; (d) visiting children and giving them support during divorce proceedings; (e) alerting appropriate services such as psychological counseling, schools, etc., of potential problems; (f) forwarding information to the interdisciplinary team working with the family.

human service organization	target population	paraprofessional tasks and functions
10 services to the retarded	mentally retarded adults and children and their families	*care assistant*: (a) looks after clients' well-being, including all caring functions; (b) educational functions including teaching, reading, writing, and communication skills appropriate to clients' level of functioning; (c) mediating between clients and community services; (d) helping families cope with retardation; (e) teaching families how to utilize community resources for help.

Paraprofessional roles

As *Table 2* shows, there are many paraprofessional tasks and functions that are unique to a particular field of practice or to the client population served. However, within this wide range of specific tasks, we have identified some broad roles that cut across different fields of practice and can be considered to be common to the paraprofessional in Israel. These include advocacy, caring, counseling, mediation, service catalyst, social policy formulation, teaching, and outreach.

Advocacy
Exhorting and persuading others to provide or improve services has become an important role for the paraprofessional. Often this means fighting for changes that will enable clients to obtain minimum standards of housing, health, and well-being (Perlman and Gurin 1972). This role is common in Project Renewal where neighborhood workers advocate for the rights of clients and organizing them in order that they may receive benefits to which they are entitled. It is believed that the advocacy role has become more meaningful now that community residents and indigenous paraprofessionals participate on steering committees with planners and policy-makers of both municipal and national government agencies in regard to Project Renewal. The advocacy role also

involves protecting persons who are especially vulnerable to societal strains and seeking appropriate services for them. These persons include patients discharged from mental hospitals, ex-prisoners, alcoholics, the aged, and children. For example, in one community in Israel a paraprofessional played a particularly important role in the long process of negotiating for a half-way house for retarded people.

Caring

Respondents from Israel confirmed what had been reported to us by experts from other countries regarding the crucial role of the paraprofessional in the personal social services. Without the personal care and assistance that the paraprofessional provides, many of these services would collapse. The personal caring role includes such life-line functions as washing, dressing, and feeding dependent and infirm persons in their own homes or in residential settings. A prime example would be the Meals-on-Wheels Programs that provide basic sustenance for frail elderly homebound people. For many of these people the home-delivered meal is the only regular nutritious meal they receive and, for a large number of them, the only meaningful personal relationship they are able to establish is with the person who brings it. Such caring and helping roles performed by paraprofessionals are particularly important when crisis situations arise.

Counseling

Paraprofessionals have increasingly taken on counseling roles in relation to individual, couple, and family problems. This role is not necessarily linked to formal counseling and family services *per se*, but occurs in the majority of human service agencies we have listed, as an adjunct to other paraprofessional roles. The complexity and sensitivity of problems that individuals and families face make it easier for clients to share these problems with persons who are closer to them in socio-cultural background and are more likely to be readily available. The types of counseling tasks carried out by paraprofessionals are broad, ranging from the provision of psycho-logical support to intervention in crisis situations. However, paraprofessional skills do not enable them to perform the more advanced treatment and interventive strategies carried out by professional social workers.

Mediation
Paraprofessionals are particularly skilled at linking clients to services. They learn very fast about the range of services available and how to help clients obtain them. In one neighborhood, for example, they have become expert at interpreting financial benefits available to newly married couples seeking government housing. In another neighborhood, paraprofessionals negotiated for young mothers seeking family, educational, and psychological counseling. In two studies of paraprofessionals, one in Israel (Kuperman, Terenechofsky, and Meire 1980) and the other in the USA (Katan 1974), mediation was found to be a vital element of paraprofessional functioning.

One of the major goals of the social work profession is getting services to people and helping people to use these services properly. The skills involved include advising, guiding, and actually helping people get the services they need. The mediating function relates to access which is vital to effective service delivery. As Kahn (1973: 162–63) puts it: "Many citizens never learn about rights, benefits or entitlements that would ease their lives. . . . People in need of advice go from place to place sometimes getting to the right place after inordinate expenditure." The important role of linking people to services is central to paraprofessional activities and has become an important skill in helping people in crisis situations.

Service catalyst
Paraprofessional workers not only identify problems and connect clients to services but also initiate new programs. Indigenous workers have initiated Head Start programs for the educationally disadvantaged and, as members of interdisciplinary teams, have introduced early childhood programs designed to monitor infant development. On a more general level, they have introduced new thinking into human service organizations and programs because of the particular background and expertise they bring. In a sense, they have brought about a modification of the bureaucratic stance that human service agencies typically have towards the disadvantaged. The limited influence of low income people on service bureaucracies has been well documented by Cloward and Piven:

"The bureaucracies have intruded upon and altered processes of public decision so that low income groups have fewer occasions for exercising influence and fewer effective means for doing so;

and . . . the bureaucracies have come to exert powerful and inhibiting controls on the low income people who are their clients."

(Cloward and Piven 1969: 359)

Paraprofessionals have modified this pattern. Through closeness to and knowledge of the community and its residents they are able to recommend, initiate, and organize services that are responsive to the needs of the local population.

Information gathering (related to social policy)
It has been suggested that social policy is both "a decision-making process and its outcomes concerned with social welfare, social services and closely related spheres" (Dolgoff and Feldstein 1980: 96–7). While paraprofessionals do not design or formulate social policy, they are effective in providing important data to planners. The information-gathering function enables planners to arrive at decisions that are in keeping with the cultural and ethnic values of the community.

Paraprofessionals are increasingly involved in decision-making with professionals and have helped modify professional judgments about local needs and appropriate responses to these needs. For example, the professional staff of Project Renewal have become sensitive to paraprofessionals' views on housing design. In one community, family flats were expanded to include room for grandparents and, in a second neighborhood, flats for elderly people were built in proximity to their children, both decisions having been initiated by indigenous paraprofessionals and community residents. This indigenous dimension (that is drawing upon the knowledge and expertise of persons who are closest to the cultural, religious, and ethnic temper of the community) plays an important part in effective social policy formulation.

Teaching
The teaching role permeates many of the services we listed in *Table 2*. Naturally, this differs from the formal teaching procedures found in school settings. The major teaching tasks of paraprofessional human service workers are informal, usually based on tutorial, modeling, and informal group methods. An example would be using games with pre-school children to accelerate development of

their cognitive and motor skills and instructing parents how to use these techniques with their children (Project Education and Community Development 1980; 1981).

Teaching and modeling are also used extensively by paraprofessionals who work with physically and mentally handicapped populations. In Israel there are a host of sheltered workshops for handicapped people where vocational and social skills are taught that enable these persons to enter the job market. Paraprofessionals play an important role in these programs.

Outreach

In such services as Project Renewal, social welfare bureaus, mental health centers, community centers, clubs for the aged, half-way houses, and rehabilitation programs for alcoholics, the outreach function is vital. The outreach role is intended to help persons in difficulty find help or to encourage citizens to utilize available services. In Israel, as is true in many of the countries we studied, knowledge about available services, one's rights to these services, and how to gain access to them is often lacking for those in need. For example, it is difficult for Ethiopian or Russian immigrants in Israel to be knowledgable about available cash and in-kind income maintenance programs when information about these programs is communicated in Hebrew. It is necessary to reach out to these people, inform them of sources of help, and encourage them to use these services. It also involves following up with clients to assure them of one's concern and commitment to help.

The outreach role is particularly important to rural populations if they are to be helped to obtain services. For example, in one of the developing towns in Israel's southern district, citizens who were entitled to benefits from the National Insurance Institute were unable to obtain income maintenance payments because of lack of access to the nearest office of the institute which was located in Beer Sheba, an hour's journey by bus. Through the efforts of a professional and paraprofessional team, this situation was rectified.

Role strain

Finally, it is important to recognize that many of the roles that paraprofessionals have taken on frequently place them in a difficult position *vis-à-vis* the human service agencies that employ them and the clients and communities they are expected to help. Paraprofessionals can experience conflict and role strain arising from cultural, religious, political, or organizational factors. For example, a worker's expectations for change and his own need to succeed may conflict with clients' differing expectations of the helping relationship. Religious differences surrounding such issues as abortion and family planning are additional potential sources of conflict and strain. Paraprofessionals can be susceptible to co-optation by political parties with which they are affiliated and, when this occurs, their efficacy in serving the community can be impaired. As representatives of human service organizations, paraprofessionals are often faced with pressures from citizen groups with which they cannot comply. These can range from requests for improved housing to demands for increases in income maintenance payments. In many cases, workers are placed in an organizational bind. On the one hand, they are placed in the community to be responsive to client needs and to bring about social change but, on the other hand, are severely limited in what they can do, as a result of inflexible agency policies. Feelings of hopelessness and powerlessness are often generated by such situations and it is questionable whether paraprofessionals can continue to be effective under these circumstances.

Role strains such as these are likely to be mitigated somewhat if paraprofessionals have support from other paraprofessionals. Research suggests that conflict and strain are higher in organizations in which paraprofessionals are heavily outnumbered by professionals. Equalizing the distribution of the two types of personnel and enabling paraprofessionals to play a greater role in organizational decision-making may alleviate some of the problems described above (Loewenberg 1968; Hage and Aiken 1970).

UNITES STATES OF AMERICA

As we have reported elsewhere, there is an enormous range of job titles used for paraprofessionals in the USA. Among those specifically mentioned as typical examples by respondents to our international survey were human service worker, mental health technician, social service aide, outreach worker, case manager, residential care worker, substance abuse counselor, child-care worker, case aide, activity director, therapy aide, teacher's aide, residence manager, social work assistant, and caseworker. Quite literally, dozens of additional examples could be provided. What seems clear is that in all human service settings, paraprofessionals are performing a wide variety of direct service functions.

Over the years, descriptions of the activities of paraprofessionals in a wide variety of human service agencies have appeared in books, reports, and social science journals and these have been listed and summarized in periodic bibliographies and reviews of the paraprofessional literature (for example Barker and Briggs 1966; Social Action Research Center 1978). What is clear is that there has always been strong evidence that paraprofessionals can make a valuable contribution to human service provision, if they are used appropriately, and this evidence has been cumulative over the years (see Barker and Briggs 1966; 1968; 1969; Grosser, Henry, and Kelly 1969; Sobey 1970; Gartner 1971; Hirayama 1975; Austin 1978; Alley et al. 1978; President's Commission on Mental Health 1978; Robin and Wagenfeld 1981).

In specific human service organizations, paraprofessional activities may or may not differ from those carried out by professional workers, depending on a number of factors. However, as was true with most respondents to our survey, those from the USA felt that, in general, professional and paraprofessional activities are different. For example, professionals are more likely to be involved in administration and supervision, engage in clinical treatment, and generally carry more responsibility. On the other hand, paraprofessionals tend to be involved in direct service activities of a more concrete nature (for example information and referral, supportive counseling, and care of clients in a therapeutic milieu). They are less likely to carry supervisory or administrative roles, be involved in program development, or engage in sophisticated individual or family therapy.

It has been observed that a feature that distinguishes the newer professions, like social work and teaching, from the older professions, like law and medicine, is that in the former "prestige goes to those in the careers removed from practice" while in the latter "this is by no means so clearly the case" (Hughes 1960: 58). In social work, unlike the legal and medical professions, "the higher the training, the higher up the career structure the worker starts and the faster he climbs it," and, because of the way the human services are organized, the "less trained therefore are most likely to make the first and continuing contact with the clients" (Sinfield 1970: 43).

If, indeed, the workers with the least formal education are the front-line providers of service and if, as seems to be the case in many sectors, they are functioning in key service roles, it follows that we must be clear about their functions and about the kind of organizational arrangements that will best support them in the performance of their important service roles.

Differentiating professional and paraprofessional roles

There was little attempt made in the early experiments on the use of paraprofessionals to come to grips with the theoretical issues involved in staff differentiation in the human services, beyond the idea that certain tasks usually performed by professionally trained personnel could be delegated to persons without such training or that the latter could provide certain services that would supplement the work done by the former. However, by the end of the 1960s, more systematic and sophisticated approaches to human service staff differentiation began to be explored. The first efforts tended to take one or the other of two alternative approaches: (1) differentiation by task; or (2) differentiation by case.

Differentiation by task is achieved by a system that evaluates all the tasks that have to be carried out in the course of providing a specific type of human service. These tasks are ranked in terms of the skills and knowledge needed to perform them and then allocated to appropriate personnel, the latter usually being differentiated on the basis of formal education and years of experience (Committee on Practice and Knowledge 1964). Conceptually this approach lends itself well to the idea that the paraprofessional functions as an assistant to the professional. However, the difficulties involved in accomplishing a realistic evaluation of human service tasks and relating them to levels of assumed skill are enormous and, besides, the premise that the multiple needs of a given client can be compartmentalized and performed by different workers has been questioned (Barker and Briggs 1968). In practice this approach to human service staff differentiation is less frequently used than the case differentiation approach.

The case differentiation approach assumes that the needs of certain client groups can be met only by the professional worker while there are other clients whose needs can be met adequately by paraprofessionals (Heyman 1961). Among the problems with this approach is determining accurately which clients need the ministrations of a professionally trained worker and which can be effectively helped by a paraprofessional. Barker and Briggs identify another major weakness of the case differentiation approach:

"The professional on those cases that were assigned to him would have to perform all tasks that would be necessary to meet the needs of the case. He would thus inevitably be called on to perform many tasks which do not require his level of skill and knowledge. This would be under utilization of the professional person and, therefore, would not really be more efficient. Conversely, the subprofessional would be responsible for meeting all the needs of all his clients, some of which would exceed his ability, skills, and knowledge to fulfill and would go unmet."

(Barker and Briggs 1968: 43)

Nevertheless, despite its shortcomings, the case differentiation approach to human service staff deployment is widely used in practice and especially where professional workers are in short supply. It approximates what we characterized as the "autonomous" model of paraprofessional staff deployment in the introductory chapter.

In its search for a model of staff differentiation compatible with practice needs in the field of mental health, the Southern Regional Education Board (SREB 1969: 4) developed an alternative to the above approaches that it designated the "developmental" approach. A major fault with the existing models, SREB noted, was that they tended to perpetuate traditional models of service whether or not these models were meeting client needs. The developmental approach, on the other hand, starts with client needs and problems and moves from there to a determination of activities that need to be performed to meet them, regardless of who now performs such activities or whether they are being performed at all (see also Fine and Wiley 1971). Depending on actual client needs, clusters of activities are arranged to form the jobs to be performed by various kinds and levels of worker. SREB (1969: 6) acknowledged that the developmental approach to human service staff differentiation is more difficult to operationalize than the other approaches but insisted that it is more likely to produce jobs "that are more responsive to client needs, that are more challenging to job holders, and that allow the professionals to extend their knowledge and competence as widely as possible without becoming hung up on traditional role models."

The developmental or functional approach was subsequently elaborated by Teare and McPheeters (1970) who promulgated a model of human service personnel deployment that viewed work in that field as a blend of specific activities and tasks that could be clustered into major functional roles, for example, advocacy, instruction, changing behavior, processing information, providing care, mobilizing resources, and administration. Depending on particular client needs, these functional roles could be performed by persons with different types and levels of knowledge and skills. Allocation of work among staff with different levels of skill is based on the complexity or difficulty of the work to be performed and the degree of risk involved for the client if the worker is unable to help. (For consideration of differentiation criteria related to these, see Briggs, Johnson, and Lebowitz 1970, regarding "complexity/ responsibility.")

The team approach to personnel deployment

While these attempts to distinguish between professional and paraprofessional roles and tasks were going on, other members of the social work profession were advocating experimentation with the team model of social service staff utilization (Kahn 1964; Brieland, Briggs, and Leuenberger 1973; Brill 1976). Although research was limited, good results were reported from the use of social work teams in mental hospitals (Barker and Briggs 1969) and public welfare settings (Schwartz and Sample 1967). Based on their extensive studies on behalf of the National Association of Social Workers into differential use of social welfare personnel, Barker and Briggs (1968) developed a fairly sophisticated conception of how the team would work, and they offered it as an alternative to previously specified models of staff differentiation and utilization. Instead of using the case or the task as the unit of differentiation, they proposed the use of a concept they called the "episode of service." They described this as "cluster of activities that go together to achieve a social work organization's specified goal" (168).

"The means chosen to achieve the goal should be the most
efficient of those that the workers are competent to perform. The
episode of service is assigned to the social work team, whose
leader allocates parts of the activity to the members of the team
whom he recognizes to be most qualified and capable of performing them."

(Barker and Briggs 1968: 168)

Barker and Briggs claimed that the episode of service as a unit of
differentiation was "a more defined and thus more advanced unit
than the case" and that it was "more flexible and less arbitrary than
the single social work task" (68). In providing service to clients or
client groups, the members of the team would work together to
accomplish a stated goal for and with the client.

Although it is far from providing all the answers to the question
of differential staff utilization in the human services, the team
approach seems to have the potential for making the best use of
available personnel resources, including paraprofessionals (Brawley
1978). Of course, it leaves open to the good or bad judgment of the
team leader the problem of matching team resources to client needs.
However, this is not a completely new problem for professional
workers, who are always faced with the task of assessing the needs
of a client or situation and meeting them from their own repertoire
of skills. The novelty and difficulty lie in applying the criteria for
staff differentiation described above and the communication and
coordination patterns that have to be developed within the team.
The team members would presumably possess a variety of areas of
expertise, the exact mix depending on the nature of the practice
setting and the overall function of the team. The team leader would
be responsible for coordinating and giving direction to the activities
of the team.

Beyond the team leader's function, which can take various forms,
there could be an effort to move away from the current tendency to
view the skills and knowledge of the different team members in
terms of a simple hierarchy of competence. Each team member
would be viewed as possessing – and would be expected to
develop – his or her own areas of special competence rather than
being viewed as having a specific level of competence within a
unidimensional view of that concept. The worker providing help to
a client with intrapsychic conflict would not be regarded as
providing a service of greater intrinsic value than the worker who

helps a client deal with a recalcitrant landlord. The former function is relatively abstract and complex and ordinarily would be carried out by a worker with substantial formal (probably professional) preparation while the latter function is more simple and concrete (although not necessarily less difficult) and could probably be carried out by an agency-trained worker or other paraprofessional. However, each function can be carried out with greater or lesser degrees of competence and effectiveness. Besides, no one can say which activity is of greater value to any client or to clients in general.

The particular talents and competencies of individual paraprofessionals are undoubtedly already being recognized and utilized effectively in many settings. However, it is suggested here that individual potential is probably not being fully maximized at present on account of our tendency to take a unidimensional view of what constitutes practice competence. At any rate, that is the impression given by much of the literature on human service staff differentiation and by the respondents to our international survey, many of whom tended to limit paraprofessionals arbitrarily to the performance of a narrow range of routine, concrete tasks.

While nobody likes to perform narrow, routine tasks, most people like to feel they have some unique talent or ability. Organization research reveals that a division of labor based upon task specialization lowers worker morale while division of labor in which workers are assigned to functions for which they feel they have particular expertise seems to increase worker morale (Price 1968). However, it is not suggested here that individual jobs in the human services be created out of single roles that a worker may be best able to carry. This would tend to lead toward overspecialization and consequent fragmentation of services to clients. Nearly all jobs in the human services should be a blend of what Fine and Wiley (1971) call "functional roles." The blending of roles and their priorities in particular settings would have to be determined by each organization on the basis of actual client needs.

Beyond its possibilities for making sense out of human service staff utilization problems, the team approach, if structured in a certain way, can make human service agencies more responsive to community and client needs, and is potentially more conducive to high staff morale and productivity.

The dysfunctional aspects of large, complex organizations have been well documented (Merton 1958). The hierarchical form of organization that characterizes the bureaucracy and is typical of social agency structure was developed for the efficient accomplishment of tasks determined by those at the apex of the structure. The bureaucratic organizational model is preoccupied with control, and consequently has tended to curtail the flexibility and creativity of persons located in lower ranks of the organization (Thompson 1964). The decentralization of control implicit in the team approach to human service provision would tend to mitigate some of the dysfunctional aspects of bureaucracy. Of course, the degree to which the team would be the locus of decision-making about service activities could vary tremendously among agencies, but it is fairly clear that some decentralization of control would inevitably result from the adoption of a team approach to human service staff deployment.

If the team itself were to be organized on a horizontal rather than a vertical basis, this would further de-emphasize hierarchical control, enhance participative decision-making at the team level, and promote greater responsiveness to client and community needs. Bennis (1969) has suggested such an organizational structure as an alternative to the bureaucratic one. This model, which he calls "organic-adaptive," would be comprised of "task forces organized around problems-to-be-solved." The problems would be solved by groups or teams comprised of individuals with diverse skills. The team would be based on "organic rather than mechanical models" and would respond to clearly identified problems rather than to programmed role expectations. Team members would be differentiated "not vertically, according to rank and role, but flexibly and functionally, according to skills and professional training" (2). Although Bennis was concerned primarily with teams composed of members of various professions, the model he proposes could have equal utility for a team comprised of different kinds and levels of human service practitioners.

Setleis (1969: 149) has observed that the manner in which a social work agency is organized "reflects its values, defines relationships and determines the nature of its activity." He asserts that a hierarchical structure "limits an agency's ability to be responsive to itself, to the community, and to the client group" and "by its positioning of personnel creates antagonisms that are inherent in the positioning, rather than in the functional roles they have." Lest we envisage a form of organizational anarchy resulting from the abandonment of hierarchical control, Setleis assures us that a horizontally structured organization does not eliminate functional responsibility; it merely alters the manner in which it is carried out. The critical question is the degree to which the human service agency can give up some direct control of its members without abdicating its responsibility for the quality of service it provides. In this regard, it is useful to bear in mind Child's (1970) differentiation between the locus of decision-making and the source of authority within an organization. An organization may manifest a high degree of decentralization of decision-making without necessarily giving up its authority to hold organization members accountable for their actions.

If members of the community or client group the organization seeks to serve are included in the team and if these persons are regarded as full members of the team with their own areas of expertise, the democratization and responsiveness of the organization is likely to be further enhanced.

In summary, research on human service staff utilization in the USA has produced some promising concepts for differentiating professional from paraprofessional functions, for example, the complexity or difficulty of the work that has to be accomplished and the risk to which clients are exposed. There are also ways of organizing human service personnel that are likely to result in efficient use of available resources as well as effective and responsive service, for example, using teams of mixed professional and paraprofessional personnel to carry out episodes of service. Based on our analysis of these research findings, we suggest that, when appropriate concepts are used to distinguish professional and paraprofessional functions and these are applied within a team model of human service staff deployment that is horizontally organized and that recognizes the particular areas of competence of its paraprofessional members, the contribution of the latter to human service goals is likely to be maximized.

DISCUSSION

We had found in our international survey that paraprofessional human service workers are employed in a wide range of settings performing a multiplicity of tasks. This was no less true in the four countries that we studied in detail. In all four countries paraprofessionals are engaged in front-line service activities with children, youth, families, the elderly, physically and mentally disabled people, the disadvantaged, mentally ill people, and delinquents. In their work with these populations, their activities range from carrying out simple routine tasks all the way to the performance of relatively sophisticated procedures that are indistinguishable from those that are normally considered to be within the domain of professionally trained workers. These tasks or functions are distributed along a continuum from the provision of information and concrete aid and advice, through tending or caring for dependent populations, to supportive counseling, mobilizing community resources, acting as advocates for clients and communities and (in some instances) the performance of quite complex treatment, supervisory, and organizational roles. The activities of some paraprofessionals are clustered at the lower end of this scale, others function in the middle range, and yet another group is operating in the upper reaches of the continuum. However, in all countries, paraprofessionals tend to be the workers who have the most frequent and regular face-to-face contact with clients.

While there is a great deal of overlap in the types of roles and functions carried out by paraprofessionals in the four countries we studied, there are some examples of paraprofessional activity that are unique to specific countries. For example, in India the role of village-level workers in helping rural communities cope with threats to their survival (flood, drought, famine, and so on), the *anganwadi* workers who play a central role in child development, nutrition, and health care and the front-line workers who work with village women to help them improve their status and economic situation are all noteworthy.

Israel's indigenous paraprofessionals who work with multi-problem families in a nationwide urban and rural community renewal program are unique. Under professional supervision they perform a wide range of functions, many of which are quite complex and demanding. They are viewed as having played a key role in the social and physical rehabilitation of 80 disadvantaged neighborhoods out of the 160 that have been targeted for renewal in Israel.

In Britain the bulk of the work that has to be carried out by the local authority social services departments is considered to be appropriate for paraprofessionals to perform. Many of these paraprofessional functions are similar to those found in other countries but some are less common or significant elsewhere than they are in Britain. For example, the role of home helps in maintaining the health and safety of elderly and disabled people who live at home is particularly significant.

It is estimated that about half the staff of community mental health centers in the USA are paraprofessionals. In these settings, they are performing a variety of therapeutic functions in day treatment, group counseling, after care, and community outreach. Although paraprofessionals are found in all human service settings in the USA, the paraprofessional movement has been closely related to the community mental health movement.

One of our purposes in looking at paraprofessional tasks and functions in different countries was to identify promising conceptions of how human service activities can best be divided between professionals and paraprofessionals. Our assumption is that clarity about professional and paraprofessional tasks and functions and the distinctions between them will result in efficient use of available resources and will contribute to effective service provision. A major problem that was encountered in seeking such definitions and distinctions is a general lack of clarity in all countries about the nature of both paraprofessional *and* professional tasks and functions. While the more simple and concrete paraprofessional activities are easy to differentiate from those activities that call for professional training, this is not so true when one looks at the more complex functions that many paraprofessionals perform. In many instances, there is a great deal of overlap between professional and paraprofessional roles.

Sometimes distinctions seem to be more a function of the type of population being served, the setting in which service is provided, or the geographic location of service than being based on any formal assessment of the needs of the people being served and the skills needed to meet their needs effectively. For example in Britain professionally trained personnel are more likely to work with families and mentally ill people while paraprofessionals tend to be the primary workers with elderly and disabled people. In both Britain and the USA paraprofessionals provide almost all the care and treatment to people in residential settings, since the latter are apparently not attractive to professionals. In India paraprofessionals are the front-line service providers in poor urban and rural communities, while professionally trained workers tend to be clustered in more affluent urban centers, serving less deprived client groups. In Israel paraprofessionals constitute the majority of social service workers in rural areas; they are the primary care-givers in the personal social services; and they tend to be closer to the community than professionals. When professionals are employed in rural settings, their turnover is usually quite high. While professionals do serve deprived groups, they are more frequently interested in providing services of a therapeutic or clinical nature. All of these patterns of personnel deployment appear to be the result of accident, professional preferences, or expediency rather than careful assessment of what is appropriate.

Nevertheless, we found some promising theoretical approaches to differentiating between professional and paraprofessional functions. In the USA the work that has been done in developing systems of allocating workers to episodes of service within social service teams based on their ability to take responsibility and handle complexity suggests some potentially productive approaches to staff differentiation. Similarly research in Britain on those social service functions that require a situational response or careful analysis based on professional training and judgment and those that can be largely prescribed ahead of time and, therefore, are appropriate for paraprofessionals can move our thinking forward about how work can be properly distributed between professional and paraprofessional personnel.

In our introductory chapter, we noted that there were at least three broad conceptual approaches to the deployment of paraprofessional workers. In the first case, it is possible to view them as assistants to professionals, carrying out simple, routine tasks that contribute to the work of the professional, under the latter's supervision. In spite of the fact that this is an appealing model conceptually, there is not much evidence that this is a model that is widely used in practice. Even those workers with the formal title of "social work assistant" in Britain more often than not carry responsibility for their own cases, rather than assisting professionals with the latter's cases.

The second approach to paraprofessional personnel deployment is simply to have them function as the primary and relatively autonomous front-line providers of service. This practice is fairly widespread in all four countries that we studied in detail and, of course, in remote rural areas of a country like India such an approach is inevitable since there is a severe shortage or, in many instances, a complete absence of professionally trained workers in these settings.

A third alternative is to view professionals and paraprofessionals as having distinct but complementary functions that can jointly be brought to bear upon the needs of people and communities. In this approach, they work alongside each other in a partnership or team model of service, each carrying out those tasks for which they are best suited. This has been an appealing conceptual model in all countries although its application in practice is not as widespread as its appeal would suggest.

It must be acknowledged that each of the above approaches to paraprofessional personnel deployment may be appropriate in particular situations. However, under ideal circumstances (for example, where both professional and paraprofessional staff are available and the latter can be offered training that will optimize their contribution to service goals) the team model is probably the most promising approach. It seems to have the greatest potential for making the most efficient use of available resources and, under certain circumstances, can lead to more extended and effective services. For example, evidence from Britain, India, Israel, and the USA suggests that decentralized community- or neighborhood-based teams can be particularly responsive to client or community needs if they include paraprofessional personnel who are drawn from the local community. In general, we would conclude that team models of human service personnel deployment based on appropriate distinctions between professional and paraprofessional functions are most likely to maximize the contribution that the latter can make to human service systems.

Professional–paraprofessional relationships

6

The nature of the relationship between professional and para-professional personnel in each country is examined in this chapter. Comparatively speaking, professional social workers in Britain have adopted a generally constructive posture towards their para-professional colleagues while in India, Israel, and the USA there is some degree of tension between professionals and paraprofessionals. Types and sources of strain and conflict are examined in order that they can better be understood and perhaps resolved, and potentially constructive approaches to dealing with areas of tension between professionals and paraprofessionals are identified.

BRITAIN

Distinctions between professional and paraprofessional social service personnel are of fairly recent origin in Britain. Prior to 1970, the paraprofessional (or more accurately in the British context, the unqualified or untrained) worker was the norm. It appears that as professional social work has grown in importance, there has been a corresponding or parallel recognition of the potential contribution that can be made to the social services by the person who does not have, and does not need, professional social work training. Consequently the position of the paraprofessional social service worker is fairly well recognized and accepted in Britain among government bodies, employers, and professional social workers alike. This does not mean that there are no areas of ambiguity, tension, and disagreement. It is simply that most discussion of contentious issues takes place in a climate that is generally supportive of paraprofessionals and that accepts the legitimacy of their place in the social services.

In the following discussion, we present a brief overview of professional–paraprofessional relationships in the British social services, examine the general climate that exists, and identify some areas of tension or controversy and some current trends.

Overview

In considering the relationship between professional and parapro-fessional social service personnel in the British context, it is useful to examine the way in which specific categories of workers function in relation to professional social workers. The three typical working relationships are as follows:

1 Paraprofessionals work for or assist social workers.
2 Paraprofessionals work alongside social workers.
3 Other professionals work alongside social workers.

In principle, social work assistants fall into category (1) but in practice they have tended to function under category (2). Many senior residential care staff, including directors of institutions, have tended to be viewed as belonging in category (2) but, in some regards, they can now be viewed as making some progress toward category (3). The same applies to home help organizers who have tended to be viewed as belonging in category (2) but recently have been making strong claims that would place them in (3). In summary, there have been some pressures in Britain in recent years to upgrade a number of categories of paraprofessional social service personnel, in many instances from particular groups themselves. This impetus for upward mobility has taken several forms, including a movement of paraprofessionals out of subordinate roles into parallel roles in relation to social workers, becoming social workers themselves, or becoming distinct professional groups that also work alongside social workers. These developments are by no means uniform or clear, nor are they necessarily widely recognized by other interest groups, for example social workers or employers. However, as a result of these developments, there is at least the potential for tension between social workers and these other occupational groups in the social services.

General acceptance of paraprofessionals

Since those persons we are calling paraprofessionals preceded the relatively recent appearance (in large numbers) of professional social workers in Britain, the issue of professional acceptance of the paraprofessional is complicated. Most British respondents to our international survey felt that the social work profession in general has accepted the paraprofessional. Although there may be reservations in some quarters, any resistance is considered to be quite small. Since its formation in 1969, the British Association of Social Workers (BASW) is reported to have been preoccupied with its own identity problems and to have paid very little attention to the paraprofessional. However, it seems to have endorsed the idea that many kinds of personnel are legitimately engaged in social service provision and that there is considerable overlap in the roles of these workers and in the training they need.

> "there is no rigid boundary between the practice of social work and social service and between the relevant forms of training . . . social workers and other social services staff should unite in the common task of helping people with problems, but the range of activities involved in offering such help is such that not all staff have to be trained in the same way or to the same extent."
> (Cypher 1979: 209)

Similarly the Central Council for Education and Training in Social Work (1975) sees the training and use of diverse kinds of social service personnel as contributing to the important work that social workers undertake.

> "The case for providing training related to the increasing diversity of staffing patterns within the social services in no way detracts from the key role of social workers. On the contrary, it reinforces the need to enable them to contribute their expertise within mixed staff teams."
> (Central Council for Education and Training in Social Work
> 1975: 19)

The value of using teams of different kinds of social service personnel to respond to people's needs is being increasingly recognized in Britain. For example Payne (1982: 26) asserts that "teamwork can . . . produce better work in the social services than other systems." He notes that much of the impetus for team models of social service delivery in both the USA and Britain has arisen in response to increased use of paraprofessional personnel (24). In Payne's view the most collaborative (and consequently most effective) teams are those in which the paraprofessionals are viewed as having a special contribution to make (32). He has suggested that the experience of working alongside paraprofessionals tends to have the effect of making social workers "less precious about so-called professional skills," resulting in some reassessment of the nature of the work that needs to be done to respond appropriately to clients' needs (24). This demystifying effect is reported by Cooper in relation to the performance of paraprofessional workers in the North of England.

> "If evidence is needed to demonstrate the quality of care or degree of responsibility able to be exercised by [these paraprofessionals], it is abundantly available in the tasks achieved by this group of workers. By force of sheer ability they have equalised the status difference between themselves and the qualified staff and refer to such staff mainly for information and departmental backup. Their achievement effectively undermines any pretence at professional mystique by qualified social workers."
>
> (Cooper 1980: 35)

As noted earlier, the Barclay Report (1982) on the role and tasks of social workers in the British social services endorsed just such a model of social work practice and social service provision utilizing community-based teams composed of social workers and different kinds of paraprofessional personnel. The report noted that the work that comes into a social service agency is such that it must be allocated appropriately among a diverse group of staff. In some specialized agencies the work might be such that most or all of it must be assigned to qualified professional social workers. In most instances, however, the volume and variety of work coming into an agency will probably be such that it is "appropriate to differentiate between the tasks according to the knowledge, skill, training, and experience required to carry them out" and will entail the use of a range of personnel carrying such designations as "social work assistant, welfare assistant, home help, care assistant, social worker, senior social worker and so on" (Barclay Report 1982: 137).

The above brief review sketches the type of support that exists among British social workers for the paraprofessional social service worker and outlines some recent trends that suggest that the paraprofessional will continue to play an important role in community-based social service teams. However, there are critics of these trends in British social work. For example in his dissenting addendum to the Barclay Report, Pinker (1982) criticized the type of community social work based on shared professional–paraprofessional responsibility recommended in the report and its implicit de-emphasis of conventional casework models of practice. Asserting that "social work and social casework are virtually synonymous" (239), Pinker stressed that "the powers and responsibilities of social workers cannot be brushed under the carpet of egalitarianism" (240). His opposition to the community-based team model of social work practice was summed up in quite graphic terms:

> "It conjures up the vision of a captainless crew under a patchwork ensign stitched together from remnants of the Red Flag and the Jolly Roger – all with a license and some with a disposition to mutiny – heading in the gusty winds of populist rhetoric, with presumption as their figurehead and inexperience as their compass, straight for the reefs of public incredulity."
>
> (Pinker 1982: 262)

M. Brown (1982) and Klein (1982) are also critical of the Barclay Report and are generally supportive of Pinker's position that, rather than move toward some kind of community-based practice, the social work profession should concentrate on refining its core (that is casework) skills in order to enhance its professional standing and public recognition. However, at present these views seem to represent the minority position. The tide of professional opinion would appear to be more in accord with Allen's posture:

> "I believe the time has come to reconsider the boundaries of social work. It appears that influential representatives of the profession are unwilling to contemplate this lest any 'watering down' of the profession in this country makes it lose status in the

EEC or across the Atlantic. To me this is an insufficient reason for resisting a re-think. If social work is unwilling to contemplate admitting to its rank large numbers of people engaged in very closely related activities it risks being stranded on the beach like a large whale while the other creatures of the sea continue their evolution by swimming with the tide."

(Allen 1984: 21)

Some contentious issues

Given the generally supportive posture of social workers toward the paraprofessional, it should not be surprising that there appears to be very little antagonism towards social workers on the part of paraprofessionals. Of course, this does not mean that paraprofessionals bear uniformly favorable feelings about their role, status, and opportunities for recognition. As we have already noted, the policies and practices of both the central and local governments gave a central role to qualified social workers in the development of the new consolidated social services departments (SSDs) that came into existence in the early 1970s. As a reflection of these priorities, personnel practices and training policies appear to have been more beneficial to social workers than to other categories of personnel. At any rate, as Hey (1975: 11) has noted, "the system is felt by non-social workers to be weighted against them."

A 1978 study of social service teams revealed considerable ambivalence among paraprofessional team members about their role and status. There was "a tension between the [social work] assistants' stated and evident enjoyment of, and commitment to, their work and their feelings of resentment about their status and job opportunities" (Hallett 1978: 155–56). Interestingly both the social workers and the paraprofessionals in the teams studied felt that the latter did not receive the recognition they deserved.

"There was . . . the feeling that they were undervalued – not by their immediate colleagues but by the hierarchy. As one social worker said:
    'If they packed up tomorrow I don't know what would happen.'
Another said:
    'Social work assistants are not recognized as doing social

work with the elderly and handicapped; if they were to apply for upgrading they would be told they should not be doing this type of work.'

An assistant who was about to train as a social worker, summed up the assistants' feelings:

'I think social work assistants are very undervalued, and underpaid, and I don't think it is appreciated just how much they do and how good they are as well. I can say that now I'm not going to be one.' "

(Hallett 1978: 159)

While the roles and tasks of most paraprofessional social service personnel in Britain (home helps, care assistants, wardens, and so on) are quite distinct from the work performed by professionally trained social workers, the same cannot be said of social work assistants who, as Hey (1978: 22–3) has noted, frequently carry cases that need "the systematic application of social work knowledge and skills if they are to be handled requisitely." Given the overlap of roles between social workers and social work assistants and the reported disparities in status and reward between the two groups, it is in the relationship between these two groups that tension and resentment are likely to be most acutely felt. However, as Hallett (1978: 159) notes, the frustrations of social work assistants seem to be directed more toward "the system" than to their professional colleagues.

Just as the position of social work assistants in area social service teams contains some contradictions and sources of inherent or overt tension or conflict, similarly there have been some structural tensions inherent in the relationship between holders of the Certificate of Qualification in Social Work (CQSW) – professional social workers – and those who hold the Certificate in Social Service (CSS) qualification. Fortunately some positive steps are being taken to resolve these problems. Since the great majority of what are called "field social workers" now have professional social work (CQSW) credentials, the CSS was intended to provide a parallel qualification for those social service personnel who are primarily engaged in such activities as the administration of residential and day care programs for the elderly, young children, and mentally impaired people, organizers of home-care services for the aging and infirm, some types of community work, and some administrative functions. In fact CSS holders tend to be concentrated in day and residential care, with only a minority engaged in field services (for example in the work of area social service teams).

When it introduced CSS training in the mid-1970s the Central Council for Education and Training in Social Work (CCETSW) asserted it was different from but equivalent to professional social work training (Ash et al. 1980). This led to some confusion about the exact nature of the differences and similarities. There has clearly been a status difference between the two which is reflected in many ways, including the tendency for most professional social workers in Britain (including most of the respondents to our survey) to regard holders of the CSS credential as paraprofessionals, despite the fact that those CSS holders who are employed as social workers are eligible for membership in the professional association. Similarly, because CQSW training has occurred primarily in university or polytechnic settings while CSS training has taken place in technical colleges and colleges of further education, the status differences between the two tend to be reinforced (Hartnoll 1984: 26). While they are purported to be parallel and, in some senses, equal, holders of the CQSW are not only accorded higher status but also frequently earn higher salaries. This has been a matter of concern, especially in departments where some CSS and CQSW holders are performing similar jobs (Bessell 1982). In general, the precise relationship between the professionally trained social worker and the person with the CSS credential has been a somewhat contentious issue.

There is a significant body of opinion that asserts that the two credentials should be viewed as equivalent, that they are simply different routes to the same end. For example, Bessell (1982: 17) claims that there is no clear difference in skills between CQSW and CSS holders. He notes that, "while there are, no doubt, variations in standard between one CSS course and another, as there are between CQSW courses, I can discern no general difference in the ability or knowledge of students graduating from either type of course." He has advocated a move toward regarding the two credentials as equivalent and interchangeable, citing previous efforts to create different levels of social work practitioners which had undesirable consequences, including invidious status differences, and a variety of other inequities. A major danger in maintaining what he considers to be unsupportable distinctions between CSS and CQSW holders is, according to Bessell, the inevitable distrust and rivalry created.

In fact, following an extensive review of CQSW and CSS training and the relationship between them (Central Council for Education and Training in Social Work 1983c), CCETSW (1985a) has taken steps toward consolidating the two, that is, having the two types of training lead to the single credential – the Certificate of Qualification in Social Work. At the time of writing, this has not been finally settled but appears to be well on the way to being accomplished.

Summary

It would appear that the paraprofessional has a more firmly established place in the social services and enjoys more acceptance and support by social workers, employers, and government agencies in Britain than is the case in some other countries in our study (for example the USA). This does not mean that there are no unresolved issues or that the working relationship between the professional and paraprofessional could not be improved. However, from the evidence we have been able to gather, it seems that the general posture of all concerned is to seek constructive resolution of those issues that remain.

INDIA

In this section on professional–paraprofessional relationships in India, we review the status of the social work profession and the fact that it is not yet well-established. It appears to have paid little heed to paraprofessionals and yet is somewhat threatened by these workers. We examine the sources of strain between the two groups and identify some positive aspects of the situation.

The social work profession in India

Indian respondents to our international survey indicated that the social work profession in their country had shown only limited support for paraprofessionals, having accepted their participation in the human services with reservations – in some cases, grave reservations (Brawley and Schindler 1985). We were interested in

of welfare work among the handicapped and deprived groups is done under voluntary auspices. Voluntary agencies are the implementing bodies of welfare schemes sponsored by the government."

(Ranade and Chatkrjee 1982: 9)

As we noted in an earlier chapter, the work of these voluntary organizations is guided and supported through grants-in-aid by the Central Social Welfare Board. The range of services provided by these government-supported voluntary organizations is enormous and includes programs directed to the welfare of women, children, and physically handicapped people, supplementary child nutrition programs, nursery schools and mobile creches, and counseling services for mentally handicapped people (Central Social Welfare Board 1985). All of these programs, which in many ways can be viewed as representing the mainstream of social welfare activity in India, are staffed predominantly by paraprofessional personnel.

Another aspect of the gulf between professionals and paraprofessionals is the fact that professionally trained social workers appear to practice primarily in major urban centers and in services that do not address the most dire needs. D'Souza (1982: 22) has gone so far as to state that "the role of professional social work has in fact to a large extent been dysfunctional to the existent problem situation in India. . . . we have not been able to generate front-line workers to meet the manpower needs of the country for social development." Indeed the Ministry of Social Welfare (1982: 33) has recently indicated that "the future development of welfare services will have to give greater attention to the needs of rural areas, tribal areas, urban slums and the underprivileged sections of society." It is the general view in India that this role will be taken on primarily by paraprofessionals, thereby further widening the gap between professionals and paraprofessionals in terms of their areas of major activity.

Another aspect of the distance between professionals and paraprofessionals is the increasingly activist role that the latter are taking in India, a trend that academics and other observers expect will accelerate over time. These developments are creating tensions that permeate the social welfare field, professional groups, and voluntary human service organizations. There has been a shift in emphasis among front-line workers from the provision of ameliorative services and the promotion of infrastructural development to social and political action on behalf of disadvantaged groups or communities, the purpose of which is to "fight exploitation and secure justice as perceived by them" (Kulkarni 1977: 20).

"Thirty years of political independence has made people aware of what their basic rights are under the Constitution and under the law of the land. When they find they have not fair or even access to benefits of development but also are not able to exercise and enjoy their basic rights the culture of silence starts turning into a culture of protest. Certain individuals either out of intellectual conviction or out of personal experience or both begin to intervene in the seething discontent in order to organize and direct it into a conscious force of social transformation."

(Kulkarni 1977: 20–1)

An increasing number of social action groups is emerging in relation to the unorganized poor. Rather than concentrating on social development programs like sinking wells, building reservoirs, or developing health services, they aim at awakening the people to their rights. The types of issues addressed include the enforcement of minimum wage legislation for agricultural laborers, land reform laws and government policies in regard to rural employment, and the assertion of people's rights over forest lands and products. The ultimate goal of many of these activities is to build mass democratic organizations of the poor. In some cases, these activities have been initiated by persons from outside the community in question but in many instances they are grassroots movements. In either case, front-line paraprofessional workers are frequently involved.

It should be mentioned that the desire for greater action on behalf of people's rights is supported by some members of the social work profession since they see the possibility of bringing about positive social change through such methods. These persons advocate the Gandhian approach to change based on civil disobedience. It is anticipated that the issue of activism will be a growing source of controversy and conflict in the human services in India in the years ahead.

An additional source of strain between professionals and paraprofessionals is the competition for jobs that exists, particularly in some urban areas, despite the occupational distance that exists between the two groups as a general rule. Because many state governments have established their own institutes or centers for the training of paraprofessionals, these types of personnel are often preferred to professionals because of the particular training they have received and their lower cost. The matter is compounded by the fact that professional social work education in India occurs primarily at the postgraduate level and, therefore, it is frequently suggested that social workers with master's degrees are overqualified for many jobs, thereby limiting their employment opportunities.

Positive elements and developments in the relationship

The above factors indicate that the social work profession has organizational and identity problems that place it at some distance from the paraprofessional. At the same time, there are issues that tend to further alienate the two groups from each other. Nevertheless, there are some positive aspects of the situation and some developments under way that may bring them closer together in the future.

In general, there is considerably less conflict between professionals and paraprofessionals in India stemming from competition (real or perceived) for jobs than is the case in other countries we studied, for example, the USA and Israel. This is attributable, in large measure, to the relative scarcity of professionals in India. Similarly, some of the role strain that exists for paraprofessionals in human service agencies in other countries is less evident, again because of the absence of large numbers of professionally trained front-line workers and also the decentralized nature of many of the human services in India.

Hage and Aiken (1970) have suggested that in organizations openness to change is inversely related to the degree to which roles are formalized and decision-making is centralized. This means that, if human service agencies are to be responsive to client and community needs, staff functions must be reasonably flexible and decision-making has to be relatively decentralized. In fact the absence of professional workers in front-line roles and the relative decentralization of services in India, particularly in rural areas, does seem to allow paraprofessionals to be more responsive to client and community needs than is the case in other countries. For example in Israel there appears to be more co-optation and control of paraprofessionals by their professional colleagues and by their employing organizations than is the case in India.

These observations do not lead us to conclude that the work of paraprofessionals is more effective in India than in Israel but we did note that bureaucratic and professional controls on paraprofessionals in India, especially those working in rural areas, are quite limited. This seems to permit greater sensitivity and responsiveness to the needs of local populations on the part of these workers and leads them to be more spontaneous, innovative, and open to the contribution of others in the helping process than is true in the more professionalized and bureaucratized services of other countries.

As we mentioned elsewhere, the Association of Schools of Social Work was established in India in the early 1960s. Its growth since then has been significant, encompassing as it does over forty schools of social work at this writing. The recent Review of Social Work Education carried out by an expert group appointed by the University Grants Commission (1980), in addressing the need to upgrade the academic standards of schools of social work, also revealed the need for a standard-setting or accrediting body that would take leadership in this task. It is anticipated that the Association of Schools of Social Work will be given this responsibility and will be expected to take a comprehensive approach to social welfare personnel development.

Within this comprehensive training system, the place of paraprofessional training has been clearly enunciated: "The paraprofessional worker should be the first level field worker. This stage is self-contained and terminal in itself. . . . Paraprofessional training should be . . . one of the major streams at the higher secondary level such as commerce, technical and home science courses" (University Grants Commission 1980: 69–70). Desai (1985), the author of this seminal document, indicates that many schools are now preparing professional social workers to work with paraprofessional personnel and, in some instances, the latter are being directly trained within universities, through educational extension programs. Thus the association and its constituent members are beginning to adopt the recommended comprehensive approach to educational planning which includes paraprofessional training – a step that has not been characteristic of higher education in India in the past. At least in principle, this establishes the place of paraprofessional personnel within the mainstream of social work education. Perhaps more importantly, it creates a degree of educational accountability, continuity, and credibility which is often lacking in in-service and ad hoc training programs. It also opens up the opportunity for educational advancement for the paraprofessional within the structure of higher education.

Whether the initiative taken by the association will really bring the paraprofessional into the mainstream of social work professional concern remains to be seen. One of the problems relates to the diversity of human service training that exists today for paraprofessionals in India. There is an enormous and growing number of human service organizations that employ paraprofessionals who have received their training under a variety of auspices. These include the Association of Moral and Social Hygiene, an organization which addresses the problems of prostitution, the Family Planning Association, and the Integrated Child Development Program, all of which operate independently and separately from universities. It has been suggested that these human services may operate in ways that have little in common with the practices of the social work profession:

> "Although these organizations have contributed considerably to the furtherance of social work on a professional basis, we cannot call them professional organizations in social work as they are primarily interested in the promotion of a wide range of programs and activities of social welfare and are administered and controlled mainly by social workers who have no formal training in social work. . . .
>
> Even though these organizations at times subscribe to the traditional concepts of social work, based upon the ideas of self-sacrifice, personal dedication and constructive work under the influence of their policy making bodies, [they] have little commitment to professional social work ethics."
>
> (Nagpaul 1972b: 400–01)

However, despite cautionary notes such as these, the efforts by the Association of Schools of Social Work and its member schools to bring paraprofessional training into the mainstream of social work education is noteworthy and, if successful, could go some way towards narrowing the gulf between professionals and paraprofessionals in India.

Summary

The social work profession in India appears to have been too preoccupied with its own concerns to devote much attention to paraprofessional human service personnel. This professional distance may have been reinforced by the structure of human service employment in India. For example, the fact that over half of professionally trained social workers are employed in industrial welfare jobs tends to separate them from typical core areas of paraprofessional activity. Another contributing factor relates to the separate auspices of training. Professionals are trained in graduate schools in universities while paraprofessionals receive their training under the auspices of a variety of specialized government or voluntary organizations. Paradoxically, in spite of this distance between the two groups, they are sometimes in competition with each other for jobs in urban areas which creates additional strain. The complexity and urgency of social problems in India may be bringing about a more aggressive stance on the part of many paraprofessional workers, further widening their ideological and service distance from professionals.

However, there are positive elements in the situation. There is generally less conflict between professionals and paraprofessionals stemming from competition for jobs and paraprofessionals seem to be subject to less professional and organizational control and co-optation than their counterparts in other countries. The commitment of the Association of Schools of Social Work and its member schools to take a more comprehensive approach to social welfare training holds some promise of bringing professional social workers and paraprofessional human service personnel into a closer and more harmonious relationship, although it remains to be seen whether these efforts will be successful.

ISRAEL

The social work profession in Israel

In Israel social work is in the process of striving for professionalization. Its boundaries and domain are not yet well defined. It is searching for recognition through the development of its professional association but, as yet, it is not protected by law.

In 1958 Israel's parliament, the Knesset, enacted welfare legislation,

Chok Hassad, requiring local communities and municipalities to provide social services for those in need. In an address to parliament in 1956 the assistant minister of social welfare stated that "the first principle of social welfare is the need and necessity to provide social services for citizens in every community" (Divre Haknesset 1956: 1,996). The minister encouraged persons who had the knowledge, compassion, and understanding to help the indigent and needy. The social work profession was mentioned by inference. However, up until the present time, social work can still mean a range of ideas and functions to the general public that do not necessarily correspond to definitions of professional social work practice by those who are members of the profession. As a consequence, the social work profession has looked inwards in order to strengthen its organizational base and to project its professional image to the public. Indeed, once a loosely knit organization, it has become much stronger in recent years and is now, in effect, the gatekeeper to professional entry. Only through possession of a recognized social work degree can one enter its ranks. In many respects, it has achieved a standard-setting role in the welfare arena through and on behalf of its 4,000 members.

The association has made some effort to gain legal recognition for the social work profession, following the example of the psychological association which achieved passage of legislation in 1977 that permits only professionally qualified psychologists to practise in the public and private sectors. But such effort has been minimal. The social work profession's main objective in seeking such a law is to become a legally recognized and sanctioned profession that can control who may practise social work in Israel. The stated purpose of these efforts is to ensure that a high quality of service is maintained.

In addition to the role played by the Israeli Association of Social Workers, the schools of social work within higher education have strengthened the professional identity and practice of social work. There are now five schools of social work in Israel – two in Tel Aviv and one each in Hifah, Beer Sheba, and Jerusalem.

Professional reservations about paraprofessional employment

The reaction of professional social workers to the employment of paraprofessional human service workers has been both negative and positive. Because of the social work profession's relative newness there is a natural tendency to be protective of its status and role. Although all indicators reflect growing social problems in Israel and shortages of trained personnel who can deal with these problems, plans for producing the needed personnel have not been developed. The social work profession has concentrated on establishing itself as a group that, on the basis of its expertise, can claim an exclusive right to perform particular kinds of work in the social welfare field.

Many social workers express the view that the employment of paraprofessionals adversely affects the quality of social service provision. They take the position that most human service tasks demand a full understanding of the client's situation and the ability to recognize problems. For example, the director of a community service program near Tel Aviv expressed reluctance to employ paraprofessionals because of her fear of "shortchanging" the clients of her program. She suggested that paraprofessionals lacked professional standards of accountability in dealing with clients. Although the life experiences and other attributes of paraprofessionals were recognized as being valuable, they were not seen as substitutes for professional expertise.

It has been suggested that the employment of indigenous paraprofessionals tends to make human service agencies more accountable to the client community. However, this conflicts with traditional accountability patterns in professionally directed and staffed agencies where professional self-regulation and accountability are the norm. For example in Project Renewal nonprofessionals from the communities served were added to the steering committee with the purpose of gaining the viewpoint of the client community. This had the effect of making professional social workers and other staff more accountable to the client population and while this innovative idea was recognized as being sound, it was also threatening to the professionals involved.

Other reasons given by professionals for their reticence about the employment of indigenous paraprofessionals include arguments to the effect that paying community residents to carry out human service and community development functions could discourage the development of lay leadership and that the employment of people who have not undergone the rigorous university education needed to qualify as a professional social worker is unfair to those who have.

Finally, one cannot ignore the realities of the job market in Israel. As we mentioned in the last chapter, there have been increasing numbers of redundancies in the human service sector. With a recent cut of 300 jobs in the human services, occurring primarily in local welfare departments, one can easily understand the anxiety experienced by social workers. The employment situation is particularly serious in the urban areas, less so in rural settings.

Professional support for the paraprofessional

While there are reservations in some sectors of the social work profession about paraprofessional employment, the response of other social workers is positive and paraprofessionals are welcomed as valuable participants in the human services. In-depth interviews with a large number of professionals who have either trained, supervised, or worked in some capacity with paraprofessional personnel revealed a generally positive attitude towards paraprofessionals and the view that they play a vital role in service provision (Schindler 1982). To begin with, it is recognized that many human services in Israel simply could not function without paraprofessional staff. In the personal social services, their contribution is seen as being especially important. In Chapter 4 we mentioned the crucial role of auxiliary personnel in programs and services addressed to the needs of elderly people. The situation is even more pronounced in the field of mental retardation and rehabilitation. According to Sadan (1985) there are over 3,000 paraprofessionals serving this client population. Whether as house parents in residential settings or teachers in vocational rehabilitation programs, their presence is vital. The value of their work is also recognized in neighborhood and community centers where the majority of the staff are nonprofessionals, including center directors, teachers, and group leaders.

The unique contribution that indigenous paraprofessionals can make to services for certain clients and communities because of their closeness to client populations and first-hand knowledge of their needs is also widely acknowledged. Israel epitomizes the concept of cultural diversity since its population is drawn from some seventy countries. Providing human services to this population in ways that are acceptable and effective requires understanding of the cultural dimensions involved in helping different groups. In many instances paraprofessional personnel bring this essential cultural expertise to the human services. For example Jews from the Yemen react differently in regard to self-help, the extended family, and welfare benefits than immigrants from Eastern Europe. The case of a Yemenite family facing an economic crisis illustrates this point. The father's unemployment was causing great hardship to the family but income support in the form of unemployment insurance was rejected because of the perceived stigma that this would entail. The oldest child wanted to leave school to support the family. However, a paraprofessional worker was familiar with the family and called a meeting of the extended family that totalled some thirty relatives. Within two weeks of this meeting, a job had been found for the father, the child was able to remain in school, and the economic crisis was resolved.

The importance of understanding and being able to work with ethnic and cultural minority groups is also illustrated in the case of the Ethiopian community. The arrival in Israel of large numbers of Ethiopian Jews in 1984–85 brought a host of problems that have not yet been fully solved. However, paraprofessional human service workers who had come to Israel from Ethiopia ten years earlier have played a vital mediating role between the authorities and the new immigrants and have helped to clarify many complex issues. While problems remain, these indigenous workers continue to play important front-line roles as interpreters and negotiators.

A recurring theme in the responses of professional social workers to the employment of paraprofessionals concerns the value of involving current or former recipients of service in service-providing roles. Certainly, the special insights and skills of ex-prisoners and former alcoholics in working with persons who are struggling with the problems that they themselves have faced are generally recognized. This point is also relevant to such programs as Project Renewal. One social worker summarized the unique value of capitalizing on the perspective of clients or consumers of services in the following terms: "Only they can really tell us what physical and social changes are sought. Only they can really bring about true change" (Schindler 1982: 16). In the past, democratic participation was limited to electing representatives to the municipality and the parliament every four years. In Project Renewal community residents have a taste of direct democratic decision-making. For the first time, they are participating in decisions about what goes on in their own neighborhoods. Being part of a Project Renewal team, either as steering committee members or as paraprofessional block workers, brings new-found status and influence. Decisions formerly taken in Jerusalem are now taken together with community residents in their own neighborhoods. Many paraprofessionals speak for their block groups and others have a say in a variety of policy spheres.

However, local community decision-making can create problems in some instances. In one development project, the independence of the local residents was extreme. They opposed the government on every issue. In fact, they were so independent that their neighborhood committee had concentrated all road improvements and the construction of play areas in their immediate vicinity, to the neglect of other equally needy areas. Obviously a more balanced approach was called for in this case. On the other hand, it should be noted that the recommendations of paraprofessionals are simply ignored in many instances.

An additional value of paraprofessionals mentioned by professionals is the level of caring and commitment they bring to their work in the human services. There was a consensus among the professionals interviewed that social work is becoming excessively clinical in focus, with treatment as the major approach to solving people's problems. The traditional humanitarian and social reform functions of social work and the importance of self-help are being given less emphasis by the profession. This is not a new issue, having been raised by Katz and Eisenstadt (1960) in regard to professions in general and specifically in relation to social work by Carr-Saunders (1965). The latter notes that, at the turn of the century, social workers took a comprehensive view of society's problems whereas today the focus is on very specific problems that individuals are facing.

"We find specialist social workers of many kinds such as probation officers, hospital social workers. . . . The professional man no longer takes a comprehensive interest in his client. He feels that he has no general responsibility for those who come under his care and the personal relationship between practitioner and client is weakened."

(Carr-Saunders 1965: 283)

Bisno (1956) was similarly critical of the social work profession in the USA when he talked about the displacement of social work's goals from social reform to the application of specific treatment techniques and methods. There is a belief among some social workers in Israel that paraprofessional personnel can counter these trends.

A final factor mentioned by social workers in support of paraprofessionals is that adequate social services cannot be offered in many communities without their participation. The lack of professionally trained workers has been a particular concern in Israel's developmental towns where it has adversely affected the ability to provide adequate social welfare, health, and educational services. If service is offered at all, what occurs is referred to as the commuter phenomenon where professionals travel daily to developmental towns from major cities to teach or provide other services and return home at night. The general opinion is that the professionals involved gain more from this than their clients who are deprived of ongoing services. The problem of access to service is especially acute in the evenings and on weekends. Strong dissatisfaction with availability and continuity of services has been expressed by residents of developmental towns and other isolated communities. Interviews by one of the authors with residents of a developmental town in the north revealed deep frustration with the limited access to educational, cultural, health, and social services.

Situations causing role strain for the paraprofessional

One of the unique features of Project Renewal is the concept of twinning rural and urban communities in Israel with Jewish communities in the USA. This twinning program includes the receipt of financial support from the US communities involved, together with matching funds from the government. For example, the Los Angeles Jewish community is considered to be one of the most active and supportive. Not only does it provide substantial monetary assistance but over a hundred of its lay leaders have visited its twin, the Mussrara neighborhood in Jerusalem. This cooperation is admirable but it also creates some dilemmas for paraprofessional workers in carrying out their dual functions as service providers and service recipients or their representatives in these communities. They are frequently placed in the position of having to balance their loyalties to the agency that employs them and the community they represent. If they are open and frank in their criticism of the organization, they realize that this might jeopardize the development and financial support of future projects. If they fail to express their honest assessment of the needs of the community and the organization's effectiveness in meeting these needs, they are shortchanging the community. This places them in an organizational bind with little room for maneuver. (See also Grosser 1966 in regard to comparable conflicts facing paraprofessionals in the USA.)

Paraprofessionals in Israel, like many of their counterparts in other countries, work in diverse settings, ranging from public welfare agencies to community centers, from Head Start programs to after care services. In many of these settings, paraprofessionals claim that professionals pay lip service to involving them in decisions about service needs and activities but in practice severely limit their participation. In many cases, a process of co-optation or perhaps more accurately what Etzioni (1964) has called simulated co-optation takes place in which professionals use paraprofessionals to soften problems that may arise between the human service agency and its clients, limit confrontation while appearing to increase communication, with full knowledge that substantive issues have not been addressed. Austin (1978: 165) suggests that "such co-optation can lead to the paraprofessionals' loss of touch with the community." This problem is exacerbated in human service organizations where professionals outnumber or otherwise dominate paraprofessionals. In these situations paraprofessionals are more likely to adopt professional attitudes and modes of behavior and in the process lose those attributes that make them especially sensitive to and effective in working with disadvantaged clients and communities. In other words, their intuitiveness, spontaneity, and identification with their community is weakened (Loewenberg 1968).

These findings have prompted some human service agencies to exercise greater selectivity in the recruitment process. Paraprofessionals are sought who identify strongly with the community and its needs. Nevertheless, the pressures on the paraprofessional are the same and may even be increased in these circumstances. Negative judgments and poor job performance ratings can be made about paraprofessionals as a result of their dual status as staff members and community residents. Strong identification with the community can be seen as weakening objectivity and effectiveness in carrying out agency policies while membership in the organization and adoption of its values reduces identification with the community and the ability to work effectively with its residents. These problems are less critical in settings where paraprofessionals predominate (for example, services to the elderly, children, prisoners, alcoholics, retarded people, and multi-problem families) but where membership in the community is an important attribute of the paraprofessional personnel involved, as in Project Renewal, role strain is inevitable.

Finally, one must make note of some political realities in Israel. In rural communities in particular, a person's political affiliation will often determine whether or not he or she is hired as a paraprofessional human service worker. Political allegiance can also play a part in how effective one is in meeting people's needs. If a paraprofessional's political affiliation corresponds to that of the people in power, then a more certain and rapid response to requests for social change or specific services can be expected than would be the case if affiliations differed. For example, a group of village representatives reported in a meeting with one of the authors that they were faced with inordinate bureaucratic obstacles to the provision of needed services because their efforts to obtain these services were organized by a person whose loyalties were not with the dominant political party. These kinds of situations clearly impair paraprofessionals' effectiveness as advocates for their clients.

At times, political parties exert pressure on paraprofessionals and exploit any vulnerabilities they may have. A good case in point is a situation that arose with some of the paraprofessionals who worked with recent Ethiopian immigrants. As we already mentioned, the arrival of the latter group was accompanied by a number of problems and cultural strains that could not have been eased without the help of Ethiopian paraprofessionals who had come to Israel about ten years earlier and were able to serve as mediators between government agencies and the Ethiopian community. However, some of the younger members of this group were persuaded by political promises to pursue courses of action that were, in some cases, clearly not in the best interests of the Ethiopian community. In these cases, the welfare of the people became secondary to sectional political advantage.

Political affiliation is not as salient in urban areas as it is in rural communities, partly because there is less dependence on patronage and a greater range of employment opportunities in the cities. However, political pressures of one kind or another frequently cause conflict or strain for the paraprofessional in Israel.

Summary

The social work profession in Israel has concentrated on developing a strong professional association and is currently attempting to achieve legal control over who can practice social work. This is a long-term goal but one that has been consistently articulated over the years. These professional priorities and the realities of the work that has to be done in the human services are reflected in the mixed responses of professional social workers to the employment of paraprofessionals. On the one hand, there are reservations or, in some cases, strong resistance based on such issues as the need to maintain high standards of service to people and fear of competition with paraprofessionals for jobs in a shrinking human service employment market. On the other hand, many professionals recognize that large sectors of the human services in Israel could not operate without paraprofessional staff and that indigenous paraprofessionals have knowledge and skills that are valuable in the provision of services to ethnic minority and other disadvantaged groups. Finally, in this section, we identified a number of sources of strain (professional, organizational, and political) that can impair indigenous paraprofessionals' effectiveness in serving their clients and communities.

UNITED STATES OF AMERICA

The social work profession in the USA

Like all the newer professions, social work has been preoccupied with its status in the professional hierarchy (Vollmer and Mills 1966). Since Flexner (1915) asked, "Is social work a profession?", at the 1915 National Conference of Charities and Corrections, US social workers have striven hard to demonstrate that they have all the necessary attributes of a profession.

If we accept the criteria used by Greenwood (1957) and others, we would have to conclude that a fair degree of professionalization has occurred in social work in the USA. Social workers claim to have developed a theoretical base of knowledge and a repertoire of practice skills which derive from that knowledge. They have achieved control over access to this knowledge through accreditation of professional education. The professional association controls, to some degree, social work practice through licensure or certification of qualified practitioners in a growing number of states (*NASW News* 1984).

However, in spite of all its efforts, social work has remained a relatively low-status profession in the USA. Its knowledge base, in common with most of the social and behavioral science professions, is both broad and vague. As Wilensky has observed:

> "All occupations in the human relations field have only tenuous claim to exclusive competence. This results not only from their newness, uncertain standards, and the embryonic state of the social and psychological sciences on which they draw, but also from the fact that the types of problems dealt with are part of everyday life. The lay public cannot recognize the need for special competence in an area where everyone is 'expert.'"
>
> (Wilensky 1964: 145)

Specifically in relation to social work's plight, it has been observed that it "has had to fight a constant rearguard action against the pervasive notion that any man with love in his heart can do the job" (N. E. Cohen 1955: 233).

More severe critics of social work deny its claim to any unique body of knowledge. Proponents of this point of view would relegate it to the status of a semi-profession within Etzioni's (1969) typology which differentiates the life-and-death and knowledge-producing professions, like law and medicine, from the service-giving or knowledge-using professions, such as nursing and teaching. Public identification of the social worker with a low-status clientele has added to social work's status problems since a profession with a predominantly low-status clientele is unlikely to be accorded high status by the dominant groups in society. Finally, the threat to the status quo implicit in social work's social reform heritage – regardless of the relatively small part this has played in recent social work practice – has tended to differentiate it from the higher prestige professions which, according to Lipset and Schwartz (1966: 302), are "among the more conservative elements in society" in that they manifest "satisfaction with the status quo and opposition to change."

Therefore, despite the progress that social work has made in the USA in developing the basic attributes of a profession, it is neither widely recognized nor highly regarded by the public at large or by influential groups in society. Consequently it remains somewhat insecure and defensive and its posture toward the paraprofessional social service worker must be viewed in that light.

Social work's response to the paraprofessional

As is true in the other countries in our study, large numbers of untrained personnel have always been employed in the human services in the USA. However, it was during the 1960s that a number of forces joined together to focus attention on paraprofessional personnel and their particular role in social service provision. A continuing shortage of trained social workers, a restructuring of the social services, and a national policy of employing the poor in human service organizations all led to the introduction of large numbers of minority group and low income paraprofessionals into social service employment during the 1960s. The social work profession affirmed the necessity and desirability of this trend, not only as a means of solving personnel shortages but also because many of these new entrants to the field of social work were indigenous to the client groups that social work sought to serve and they had attributes and skills that enabled them to work effectively with these groups.

In fact the organized social work profession in the USA through both its practice arm, the National Association of Social Workers (NASW), and its educational standard-setting body, the Council on Social Work Education (CSWE), engaged in a wide range of activities that recognized and supported the contribution of the paraprofessional. These activities reflected a desire on the part of NASW and CSWE to play an active and constructive role in the specification of an appropriate place for the paraprofessional in social service provision and the development of necessary training programs and opportunities for career advancement for this category of personnel.

However, as the problems and promises of the 1960s receded into history, the social work profession's support for the paraprofessional in the USA largely disappeared (Brawley 1980). Efforts to specify appropriate practice roles for the paraprofessional and support for their training have all but ceased. Recent personnel policies of NASW ignore this level of worker, as do its licensing and other regulatory efforts. In the educational sphere, CSWE now provides none of the tangible services or assistance (such as the faculty workshops, publications, or technical assistance) to paraprofessional training programs that it formerly did.

Aside from a general tightening of the human service employment market (Hardcastle and Katz 1979), a major force working against social work's continued acceptance of the paraprofessional has been the "deprofessionalization" or "declassification" movement in the social services that began early in the 1970s and is still a major concern within the profession. NASW (1971: 3) warned its members that representatives of the national government were repeatedly expressing the opinion that "there is little, if any, correlation between a master's degree in social work and the kind of services that this country needs" and that "people with less education and a different kind of education are required in the new delivery system." These early warnings were confirmed by a series of court decisions that caused some states to eliminate the need for professional social work qualifications for certain jobs because they could not demonstrate that these qualifications were necessary for adequate job performance (Pecora and Austin 1983).

The declassification issue has remained a contentious one throughout the 1970s and into the 1980s and NASW has attempted to combat the threat that it represents by, among other things, devoting substantial effort to the achievement of legal recognition or licensure of social workers. This involves legally restricting the practice of social work to professionally trained social workers. NASW reports considerable progress toward this goal (NASW News 1978a: 11). At the same time, NASW (1982) has promulgated a new set of standards for classifying the social service labor force that replaces the previous NASW (1974) standards and eliminates the two pre-professional or paraprofessional levels that the 1974 policy contained.

Another aspect of the fight against declassification is NASW's effort to develop procedures for the "validation" of social work. To counter moves to declassify social work positions in social agencies, that is to open them to non-social workers, NASW has recently given high priority to projects that validate social work, that is demonstrate to state civil service systems why social service jobs require professional social workers (Teare *et al.* 1984).

While these activities do not, on their face, say that paraprofessionals are to be prevented from participating in the provision of social services, the intent clearly is to curtail the employment of paraprofessional personnel. Minimally the psychological climate created is an adversary rather than supportive one.

Systemic barriers to optimum use of the paraprofessional

While the declassification issue, together with a less expansive job market for social service personnel, may explain the present unsympathetic attitude toward the paraprofessionals, there are other less obvious factors that should also be considered. For example, there is some evidence that, even when the social work profession was most committed to the use of paraprofessionals, there were systemic barriers to the full acceptance and optimum use of this type of worker.

In a study of the impact of the paraprofessional on the professional's role in a variety of anti-poverty programs in the 1960s, Denham and Shatz (1969) found that the professionals involved experienced a high level of anxiety and reacted negatively towards their paraprofessional colleagues for a variety of reasons. For example, the frequent argument that the use of the paraprofessional for performance of simple routine tasks would free the professional for performance of previously undone tasks requiring a high degree of skill or the assumption of new tasks was not realized in any patterned or sustained fashion in the programs studied. In many agencies, the professionals had historically performed a multiplicity of tasks, many of which were of a simple routine nature, so that they had "had little opportunity to use, let alone develop, the more highly technical skills" and furthermore "had become accustomed to performing routine functions" (Denham and Shatz 1969: 181). In addition to the expectation that they would function as "expert practitioners" the professionals were often expected to take on the role of "training supervisors" of the paraprofessionals. This was also a role for which most were unprepared and to which they reacted "with considerable anxiety, much of which was displaced on the aides, who were accused of being trouble-makers and interfering with the old order" (181).

A major systemic problem which the Denham and Shatz (1969) study revealed and which has particular relevance for this discussion, is that in the programs they studied, which are probably not atypical, lack of clarity about roles and functions led to a "deprofessionalization" of services (that is direct service activity was carried out almost exclusively by nonprofessionals) rather than the more appropriate and supportable "differentiation" of services among various types of personnel. It is not difficult to see why the professionals involved, leaving aside anxieties arising from their own insecurity, would find reasons to turn against the paraprofessional. When services are performed exclusively by paraprofessionals, questions of quality inevitably arise and, in the absence of incontrovertible data to the contrary, such service will be, by professional definition, inferior service.

It is hard to determine how widespread and persistent the problems identified by Denham and Shatz are but some more recent studies suggest that they are not at all uncommon. In the study of indigenous nonprofessionals and associate degree technicians in community mental health centers and neighborhood health centers cited earlier, Hirayama (1975) found that, among other things, the definition of paraprofessional roles and functions was not the result of careful assessment of the paraprofessionals' capabilities but was based on expediency. For example, "the fewer the professional workers available, the more the indigenous paraprofessionals and associate degree technicians are expected to carry out responsibilities ordinarily carried out by professionals" (138).

It seems fairly clear that many social agencies have failed to organize their services around differential job and role assignments (Teare 1981). We seem to have two extremes: a movement towards declassification of "professional social work" jobs on the one hand and a complete failure to establish appropriately differentiated job classifications on the other. Neither approach is justified. The first is based on the argument that, since social work has so far failed to differentiate clearly between the competence of the MSW (Master of Social Work) and the BSW (Bachelor of Social Work) and between the BSW and the paraprofessional, it may not be possible to distinguish between any amount of training in social work and no training at all. The logic of this argument may be appealing in its simplicity but it is not very responsible.

The other approach assumes that the complete "professionalization" of the social services is the most desirable state imaginable and that such a state is attainable if we put our minds to it. In the meantime, we should just ignore the paraprofessional until he (or more correctly she) disappears from the social work scene. However, even if a totally "professionalized" social service system were desirable and practical (which is highly questionable), the likelihood of such an eventuality is quite remote. Despite the insecure status of paraprofessionals, they still constitute a significant portion of the social service work force and are not likely to disappear soon (President's Commission on Mental Health 1978; Robin and Wagenfeld 1981).

Current issues

In his study of professionals and paraprofessionals employed in family, neighborhood, and community health services in six US cities, Austin (1978) found that the paraprofessional workers in the human service agencies studied were predominantly female and most likely to be members of racial or ethnic minority groups, although he notes that entry into employment as a paraprofessional social service worker appears "to be more a matter of economics than of race" (173). Consequently, while the impact of the paraprofessional can be evaluated in many ways, on the most basic level, "they have integrated – racially and in terms of social class – the staff of many social service agencies" and on a more complex level "they have influenced the practice of social work by providing a new source of knowledge about the realities of the client's world" (221).

Professional social workers in the agencies Austin studied "accepted both the presence of paraprofessionals and their performance of many duties that professionals in the past had thought of as part of their monopoly," but he was at a loss to understand "why it is taking agencies so long to adapt administrative practices to this new personnel thrust" (237–38). In the absence of the necessary systemic changes, the status and survival of the paraprofessionals will either continue to be threatened, as Hirayama (1975) suggests, or they will turn to other sources of recognition and support. Either outcome would be regrettable since Austin (1978: 187) found that "given a hypothetical choice of careers and asked to assume that they had all the necessary qualifications, paraprofessionals overwhelmingly (70 per cent) selected the social work profession." The very high proportion of female, minority group, and low-income persons among the paraprofessional ranks is quite clear, providing social work with a prime opportunity to involve these groups in social service roles and, subsequently, to welcome many of them into full professional membership.

Despite their apparently strong identification with social work, there are some signs that paraprofessionals are turning to other groups for support and guidance. For example, in the absence of the kind of support and leadership that NASW and CSWE provided in the late 1960s and early 1970s but have failed to provide in recent years, other groups (for example, the Council for Standards in Human Service Education, and the National Commission of Human Service Workers) have stepped into the void and expanded their supportive activities, including the development of standard-setting mechanisms. As a consequence a group of workers who constitute a substantial proportion of the social service work force seem likely to have their preparation for practice guided by a body over which the social work profession may have little influence.

Another sign of the paraprofessionals' alienation from the social work profession and their search for other sources of support is their rapidly increasing membership in the public employee unions. While it is true that both professional and paraprofessional social workers are joining unions, the latter constitute the overwhelming majority of social service union members (Shaffer 1979). In their social work licensing and validation efforts, state chapters of NASW have frequently found themselves in conflict with these unions which are naturally concerned about protecting the job security of their primarily paraprofessional membership and resist the threat of displacement by licenced professional social workers. Union opposition has blocked social work licensure efforts in a number of states (Karger 1983).

The consequences of these developments are difficult to predict but it could be that social work will have to deal with a significant group of social service workers who have their own distinct identity, a separate educational and credentialing system, and their own power bases. If, as appears to be the case, this group is made up largely of those social service workers who are drawn from lower-income and minority groups and is unionized and opposed to some of the goals of the profession (for example licensure), this could put social work in a difficult position, philosophically and politically.

In summary, we believe that any assumption that the paraprofessional will disappear from the social service scene is unrealistic and fosters an irresponsible attitude toward appropriate social service staff differentiation. Failure to address the issue of the place of the paraprofessional in the social services or, worse yet, antagonism toward this group of co-workers (who have been well identified with social work), will simply force them into other alliances that are likely to reduce the possibility of optimum professional–paraprofessional collaboration in the future and could make it more difficult to develop appropriate and effective approaches to social service staff differentiation and optimum patterns of service delivery.

DISCUSSION

As we had found in our 1983 international survey, there is some degree of ambivalence on the part of professionally trained social workers toward paraprofessional personnel in all countries. This can take the form of relatively mild reservations among a minority of social workers, as is the case in Britain. It can manifest itself in more obvious role strain and mutual suspicion between professionals and paraprofessionals, as we found in India and Israel. Or it can involve fairly strong resistance to the employment of paraprofessionals on the part of influential segments of the social work profession, the situation that we found in the USA.

In looking at the situation in Britain in some depth, we found that paraprofessionals are seen as having a valuable role to play in the provision of the country's social services. Their legitimacy is not questioned. Whatever reservations exist concern the degree to which they should be regarded as full partners with professionals in social service provision, particularly in the new "patch" or community-based social service teams. Related to this question are issues of role or task definition, appropriate training, opportunities for career advancement, and equitable treatment in terms of status and remuneration. There is some evidence that paraprofessionals feel undervalued and under-rewarded and that they have fewer opportunities for training and career advancement that their professional colleagues. Unless these issues are resolved, some degree of strain between professionals and paraprofessionals could result.

In India the professional social work organization has virtually ignored the paraprofessional. However, there is concern among some social workers that the widespread use of paraprofessionals will jeopardize the progress that has been made in gaining recognition for social work as a profession. In practical terms, professionally trained social workers and paraprofessionals operate in such distinct spheres and at such social and geographic distance from each other that the causes and degree of strain that are evident in more developed countries are less evident in India. This is so regardless of the fact that, in certain urban areas, professionals and paraprofessionals may occasionally compete for the same jobs.

The social work profession in Israel has made substantial progress in achieving formal recognition, that is in establishing the requirement of professional qualifications for employment as a social worker. The profession controls access to membership and, to a significant degree, to the social service employment market.

In spite of this, the contribution that can be made to social service provision by paraprofessionals is widely recognized by Israeli social workers. This is especially the case where paraprofessionals share cultural and other characteristics with disadvantaged clients and communities. The fact that there is often a shortage of professionally trained workers in these communities tends to reduce potential strains that might flow from perceived paraprofessional encroachment on professional roles and functions. Nevertheless, some areas of tension are evident.

For example, some Israeli social workers feel that all clients are entitled to the most skilled professional help and that nothing less will do. Others feel that all persons who are employed in social service jobs should go through the same rigorous training process. There is also a concern in some quarters that the use of paid paraprofessionals may discourage the development of voluntary community leadership. It is interesting that these same professional social workers do not as readily make this argument against their own employment.

Other strains result from the way paraprofessionals are used by human service organizations. For example, instead of serving as bridges between the organization and the community it seeks to serve, paraprofessionals may function as buffers. They are often used by their employers and professional colleagues to soften community issues and demands, to deflect confrontation, and in general to serve as symbolic community representatives without much commitment on the organizations' or the professionals' part to address substantive client or community service issues that the paraprofessionals can bring to their attention. Added to this is the pressure that paraprofessionals are often under to adopt points of view, attitudes, and behavior that are acceptable to their employers and professional colleagues. This often tends to result in increased social distance between paraprofessionals and their communities and reduces their special value in social service provision.

Although social work has achieved a fair degree of recognition in the USA, it is still a relatively low-status and insecure profession. Therefore its posture toward the paraprofessional has been variable and at present it is defensive, at best. When social programs were expanding rapidly and there were serious shortages of trained workers in the USA in the 1960s, social workers welcomed paraprofessionals and affirmed their value in social service provision. As expansion has ceased and employment opportunities for professionals and paraprofessionals alike have become more limited in the 1980s, professionals have become less supportive of paraprofessionals and, in some instances, are antagonistic towards them.

Lack of clarity about the roles and functions of professionals and paraprofessionals has contributed to the problems. Human service organizations have not done a good job in differentiating professional and paraprofessional functions and this has fueled a broad movement to open up human service jobs to people with a variety of qualifications. These developments have caused concern among social workers about the quality of service being provided in many situations and has been perceived as a serious threat to their job security. They have reacted to these developments by seeking to restrict, by legal and other means, the employment of paraprofessionals in broad categories of social service jobs.

In response to the defensiveness or antagonism of the human service professions, including social work, paraprofessionals are turning to other sources of support and recognition. For example, they are joining public service unions and forming their own professional associations. They are also pursuing opportunities for education and career advancement outside traditional academic and professional disciplines.

In reviewing the situation in these four countries, it seems that the relationships between professionals and paraprofessionals are most constructive when the roles and functions of each are clearly defined or where there are shortages of professionally trained workers. Conversely, conflict or strain is increased when there is a lack of clarity about roles and functions or when paraprofessionals are perceived as a threat to the job security of professionals. In this regard, it is worth noting that, in Britain, where the roles and functions of paraprofessional social service personnel are fairly well defined, they appear to present very little threat to professionally trained social workers. This is true even in the present relatively tight employment market. Clearly a potentially constructive approach to avoiding or reducing strain between professionals and paraprofessionals is to ensure that the roles and functions of each are well defined. In those situations where professionals and paraprofessionals are working side by side, a team model of service is probably most appropriate, especially if the paraprofessional's particular role and special contribution to the team is recognized. In addition, opportunities for appropriate training and career advancement are important ways of demonstrating that the paraprofessional's role is important, making maximum use of their capabilities, and reducing frustrations.

In all four countries that we studied there were at least some social workers who believed that social work might have become too professional, specialized, or clinical in its orientation and methods, thereby reducing its effectiveness in certain situations. The use of paraprofessionals is viewed as a means of countering this problem. Criticism of professional social work methods takes on an added dimension in India where there is concern about the fact that these methods are derived from Western industrialized (primarily North American) conceptions of social work education and practice. Arguments are advanced for developing approaches to social service provision based on Indian realities and indigenous methods of helping. It is believed that a movement in this direction could reduce the enormous gulf between the relatively small group of highly trained professionals who are serving a minute segment of Indian society and the mass of front-line paraprofessionals who are providing the bulk of service to the most needy populations, often without training or professional support.

Training and educational approaches

7

The forms, content, and auspices of paraprofessional training in each country are examined in this chapter. The diverse educational approaches that have been developed to meet the training needs of the enormously varied human service work force that ranges from village-level workers in India who may be illiterate to paraprofessionals in the USA, some of whom are college and university graduates, are identified. Examples of particularly innovative educational models that may have applicability beyond their country of origin are given special attention.

BRITAIN

As a result of the rapid expansion of social work education programs, liberal secondment policies (that is giving employees paid leave to pursue full-time social work education), and relatively generous government grants in support of social work education in Britain during the last two decades, a high proportion of social workers had received professional training by the early 1980s – more than 70 per cent of those employed in direct practice and over 90 per cent of those in management positions (Barclay Report 1982: 25). The training of paraprofessional personnel, on the other hand, many of whom perform vital social service functions, has seriously lagged (Ash *et al.* 1980: 6–10). This is true of staff engaged in domiciliary, day, and residential care programs operated by local authority social services departments and by voluntary organizations and it seems to be especially critical in residential settings where an estimated 80 per cent of the staff have not received appropriate training (Barclay Report 1982: 57). During the last few years, a number of discrete but related efforts have been mounted by national bodies responsible for overseeing the training of social service personnel to develop and promote new approaches to training for various categories of paraprofessional workers. The most significant of these models or approaches will be reviewed in this section.

Types and auspices of training

Training is available to paraprofessional social service personnel in Britain but this varies greatly according to the job that the worker occupies and the practices and policies of his or her employer. The type and amount of training range from the most basic induction or orientation to quite intensive programs leading to nationally recognized credentials.

Besides the local authority social service departments and voluntary social service organizations that employ paraprofessionals and may provide in-service training for them, there are two national statutory bodies that promote appropriate training. One of these, the Local Government Training Board (LGTB), has responsibility for establishing guidelines for the training for all manual or nonprofessional local government employees in England and Wales. This is an important body in relation to certain categories of paraprofessional social service personnel and has recently issued guidelines and recommendations governing the training of home helps, care assistants in old people's homes, and wardens of sheltered housing for the elderly.

The other body, the Central Council for Education and Training in Social Work (CCETSW) is the national accrediting body for social work training. It also promotes and approves a variety of types of training for paraprofessional social service personnel. These training programs are more generic in nature than the training promoted by the LGTB and are addressed to a broader range of paraprofessional staff in domiciliary, day, and residential services for all client groups – children, the elderly, families, mentally handicapped and physically disabled people, and so on.

Participants attend local educational institutions and follow a training program approved by CCETSW. Upon successful completion of the program, they receive a nationally recognized credential. Each of the above training approaches will be described briefly below.

National models of employer-provided training

Training of home helps

As already mentioned, the Local Government Training Board (undated b) has responsibility for determining the type of training needed by certain categories of workers employed by local authorities in England and Wales. Included are the home helps employed by local authority social services departments. In recognition of their important supportive, linking, and monitoring functions, steps have been taken by some local authority social services departments to upgrade their skills by providing appropriate in-service training. However, until recently only about 15 per cent of social services departments provided systematic training for home helps and, in general, this training was quite limited. In order to rectify this situation, the LGTB has recommended that all departments undertake systematic training of home helps since "the efficient operation of the service and the job satisfaction of those employed in it can both be improved by properly directed training programmes" (Booler undated: 2).

The LGTB has recently issued guidelines for what it regards as the minimum training required for all home helps and some additional or optional training opportunities that should be made available to experienced and specialized staff. Minimum training consists of at least twelve hours of induction that all new home helps should undergo during their first month on the job and at least twenty-one hours of basic training that is expected to cover the following topics:

"1 The Home Help Service and its role within the Social Services Department.
2 The practical aspects of the home help's work.
3 The range of clients and their needs from the service.
4 The other community statutory agencies that the home helps and the clients come into contact with."

(Local Government Training Board undated b: 8)

Optional training is expected to address the needs of specific groups of home helps who have already completed basic training and who need to have their knowledge updated or their skills sharpened in order to function effectively in specialized roles. Needs would be determined at the local level, of course, but likely topics include problems of hypothermia in the elderly, working with disabled clients, responding appropriately to bereavement or terminal illness, working with vulnerable families, providing on-the-job training for new home helps, and so on (10–11).

Training of care assistants in homes for the elderly
In recognition of the important role played by care assistants in promoting the well-being of the residents of old people's homes and the variability of training available to them, the LGTB (undated a) has also taken steps to assist local authorities in developing appropriate training. It has issued guidelines for the implementation of training that is designed to help care assistants meet the increased demands of their work. Specifically the recommended training should:

"1 give them a clear understanding of the purpose of their job in the specific home;
2 help them identify their role in caring for the elderly, as part of a team;
3 provide them with the necessary knowledge and skills to do the work;
4 enable them to cope with the physical and emotional demands and stress the job entails;
5 develop a responsible attitude toward the residents."
(Local Government Training Board undated a: 4)

The board recommends a sequential model of training for new care assistants that progresses from induction, through basic training, to a program of further training. After induction, which would occur during the care assistants' first week of employment, basic training would follow, involving about forty hours of instruction during the first year of employment. This is designed to develop the skills and knowledge needed by care assistants to provide quality care to residents and to enable them to become effective members of the caring team. Further training can take two forms. It can address special problems or topics that are important to the staff of a particular home or it can be designed to contribute to the overall development of staff by refining their skills or extending their knowledge (9–16).

Training wardens of sheltered housing for elderly people

The Local Government Training Board has determined that, although some local authorities provide training for their wardens, in general little training is carried out and most wardens receive no training for the important functions that they perform. In order to make some progress in correcting this situation, the LGTB has attempted to impress upon local authorities the importance of the warden's role in sheltered housing and the necessity for providing appropriate training. It has promulgated training guidelines and encouraged local authorities to implement training programs that meet the standards that the board has recommended.

If wardens are to meet the needs of tenants appropriately and handle the many complex and demanding situations they are likely to face in carrying out their roles, the LGTB (undated c: 5) feels that they should receive training that gives them a clear understanding of their role and their tenants; enables them to promote the optimum level of independence of tenants; increases their knowledge of relevant community resources that can meet the needs of tenants; improves their practical job skills and knowledge and builds up their self-confidence and breaks down the isolation that they typically experience.

College-based models of training

Each of the aforementioned training programs is addressed to a very specific group of paraprofessional social service personnel and is provided on an in-service basis by employers – in most cases, local authority social services departments. The following training models which have been developed by CCETSW are broader in scope, addressing the needs of a wider range of paraprofessional personnel. While the training is provided on an in-service basis to paraprofessionals employed in a variety of social jobs, primary responsibility for training rests with educational institutions (colleges of further education, polytechnic institutes, and so on) although a high level of collaboration is expected to occur between the educators and local social service agencies.

The In-Service Course in Social Care (ICSC)

The In-Service Course in Social Care (ICSC) replaced earlier, more specialized training programs for paraprofessional social service personnel in Britain. Initially geared toward the staff of residential facilities and later including day center personnel, the present ICSC training program addresses the needs of a broad range of paraprofessional staff who serve "any client group, in residential care, day services, foster care, sheltered housing, special schools, hospitals, domiciliary, field and community based services and other settings so long as those workers can benefit from the course" (CCETSW 1983b: 8).

The administration of ICSC training programs at the local level is supported and authorized by CCETSW which issues regulations and guidelines governing their development and operation. Upon successful completion of ICSC training, students receive a Statement of Completion from CCETSW. Since it is issued by the national body responsible for promulgating and monitoring standards of social work education and training in Britain, this credential verifies that the holder has undergone training that meets nationally established and nationally recognized standards.

ICSC training is intended to build upon the basic on-the-job training provided by employers. Participants are exposed to a broader learning experience that seeks to develop helping skills that are common to all social service settings and that enables them to understand how their functions relate to the broader framework of social service provision, specifically at the community level (CCETSW 1983b: 6). In order to achieve their broader educational objectives and to complement agency-based in-service training, ICSC programs are generally college-based. Local colleges of further education (not unlike technical or community colleges in the USA and other countries) are the most common providers of ICSC training. Participants are usually released from work one day per week for three terms to attend training (7).

CCETSW does not mandate specific course content and teaching methods to be used in ICSC training, since it is expected that these will be determined on the basis of local needs. However, the council promulgates general principles and guidelines that are considered to be important in guiding curriculum development at the local level. These include the expectation that the following instructional objectives for students will be addressed:

> "– develop confidence in what has been learned from previous training and experience;
> – develop understanding of clients and their needs;
> – develop interpersonal skills which will enhance work with clients;
> – develop understanding and skills in work with colleagues and staff in other agencies;
> – develop knowledge and understanding of the local community and its relationship to the agency;
> – develop understanding of daily work in relation to the overall function and organization of the agency and other agencies, and wider social service provision;
> – develop the ability to apply knowledge and skills gained in the course to the work setting."
>
> (CCETSW 1983b: 20–7)

CCETSW (1983b) stresses the importance of cooperation between colleges that provide ICSC training and local social service agencies that send their employees to this training. In order to obtain CCETSW approval to offer ICSC training, colleges must show that they have consulted those agencies who are sending their staff throughout the planning, operational, and evaluative phases of the training program (10). For their part, employers are expected to release participants from their normal duties so that they are able to attend college and pay the cost of tuition, books, travel, and subsistence (CCETSW 1981). By the early 1980s between 3,000 and 4,000 paraprofessionals per year were entering ICSC training (CCETSW 1985b: 3).

CCETSW (1983b: 9) stresses that ICSC should not be used as a substitute for adequate orientation and agency-based in-service training. Rather it is seen as one component of a continuum of staff development and career advancement opportunities for social service personnel.

Training leading to the Certificate in Social Service (CSS)
CCETSW has also developed and promoted a more intensive and more structured training program for employed social service

workers that involves a combination of college instruction and directed practical experience. This program takes at least two years to complete and leads to the nationally recognized Certificate in Social Service (CSS). This training program, initiated by CCETSW in 1975, is intended for people other than social workers who are employed in social service roles; for example, the staff and administrators of residential services for various populations, home help organizers, day care center staff, and so on. There was some question as to whether this should be viewed as training for paraprofessionals or as an alternative kind of professional training. However, at least initially, most British social workers, including most respondents to our international survey, seemed inclined to regard it as paraprofessional training. Developments are presently underway that are likely to place the CSS training model unequivocally within the professional category. Nevertheless, since it has been and will probably continue to be an important training and career advancement vehicle for persons occupying paraprofessional positions in the social services, it is worth examining briefly. It also represents an interesting and unusual example of the transformation of a training program for paraprofessional social service personnel into an alternative form of professional social work education.

Each CSS training program, or "scheme" as it is called in Britain, serves a specific geographic region of the country and is planned and operated jointly by a consortium of local social service agencies and educational institutions. Following the successful implementation of five pilot schemes in different parts of the country in the late 1970s, there are now twenty-nine CSS training schemes that together cover the whole of the United Kingdom (England, Wales, Scotland, and Northern Ireland). By the early 1980s some 1,100–1,300 participants were entering CSS training schemes annually (CCETSW 1985b: 3).

In order to be approved by CCETSW, a CSS training scheme must include the following educational components or units:

A   *A Common Unit*. This includes foundation content on social policy, the organization of the social services, human growth and behavior, etc., and it is taken by all students.

B   *Standard Options*. Students must select one of the following four usual areas of concentration: children and adolescents, adults, the elderly, or communities.

C *Special Options.* These are fairly specialized units of instruction
   that address a defined range of work tasks for a particular
   student; e.g., administering community residences for the
   mentally retarded, mobilizing self-help groups, assessing
   clients' levels of functioning to determine needs for a range of
   in-home services, etc. Various aspects of management constitute
   a large number of special options.

(CCETSW 1980a: 50–5)

Each of these three units of instruction involves a minimum of 480
hours of study. The scheduling of the classroom instruction,
practical experience, and individual study periods varies among
CSS training schemes and between different units of instruction in a
particular scheme. In some instances, students spend one day a
week in college, one day in out-of-class study, and three days at
work. In other cases, they may intersperse short periods of intensive
full-time college attendance with full-time work.

Among the distinctive features of this new type of social service
training program are (1) its focus on the employed social service
worker; (2) the joint management by educational institutions and
social agencies of local schemes that is mandated by CCETSW; (3)
the relatively high degree of autonomy that local schemes have to
form consortia of educational institutions and social service
employers and to develop educational programs that address local
needs; (4) the approval and monitoring mechanisms that ensure
adherence to national guidelines and standards; and (5) the
emergence of a nationally recognized credential that has the
potential for upgrading and professionalizing significant numbers
of the untrained social service work force.

The joint planning and management that CCETSW requires of
those colleges and social service agencies that operate an accredited
CSS training scheme in a particular geographic area results in a
much stronger role for employers and practitioners in the design
and operation of educational programs than is presently the case in
some other countries (for example, the USA). In return for their
greater influence in defining training needs and designing instructional
programs, the social agencies involved are required to make a long-
term commitment to the training of their untrained employees,
including the provision of tuition and other educational costs,
released time, and study supervisors.

While CSS training is not without its critics, there appears to be broad support for the CSS movement among British social work practitioners and educators alike (Cypher 1979: 206; Ash *et al.* 1980: 95). In fact this support has been so strong that, following an extensive review of the relationship between CSS training and that which leads to the Certificate of Qualification in Social Work (CQSW), CCETSW (1985a) proposes to capitalize on the unique strengths of each and have the two forms of training lead to a single qualification in social work. In other words, a slightly modified version of the current CSS training program would become an alternative, employment-based route to qualification as a professional social worker.

Summary

Substantial progress has been made in Britain over the last ten years in ensuring that most jobs that require the skills of professional social workers are filled by qualified staff. However, the great majority of social service jobs do not require professionally trained personnel but can be satisfactorily performed by paraprofessionals, provided that they are appropriately trained. The training of the paraprofessional social service work force has not received the attention and resources that have been devoted to social work education so that most paraprofessionals have not been properly trained for the vital functions they perform. In order to come to grips with this problem, a number of training approaches, addressed to the needs of particular groups of paraprofessionals, have been developed in Britain. Each of these approaches is, in its own way, significant and has potential applicability beyond its intended target group and its country of origin. The transformation of CSS training from a form of paraprofessional training into an alternative route to qualification as a professional social worker is especially illuminating.

INDIA

Background

Historically, social work in India can be traced back to the 1920s when short-term courses were organized by the Social Service League, a voluntary group in Bombay. In the mid-1930s a training institute was established in Bombay. Originally called the Sir Dorabji Tata Graduate School of Social Work it was later renamed the Tata Institute of Social Sciences (Desai 1985). Within a short period the Tata Institute was offering a diploma in social service administration. Graduate schools of social work were to follow in Delhi, Baroda, Agra, Madras, and Calcutta. This was the beginning of a strong trend toward the expansion of social work education in different cities and states of the Indian Union. It is estimated that at present there are over forty institutions providing social work education at the postgraduate level, eleven of these offering doctoral programs. In addition, there are eleven institutions providing social work programs at the undergraduate level (Gangrade 1985).

Desai (1985) has pointed out that, while this period of expansion provided opportunities for the training of increased numbers of social workers, the schools were unevenly distributed across the country. The majority were located in major urban centers with consequent neglect of rural and tribal areas. An additional problem was their focus on the highest levels of education and a consequent neglect of training for front-line workers. The task of training paraprofessionals was left to government agencies, particularly during the 1950s and 1960s. By the 1970s some critics of this situation were pointing to the need for some adjustment in the mission of social work education programs. For example Desai asserted that:

> "Schools of social work have to move down from the masters and doctoral levels to the bachelors and auxiliary level of training. There is now a school of social work in almost every state in India. Because the need is for greater manpower at lower levels and the schools train at higher levels they have contributed very little developmentally."
>
> (Desai 1975: 15–17)

As we noted in Chapter 4, the committee appointed by the University Grants Commission (1980) to review social work education (which incidentally was headed by Desai) was critical of the model of social work practice embraced by the social work profession and the schools of social work in India. Because of its industrial and urban biases the dominant social work education and practice paradigm has tended not to address the problems faced by the most deprived segments of the population. The committee warned that, unless some reorientation occurred, schools of social work were likely to contribute little to the real needs of the country (12).

> "There is a push for growth at higher levels but very little development of the front line worker. . . . There should be a greater emphasis in these institutions to develop the lower levels of training. Unless this is done social work education will remain outside the mainstream of national development and welfare activity and will make little contribution or impact."
>
> (University Grants Commission 1980: 21)

The fact that there are more doctoral than bachelor's degree social work programs in India has caused Desai (1985) to compare the situation to an inverted pyramid that urgently needs to be turned right way up.

These criticisms of the shortcomings of the social work profession and the schools of social work in India are gaining wider acceptance and the need to adjust curricula to the needs of the most vulnerable populations in both urban and rural areas is beginning to receive more attention (Desai 1985; Gangrade 1985; Siddiqui 1985; Muzumdar 1985). Indeed, the Indian government has placed high priority on the training of front-line paraprofessional personnel and a variety of training and educational programs have been introduced to meet this need.

At this writing, there are five dominant training and educational patterns for paraprofessional human service personnel in India. These patterns are outlined in *Table 3*.

In this section we will focus on training provided by government centers, in four-year colleges, and in universities since this is more clearly defined than employer-provided training and likely to be more significant in the long term.

The training center model

By far the most common pattern of paraprofessional training found in India is based on the training center model operated or supported by government agencies like the Central Social Welfare Board. As we noted in an earlier chapter, the board was established in 1953 to coordinate, assist, and support the work of all voluntary social

TABLE 3   *Training patterns of paraprofessionals*

training patterns	length of training
pre-service (employer auspices)	one week to six months
in-service (employer auspices)	one week to one year
training centers (central and state govt)	three months to one year
four-year college	three years
university	three months to six months

welfare organizations in India (Rohatgi 1982). It also supports the training of staff for these organizations.

Exemplifying this training center approach is the training provided under the Integrated Child Development Services (ICDS) Program. The ICDS employs the largest corps of paraprofessional child health and development workers in the country and operates an extensive training program to meet their needs. The aim of the ICDS Program is to promote the development of a target group of children under 6 years of age through a comprehensive package of services that include nonformal pre-school education, immunization, health check-ups, supplementary nutrition, medical referral services, and nutrition and health education for women (Chowdhry 1985). The unique role of the *anganwadi* worker in the provision of these front-line child health and development services was described in Chapter 5.

Training programs for *anganwadi* workers, supervisors, and project directors are provided through regional training centers. The design of these training programs is based on a core curriculum in child welfare that includes the following major content areas:

"1 Community involvement in promoting children's services.
  2 Socialization of children and the formation of sound health habits through programs in health and hygiene, nutrition and preschool education.
  3 Nutrition and health services for children and expectant and nursing mothers.
  4 Preschool nonformal education for children between 3 and 5 years of age.
  5 Parent education in child development, including family life education.

  6 Identification of children needing special services and making
     referrals to specialized agencies."
(Nanavatty 1984: 222–25. For more detail, see all of Ch. 5)

This core curriculum provides a broad conceptual framework for
the training of all staff, professionals and paraprofessionals, from
project directors to front-line personnel. Within this overall
scheme, the front-line workers are specifically trained to carry out
the following functions:

 "1 Organizing preschool education programs and activities for
     children aged 3 to 5 years.
  2 Organizing supplementary nutrition services for children
     aged 6 months to 5 years.
  3 Giving health and nutrition information to mothers.
  4 Making home visits and educating parents, particularly in the
     case of children attending the anganwadi, so that the mother
     of the child can be helped to play an effective role in the
     child's growth and development.
  5 Eliciting community support and participation in running the
     progam.
  6 Assisting the primary health center staff in health checkups,
     referral services, and health education.
  7 Maintaining routine files and records to enable measurement
     of the impact of the services.
  8 Maintaining liaison with other institutions in the village."
                           (Ministry of Social Welfare 1982: 8–9)

Despite the generally favorable results achieved by this type of
center-based training, it is not without limitations. The core
curriculum appears to provide a sound conceptual base for all staff
and the specific training goals and activities designed for paraprofessionals are appropriate in most situations. However, there are
workers engaged in projects in areas that require more specialized
training. These include workers employed in tribal or other
backward areas.

In India today almost 40 million people constitute tribal
populations. The majority still live in their traditional habitat and
follow their own cultural heritage. Strong kinship relations and
high incidences of endogamy continue to exist within many of these
groups. Tribal children share all the particular hazards of life faced
by their communities, including disruptions and deprivations

resulting from shifting cultivation patterns and industrial development in the homelands. If social welfare services are to be delivered effectively to these tribal children, the impact of these changes on the traditional tribal way of life of these people has to be taken into consideration. However, at present there is only limited training for tribal front-line workers.

This is one of the shortcomings of ICDS training programs revealed by a recent evaluation carried out by Nanavatty (1984). Besides failing to address adequately the need for training that takes into account ethnic, regional, and tribal considerations in the provision of services, little attention has been given to the need for refresher courses and continuing staff development activities. Furthermore, because individual ICDS projects have tended to operate on an ad hoc basis, many trainees have found themselves in dead-end jobs. Nanavatty is critical of the government's reliance on short-term training and its failure to make a commitment to longer-term, more career-oriented training for front-line paraprofessionals (303). This is a recurring theme in discussions about the training and use of paraprofessional human service workers in India, as it is in other countries.

Despite these limitations, we were impressed with the impact of these programs, particularly in rural areas. The comprehensive rural health project that one of us (Schindler) visited in the Jamkhed area of Maharashta State and that we mentioned earlier is an illustration of an effective program of this kind.

Jamkhed, situated in a remote rural area of India, encompasses a number of small village compounds, each housing about a hundred families. Most of the villagers are illiterate or semi-literate and from this population local residents are chosen by the community to serve as front-line health workers. These paraprofessionals receive a week of pre-service and twice-weekly in-service training at the regional training center. Instruction is based on actual cases encountered in the village and emphasis is placed on the prevention of simple illnesses. There are also courses in community involvement and decision-making since village paraprofessionals must work with a variety of groups, including the local leadership, for purposes of organizing health and other community projects.

In designing educational programs it has been found that it is important to find out what paraprofessionals in a particular setting actually do and then see that they are adequately prepared for these responsibilities. Often paraprofessionals must be able to deal with the entire spectrum of health problems encountered in the village. The reality is that these auxiliaries who work alone in remote areas have to attend single-handedly to all the problems that a range of medical staff would normally deal with in the health services of less isolated areas. In addition, it is vital to understand and take into account the particular culture, beliefs, and folkways of the local community. As Arole (1985) puts it, "Training of the village worker is a two-way communication process. As the instructors gain knowledge on local beliefs and taboos, they and the paraprofessional discuss together ways and means of overcoming those beliefs and taboos of a negative nature." The capacity of relatively unsophisticated indigenous workers to benefit from appropriate training has been noted by Joshi, Krishnayya, and Gupta (1978: 41–2):

> "Given their illiteracy and earthy simplicity it is easy to underestimate the capacity of the village health worker to learn. On several occasions in the past they have stunned outsiders by the extent of their knowledge and by their attitudes. There is a danger therefore of oversimplification and too slow a rate of introduction of new topics by the trainers."

Having observed these front-line paraprofessionals at work in the village areas of Jamkhed, Schindler can attest to the accuracy of these observations. Indeed, given appropriate training, their potential contribution to the health and well-being of people in remote poorly served areas is enormous.

Social work education and paraprofessional training in four-year colleges

It is important to note that, of the five major patterns of paraprofessional training mentioned earlier, that provided in four-year colleges is a special and exceptional case since very few untrained human service workers have access to this kind of educational opportunity. However, it is worth looking briefly at undergraduate social work education programs offered by four-year colleges in India since two of the three basic models produce graduates who function at the paraprofessional level (Lakshamanna 1979; Gangrade 1985).

In the first model there is little social work content – usually three or four courses such as the philosophy of social work, fields of social work practice, and social work methods. In this first pattern the student is simply introduced to the principles and concepts of social work and, upon graduation, can seek employment as a paraprofessional or can pursue a master's degree in social work. The main drawback of this program is insufficient social work content (including field instruction) to qualify it as a professional baccalaureate degree in social work. As we have already noted, those graduates who enter the social welfare field do so as paraprofessionals.

The second model, which can be characterized as the integrated social work program, provides students with sufficient course credit in both the social sciences and social work to enable them to pursue graduate study in either stream. Courses in psychology, sociology, anthropology, and research are prerequisites for further graduate study. While it has many of the limitations of the first model, this second pattern has been encouraged since it avoids locking students into one limited career path, offering them further educational opportunities in either social work or one of a number of areas in the social sciences. Again, those students who wish to enter the social welfare field upon graduation do so at the paraprofessional level.

The third model offered to undergraduate students is the professional bachelor's degree in social work. Courses include the study of casework, group work, and community organization. The particular strength of this program is the intensive supervised field instruction that is provided. Upon graduation, students take up jobs as field-level social workers or social work assistants. However, they do not move up to supervisory positions since these are reserved for graduates of master's degree programs.

Paraprofessional training in university schools of social work

A major barrier to training for auxiliary personnel in India and other countries in our study is the difficulty of gaining entrance to professional social work education programs. In the main, paraprofessionals have not had opportunities for upward educational mobility. The completion of secondary schooling remains the major prerequisite for entering higher education. Using life experience or other alternatives as equivalents to formal qualifications for entry into schools of social work has generally not occurred. However, in spite of these difficulties, some universities have expanded their programs in continuing or extension education which paraprofessionals and supervisors of paraprofessionals may enter and, in general, there is increased university interest in and commitment to paraprofessional training. For example, Desai (1985) and other social work educators have expressed their commitment to providing the necessary leadership in the development of paraprofessional training. As she puts it, "We don't have a choice in this country. We need grass roots services. Unless the universities set the pace and give leadership who will do so?" The rationale for social work involvement in this area of training was given considerable impetus by the seminal report resulting from the University Grants Commission's (1980) *Review of Social Work Education in India* which identified two major avenues for training paraprofessional personnel within higher education:

> "1 Training should be geared at the post secondary level and should be one of the major streams of higher education. This would be comparable to community colleges in the United States. They would be certified by the boards of higher secondary schools and serve as a prerequisite for admission to bachelor degree programs by the universities.
>
> 2 Training within colleges and universities either on a year certificate or two years. Training would take place within the four year college or university setting."
>
> (University Grants Commission 1980: 69–70)

These recommendations have not yet been implemented in full, although a number of universities have begun to offer short-term training programs for paraprofessionals. For example, the College of Social Work in Bombay has instituted a short-term training program for poverty workers in slum neighborhoods and the School of Social Work in Delhi has instituted training programs for child care, health care, and correction workers (Gangrade 1985). Of course, since these programs are of a short-term nature, they do not lead to a social work qualification. Nevertheless, they represent a very positive step on the part of the universities involved.

The innovative paraprofessional training program recently developed at the University of Bombay is a case in point. This training program is directed at paraprofessionals engaged in bringing about change in slum neighborhoods. The need for the program is based on the growth of slum areas in the city of Bombay where 40 per cent of the population live in poverty. It has been estimated that, if this problem is not dealt with by the year 2000, 73 per cent of the land in Bombay will be covered by slums (Mayur and Nadkarni 1981). While problems of this magnitude cannot be solved by grassroots paraprofessionals, the development of the training program was based on the belief that "it was essential to train indigenous community personnel if we believe in the philosophical conviction that the community must be helped to work on its own problems through its own local leadership" (D'Souza 1982: 5). D'Souza, the initiator of this program, notes some of the obstacles to implementing real grassroots participation in change in slum areas: "Today the decision-making power in the slum lies with the local slumlords and traditional leaders who are economically better off. These leaders have their own vested interests." She adds that "It is imperative that an alternative structure be created" (5). It was the training program's philosophy that, given appropriate knowledge, skill, and attitudes, local persons belonging to a similar cultural milieu can be effective change agents in the slums in terms of understanding the slum culture and playing a front-line leadership role.

A total of twenty-five trainees participated in this program (fifteen males and ten females). Almost all the trainees resided in *zopadpattis* (temporary shelters) and the rest lived in *chowls* (one-room tenement flats). The following training methods were found to be effective with the paraprofessionals involved:

> "1 Moving from the concrete to the abstract, as the learners were dropouts from the formal mainstream of education.
> 2 Utilizing the experience of the trainees and thus the need to use the discussion as a basic method of teaching.
> 3 Utilizing training techniques which involve the self, as learners from slums generally tend to be more spontaneous.
> 4 Utilization of training techniques which help trainees to understand reality; e.g., drama, simulation."
>
> (D'Souza 1982: 13–14)

Because of the success of this program, steps were being taken to extend its duration and intensity and D'Souza expected that the university would develop additional paraprofessional training programs. In arguing for greater university involvement in the training of front-line paraprofessionals, she joins those other critics of existing priorities in professional social work education.

> "Our levels of training are not responsive to the kind of manpower required to meet the needs of the situation . . . Ph.D. programs appear to increase at a faster rate than the Bachelor's degree programs. . . . An analysis of the cost structure of training also indicates that while the financial investment to turn out professionals at higher levels of training is high, their relevance to the need situation in the Indian context is alarmingly low, hence the dysfunctionality."
>
> (D'Souza 1982: 22)

This important policy issue is likely to be hotly debated in professional social work circles and among social work educators, social planners, paraprofessionals, and their advocates in the years ahead.

Summary and discussion

There are a number of trends and issues related to the training and education of paraprofessionals in India that need to be underlined. First of all, there appears to be a growing consensus that schools of social work should be training social welfare personnel at all levels, including paraprofessionals. The seminal report of the University Grants Commission (1980: 177) in its review of social work education is very specific about this point: "Training at the paraprofessional level needs to be instituted in these institutions for social work education." A number of leaders in social work education have taken a firm stance on the need to reallocate resources to the training of lower-level front-line workers rather than investing in Ph.D. programs. Priorities are clearly shifting toward the education of front-line workers.

A second issue of some significance concerns the model of social work practice taught in Indian schools of social work which, of course, has relevance for social welfare training at all levels. Many of India's leading social work educators (Siddiqui 1985; Rohatgi 1982; Desai 1985; Gangrade 1970; 1985) are calling for a shift away from the essentially Western model that prevails in most schools and see an urgent need to design educational objectives and content that reflect the indigenous Indian context. This is not an entirely new plea, having been made four decades ago by Manshard (1941: 19), the initiator and director of the first school of social work in Asia, who stated that "It is quite impossible to reproduce Western experience without first submitting it to a great amount of critical analysis and scrutinizing each subject in the light of Indian conditions." However, his arguments appear to have gone largely unheeded and, by the early 1970s, the problems evident in schools of social work were being described by Nagpaul:

"The growth and development of most of these institutions have been largely influenced by the American pattern with little regard to the social, cultural, economic and political conditions prevailing in Indian society. Indian social work education can no longer ignore the question of development and the introduction of indigenous approaches to promote the goal of Indianization of professional social work."

(Nagpaul 1971: 14)

Nagpaul's argument that the principles and methods of social work education and practice are so much related to the US economic and cultural patterns of life that they have little significance for the situation in India is supported by growing numbers of his colleagues so that there seems to be increased impetus toward change.

In calling for the development of an indigenous approach to social work education and practice, Nagpaul provides examples of aspects of Indian culture that are typically not taken into account in the existing approaches.

"Indian culture contains two potential assets for the protection and promotion of better mental health: the therapeutic value of Hindu religion and Hindu psychology . . . and the use of indigenous medicine to relieve both physical and mental illness. The teaching of professional social work however, fails to take these into consideration."

(Nagpaul 1972a: 6–7)

These types of concerns are being increasingly expressed in developing countries and, indeed, in a number of developed countries also. The implications for social work education and practice of these observations is more fully discussed in our concluding chapter.

Finally, there are some Indian social work educators and practitioners who are calling for a more vigorous social activist role for the profession. For example Professor K. S. Muzumdar of the University of Bombay asserts that there are vast injustices and growing inequalities in India which are so overwhelming that drastic action is needed. She suggests that schools of social work may have to consider taking a leadership role in civil disobedience in order to bring about change (Muzumdar 1985). Siddiqui (1984) and others have pointed out the contradictions and dilemmas that confront social workers and others who seek to bring about radical change in social institutions and arrangements of which they are an integral part. For example schools of social work are dependent upon government financial support and are therefore under considerable pressure to conform to government policies. However, while Muzumdar's position may be a minority one, there is a fairly widespread belief that schools of social work and social work professionals alike must become more vigorous in their efforts to bring about needed social change.

ISRAEL

With increased national attention being given to emerging social problems in Israel, there has been an expansion in the numbers of auxiliary personnel employed in a broad range of human service fields and the development of corresponding training programs designed to prepare them for the important functions they perform. In Chapter 5 we listed ten major areas of paraprofessional activity: (1) neighborhood services in urban and rural development projects; (2) social welfare agencies; (3) mental health settings; (4) early childhood education; (5) enrichment programs; (6) services for the elderly; (7) corrections; (8) programs for alcoholics; (9) counseling and family agencies; and (10) programs for mentally retarded people. In this section we will outline the basic or core curriculum that is provided for all paraprofessionals and the specific training programs that have been developed for paraprofessionals in each of the major settings in which they function.

The Ministries of Labor and Social Welfare initiated and

continue to be the major sponsors of paraprofessional training in Israel. This support has come about as a result of government recognition of the need to address growing social problems effectively and that appropriate training programs for human service personnel can meet these needs. The training programs developed reflect the major service functions of the Ministry of Social Welfare (1977) and local welfare agencies, including services for children, youth, the family, the elderly, the community, and special populations. In fact the training curriculum is designed to correspond to these fields of practice or service areas. In addition there are special course offerings addressed to the particular needs of Project Renewal. All training programs are designed and organized by the Institute of Social Work, the educational arm of the Ministry of Social Welfare. At present, training is offered through five learning centers located in different parts of the country which currently serve over 1,000 students (Hoffer 1982; Sadan 1985).

Space limitations do not permit us to explore all aspects and nuances of the paraprofessional training curriculum. However, we will review the core curriculum which is generic to the training provided for all auxiliary personnel and describe briefly the ten training programs addressed to specific fields of service, including that provided for paraprofessionals employed in Project Renewal.

The core curriculum

The learning units in the core curriculum include principles of communication, interviewing, human growth and development, the family, and social policy and social welfare, including the study of ethnic groups. As we have already noted, these subjects are generic to all paraprofessional training regardless of specialization. *Table 4* provides an overview of the core curriculum, including major topics, content, learning objectives, and typical teaching methods.

The rationale behind this generic approach to paraprofessional education is that students should receive a broad *Weltanschauung* (world view) of helping skills and knowledge. It is also based on the belief that paraprofessionals should not be locked into a specialization but given the opportunity for job mobility and career advancement. This policy has been articulated by the Ministry of Social Welfare and is in keeping with its commitment to building a cadre of

Table 4 *Core paraprofessional training curriculum*

subject	content	objective	teaching method
communication	communication skills; listening skills; verbal and nonverbal communication; language skills; writing skills; helping clients understand paraprofessional communication; objectives of communications; double messages and interpretative skills; recording skills.	ability to understand clients and groups; creating improved communication between group members and the helping agent; developing self-awareness; ability to listen and provide feedback; ability to record, clarify, and interpret client messages; ability to express oneself clearly.	role play; group discussion; communication games.
interviewing	rules of interviewing, listening, and observing; engaging the client who seeks help; dress and behavior; the worker's feeling about his role; the worker's responsibility in his relationship with the client.	ability to conduct an interview with clients; ability to understand clients' needs and relate to these needs; ability to structure an interview with beginning, middle, and end.	role play; field practice; video presentations.
growth and development	individual biological, and psychological growth and behavior from birth to old age.	ability to understand and work with different age groups – children, teenagers, young adults, older adults, and the aged.	record material.
family life	basic needs; the family system; boundaries; intergenerational, ethnic, and cultural issues; single-parent families.	ability to help individuals and other subunits in the family; strengthen the role of parents and children in the family; ability to help people meet their physical and psychological needs; ability to support families in crisis; develop ongoing relationships with family members.	role play; record materials; field visitations.
social welfare and social services	social welfare services – history, goals, and objectives; residual and institutional programs; universal and selective services; income maintenance programs.	ability to make referrals to private and public welfare agencies; in public agencies, help client obtain in-kind services; make referrals to National Insurance Institute for financial aid.	visitations to Department of Public Welfare and National Insurance

trained human service personnel, particularly in rural areas. Systems theory is an important organizing principle permeating both the core curriculum and the areas of specialized training. This enables students to view phenomena in the part–whole dynamic, thereby providing a comprehensive view of the helping act. The paraprofessional can step aside from specific situations and view the interrelated components and the wider context of a particular problem. As Chin (1969) has noted, thinking in systems terms provides structure and stability within some arbitrarily sliced and frozen time period. While the core curriculum covers a rather broad spectrum of knowledge and interventive skills, the course material is very much related to concrete situations in practice and is client-centered. It thus encompasses both a theoretical base and practical framework for intervention.

Training directed to specific fields of practice

In addition to the core curriculum, students receive training in an area of specialization appropriate to their specific roles and the practice settings in which they are employed (Schindler 1982; Kestenbaum and Shebar 1984; Gidron and Katan 1985; Sadan 1985). The ten major areas of specialized training, including their objectives and content, follow:

● *Neighborhood workers*

Objective: Training neighborhood workers to help multi-problem families and other families in crisis.

Content: (a) Learning communication skills and how best to speak and listen to multi-problem families.
(b) Learning about social services in the community, where families can be referred for help, such as welfare bureaus for advice and the National Insurance Institute for income maintenance benefits.
(c) Learning supportive skills and how to use support systems to help persons in crisis. Learning about cultural and religious backgrounds in order to use these for support.
(d) Recognizing and learning about the needs of multi-problem families, including exploring employment possibilities for a member of the family,

teaching the family how to budget, and encouraging children to continue their schooling.
(e) Learning to work with the family in relation to various community sub-systems, such as housing and tenant committees.

Included under this category is the training provided to community or neighborhood workers engaged in Project Renewal. The specific objective and content of this training are as follows:

Objective: Training paraprofessionals to function as part of the Project Renewal team, and in particular to work with client groups affected by urban and rural rehabilitation programs.

Content: (a) Learning about Project Renewal, its goals, purposes, and philosophy.
(b) Learning to function as part of the indisciplinary team and learning the role assigned to him or her, including the role as member of the steering committee.
(c) Learning how to identify community problems, initiate new service programs, and help those in need.
(d) Learning about the specific community served, the employing agency, the various ethnic groups in the community, the role of paraprofessional worker and former client, and the relationship of this role to that of the social worker.

● *Somchot* – support aides

Objective: Training the support aide to help multi-problem families within the setting of the local welfare department.

Content: (a) Learning about the clients who seek services from the department of welfare, that is who they are, why they come to the agency for help, and what their needs are.
(b) Learning about the role of the social worker and the agency and the services they offer.
(c) Learning how to help multi-problem families in their home, particularly in teaching communication

skills; facilitating interaction among family members; and helping the children with their homework and the mother with her tasks.

(d) Learning how to help parents and children through direct assistance in solving problems or through modeling or demonstrating effective functioning, and so on.

● *Mental health aides*

Objective: Training the mental health aide to work for mental health agencies with clients who are being discharged and facilitating their integration into the community.

Content: (a) Learning basic knowledge about mental health.

(b) Learning how to be supportive to clients who are in treatment.

(c) Learning how to help clients in their daily lives, particularly when treatment has been completed, and facilitating their return to the community. This would entail good knowledge of community services, such as half-way houses, and so on.

(d) Learning to mediate between the client and the community, including making contact with employers, helping clients gain entry to learning centers, vocational training, or universities.

● *Paraprofessionals in early childhood settings*

Objective: Training paraprofessionals to work with parents and children, primarily in the home, in order to develop the latter's cognitive, emotional, and physical potential. (In Israel there are two specific programs in this area: first, *Etgar*, literally challenge, or guiding mothers in the early education of their children aged 4 to 6; and second, *Hat'v*, guidance in the development of younger children aged 1 to 3.)

Content: (a) Learning about early childhood programs.

(b) Teaching parents how to use simple teaching materials and toys to develop their children's potential.

(c) Teaching parents of older children how to enrich their reading and language skills and be sensitive to their emotional development.

(d) Learning how to conduct enrichment programs
through the use of small groups, for example how
to lead groups, facilitate group interaction, and so
on.

● *Leaders in game activities and enrichment programs*
Objective: Training auxiliary personnel to work with children
and families through games in diverse settings such as
community centers, clubs, and programs in public
housing projects. (Unlike the latter program, this
activity is directed to all ages and does not take place
primarily in the home.)
Content: (a) Learning how to use games (active and quiet) in
order to facilitate family cohesiveness.
(b) Learning how to use games with all age groups to
develop their cognitive and emotional capacities.
(c) Learning how to identify problems of individuals
and families through game activities.
(d) Learning to serve as a model for parents on how to
teach, play, and communicate with children through
game activities.

● *Paraprofessionals in services for elderly people*
Objective: Training paraprofessionals to work with the elderly
within the community and within their home setting:
(1) Community workers with the elderly; and (2)
Mativot Metabel Bait – persons who assist the elderly
in their own homes.
Content:
(1)   Community worker
(a) Learning about elderly people, their development,
problems, and so on.
(b) Learning how to help the elderly function in the
community by establishing links with other age
groups, formal and informal.
(c) Learning about the services available to elderly
people through the National Insurance Institute
and the benefits they can derive from this national
body.
(d) Learning how to use supportive and interventive

skills when needed, developmentally and in times of crisis.

(2) *Mativot*

    (a) Learning how to care for aged and chronically ill people at home.
    (b) Learning how to dress and feed elderly, and particularly chronically ill people.
    (c) Learning how to prepare food for the elderly.
    (d) Learning the various services for elderly people in the community, for purposes of referral and treatment.

● *Paraprofessionals in corrections*

Objective: Training paraprofessionals to work with prisoners who have been released. (Paraprofessionals in Israel work extensively with ex-prisoners in the community.)

Content: (a) Learning about crime, penology, corrections, and rehabilitation.
    (b) Learning how to interview clients and how to use supportive networks to facilitate rehabilitation.
    (c) Learning how to find employment and opportunities for study and growth in the community for ex-prisoners.
    (d) Learning how to work with the prisoner's family and deal with its problems upon his or her return to the community.

● *Paraprofessionals in services to alcoholics*

Objective: Training paraprofessionals to work with alcoholics with the goal of bringing them to sobriety.

Content: (a) Learning about the phenomenon of alcoholism, its causes and effects, and the steps in rehabilitation.
    (b) Learning how to make referrals and gain access to services.
    (c) Learning how to advise the individual, group, and family about alcoholism and rehabilitation.
    (d) Learning how to compile and forward information to other staff members and professionals, as part of an interdisciplinary team.

● *Paraprofessionals in counseling and family agencies*

Objective: Training paraprofessionals to work with family counselors when severe family crises emerge, for example
divorce.

Content: (a) Learning about the role of the family counselor
and issues related to court orders.

(b) Learning about the crisis of divorce and how to
provide support for the family.

(c) Learning more specifically how to provide support
to children involved in divorce procedures.

(d) Learning to follow up families after divorce,
particularly the children involved, and report
findings to the agency.

● *Paraprofessionals in services to retarded people (institutional
settings and day care centers)*

Objective: Training paraprofessionals to work with retarded
people, particularly within institutional settings, and
to develop sensitivity to their needs.

Contents: (a) Learning about human development and the
normative aspects of development.

(b) Learning about factors that lead to retardation –
organic, genetic, and so on.

(c) Learning about the various levels of retardation.

(d) Learning caring skills needed for work with
retarded people.

(e) Learning to develop interventive skills with the
retarded, on both an individual and group level.

(f) Learning how to work with the families of the
retarded.

(g) Learning how to function as a member of an
interdisciplinary team.

The training programs listed above usually take place over a three-
month period, with weekly sessions of five hours.

The role of schools of social work

A number of factors have contributed to the growing interest and
involvement of schools of social work in paraprofessional education.

These include (1) increased recognition of the role of paraprofessionals in services vital to Israeli society; (2) increased interaction between professionals and paraprofessionals in all human service spheres; (3) the recognition that social work education can make an important contribution to paraprofessional education; and (4) the attention being given to paraprofessionals in continuing education programs for professional social workers.

A few years ago, the Association for the Development and Advancement for Manpower in the Social Services was created in Israel. This semi-voluntary association has supported a number of diverse projects involving paraprofessional personnel. In addition, funds from abroad have also been earmarked specifically for paraprofessional training. For example, the Hebrew University's Baerwald School of Social Work recently received a grant from the Adenauer Fund of West Germany to offer courses in team building and supervision for groups of social workers employed by the Municipality of Jerusalem and the national government's Ministries of Labor and Public Welfare. The social workers involved have been working with paraprofessionals employed as aides to elderly people and to multi-problem welfare families (Kestenbaum and Shebar 1984).

University continuing education programs have been particularly important in focusing attention on paraprofessional activities and issues. Courses dealing with paraprofessionals, their roles and functions, and some of the structural and other dilemmas involved in their use are being offered for graduate social workers under the auspices of several universities, including the Schools of Social Work at Bar-Ilan, Haifa, Tel-Aviv, and Jerusalem. In addition, the universities are offering graduate study at both the master's and doctoral levels that includes courses on paraprofessionals and have encouraged research on this subject.

As we have already mentioned, paraprofessionals are playing an increasingly important role in a broad range of human service settings so that professional social workers frequently find themselves working alongside auxiliary personnel, in some cases as members of interdisciplinary teams and in other instances as supervisors. Many of these professional workers are seeking to learn more about their new human service colleagues. In fact, a recent study by the Association for the Development and Advancement of Manpower (1985) indicated that this is a growing interest among graduate social workers in Israel. Clearly universities can no longer ignore the place of auxiliary workers in the human services. Their presence and impact are being felt and their efficiency is being recognized at all levels so that schools of social work are gradually taking account of their important contribution to the helping services.

UNITED STATES OF AMERICA

While it is impossible to determine what proportion of paraprofessionals receive training for their work, beyond the most rudimentary orientation or induction, it is clear that a great variety of pre-service and in-service training programs have been developed in the USA and the expectation is that some kind of training or staff development will be provided to most paraprofessionals in the human services. The bulk of this training is provided by employers. It is relatively short-term, practically oriented, and designed to prepare workers to perform specific job functions or to carry out these functions more effectively. For the past twenty years, articles and reports describing specific examples of this kind of on-the-job training for paraprofessionals in such fields as mental health, mental retardation, social welfare, family service, drug and alcohol abuse, health care, and services to the aging have been appearing in the human service literature in the United States. (See, for example, Coggs and Robinson 1967; Dalali, Charuvastra, and Schlesinger 1976; Danish and Brock 1974; Ford 1972; Johnson and Ferryman 1969; Knittel, Child, and Hobgood 1971; and Thorson 1973.) In addition to training provided by employers, a wide range of short-term in-service training is also offered by educational institutions, often with the support of grants from a variety of government agencies. (See Blayney, Truelove, and Hawkins 1976; Brawley, Bruno, Feinstein, and Lynch 1980; Brawley, Gerstein, and Watkins 1981; Lauffer 1977; and Loavenbruck and Crecca 1980.) The goals, design, and duration of both employer-provided and college- or university-based in-service training programs for paraprofessional human service personnel are so varied in the USA that they defy the kind of classification that is possible in some other countries – for example in Britain where a number of nationally recognized models have been developed by standard-setting bodies.

The situation is a little clearer in the case of paraprofessional training programs that lead to formal academic credentials. The rapid development of the community colleges during the 1960s coincided with the emergence of the paraprofessional movement and a great many of these colleges initiated two-year associate degree programs for paraprofessionals in a wide variety of human service occupations. In fact, community college programs probably constitute the most important formal educational and training resource for paraprofessional human service workers in the USA. More recently increasing numbers of colleges and universities have begun to offer four-year baccalaureate degree programs in the human services. While it would be strange in some countries to include college and university graduates among the paraprofessional ranks, it should be borne in mind that, in the USA, unless they have graduated from a social work program that is accredited by the Council on Social Work Education, graduates of college and university human service programs are defined as paraprofessionals by the National Association of Social Workers. Since associate degree and baccalaureate human service education programs are less variable and less transitory than the typical staff development activities conducted by employers and the short-term varieties of training offered (usually on an ad hoc basis) by some colleges and universities, they will be discussed in some detail.

Community college programs in the human services

In order to clarify some important aspects of two-year associate degree human service education programs operated by community colleges, a brief summary of the findings of a recent survey (Brawley 1981a) follows. This study sought to update information produced by earlier national surveys of these kinds of programs (Brawley and Schindler 1972; Claxton and McPheeters 1976; True and Young 1974). The following data are based on responses from 136 of an estimated 400–500 community college human service programs in the United States.

Respondents to this latest survey listed forty-six distinct program titles, although the term human service seems to have gained some degree of acceptance by community college educators and appears in the title of sixty-two programs. The next most common titles were mental health which appeared in twenty-four program titles and social work or social service which were used by fifteen programs.

Preparation for employment was the primary goal of almost all programs, with transfer to a four-year college or university second, and career advancement for employed human service workers third in importance. Other goals mentioned included personal development and career exploration.

The student population is predominantly female, with a ratio of at least five women to each man. Exceptions are found in criminal justice, corrections, and drug abuse counseling programs where the ratio tends to be reversed. An estimated 30 per cent of the students are members of racial minority groups. Of course, this percentage is not uniform across programs; some reported that all of their students are white while several examples of programs that serve a predominantly Black, Hispanic, or Native American student group were found.

When asked what discipline, profession, or field of practice students enrolled in the their programs identified with, social work or social service was cited by the largest number of respondents, closely followed by mental health/mental retardation. Counseling, psychology, corrections, child care, and education also received significant mention.

In terms of curriculum design, all programs provide a substantial amount of instruction specifically designed to teach students skills, knowledge, and attitudes considered to be necessary for effective human service practice. This material is communicated through courses in the social welfare system, interviewing and counseling skills, group processes, group leadership, and so on. In addition, practical field work experience in one or more human service agencies is included in almost all programs. However, despite this focus on human service practice, there appears to be an effort made to provide students with something more than specialized vocational training. Two-thirds of the programs responding to the survey require students to take at least one-third of their courses from among what are usually referred to as liberal arts or general education courses, for example written and oral communication skills, human development, health and nutrition, US government, and social problems.

Given the primacy of the employment preparation goal of the great majority of these community college human service programs, the success of their graduates in finding suitable jobs is an important indicator of program need and achievement. Three-quarters of the programs reported that the majority of their graduates find appropriate human service jobs. It is noted by some respondents that not all graduates seek employment in the human service field upon completing their programs – a significant proportion continue their undergraduate education elsewhere, some seek employment in other more lucrative and more attractive fields, and some simply postpone their entry into the job market for a variety of personal reasons. However, several respondents expressed dismay about the restricted employment market for the associate degree human service worker, which they tended to attribute to decreased government spending on the human services and the failure of civil service systems or human service agencies to establish job classifications for the associate degree worker. The specific job titles of graduates suggest that they most commonly find employment in social service, child care, mental health, and early childhood education positions at the aide, assistant, or technician levels.

About one-third of the programs participating in the survey reported that more than half of their graduates transfer to four-year colleges or universities upon graduation. This is a remarkably high proportion for graduates of programs that are concerned primarily with the preparation of people for immediate employment. One might surmise that students' educational and career aspirations rise as a result of their experience in the community college. They may view a traditional college education (that is one which leads to a baccalaureate degree) as more realistically attainable than they did prior to entering the two-year college. On the other hand, it may be that, during their community college experience, they begin to perceive that the opportunities for associate degree workers to find employment, to make significant contributions to the human services, or to receive recognition for their efforts are more limited than they expected or are willing to accept. This is a topic that needs to be more fully investigated. The most popular field of study of students who progress to the baccalaureate level is reported to be social work, followed by education, psychology, and sociology.

The faculty who guide and teach in human service programs are a very diverse group, with social workers constituting only a small, though significant, minority. However, human service students identify strongly with social work. Most of those who seek to continue their education beyond the associate degree level choose to pursue bachelor's degrees in social work. On a practical level, the graduates of community college programs are becoming a significant element of the human service labor force where, in many instances, they are working alongside or under the supervision of social workers. All of these facts suggest that social work has an important role to play in regard to the education, best use, and continuing development of this group of workers.

Bachelor's degree programs in the human services

Several factors seem to have led to the emergence of four-year baccalaureate degree programs in the human services in the USA. Hokenstad (1977: 54) mentions such stimuli as the general movement from a production- to a service-oriented work force, a greater focus on career as distinct from academic education, a decline in employment opportunities for teachers, and the trend toward consumerism (greater responsiveness to student interests) in higher education. These forces have resulted in the development in US colleges and universities of a wide range of new degree programs in a variety of human service areas and the re-orientation of existing academic curricula in the social and behavioral sciences toward some form of practice in the human services. Very little is known about these programs. In order to gather some data about them, Brawley (1982) surveyed a sample and the results of this survey are briefly summarized here.

The range of titles of baccalaureate programs is quite extensive. While a few actually carry the title human service, a total of fourteen distinct titles, including behavioral technology, rehabilitation, mental health, community service, applied psychology, human resources, individual and family studies, and social science, were identified. Most program purposes are stated in rather general terms, for example, to prepare undergraduate generalists for employment in the human services.

The ratio of female to male full-time students is two to one, while the part-time student group is equally divided between men and women. Despite the broad human service orientation of most programs, students tend to identify with a specific discipline, profession, or field of service, the most popular being psychology, followed by social work, counseling, and rehabilitation.

The proportion of instructional content devoted to career preparation (for example courses in the human service system, counseling methods, group work, and so on) ranges from 12 per cent to 80 per cent, with the balance devoted to liberal arts or general education subjects (humanities, social sciences, and natural sciences). Clearly some programs are heavily oriented to career preparation while others place more emphasis on a broad general education that includes only an introduction to the human services. All programs offer a practical field experience in a human service setting for their students and approximately 90 per cent require all students to participate.

When asked to estimate the percentage of their graduates who find appropriate employment in the human services upon graduation, 96 per cent put the figure at over half, and 70 per cent estimated that at least three-quarters of their graduates find suitable employment. There is a great deal of overlap between the reported job titles of bachelor's degree workers and those reported for community college graduates. For example, behavior technician, mental health worker, mental health associate, human service worker, income maintenance worker, psychiatric technician, psychiatric attendant, social worker, caseworker, counselor, and social services worker were among the thirty-four distinct titles mentioned.

Only a small percentage of the graduates of baccalaureate human service programs are reported to be advancing to graduate education. This may simply be a function of the newness of these programs. For those students who do continue their education beyond the bachelor's level, social work is reported to be the area of graduate study that most students enter, closely followed by psychology and then counseling.

Responses to an open-ended question about anticipated developments over the next five years were fairly conservative and unremarkable. A few programs anticipated some expansion in terms of the number of courses offered, the number of students enrolled, or the development of specialized courses in such areas as substance abuse or mental retardation. A move toward greater standardization of programs, including the development of some form of national accreditation system was expected by some respondents. As is true with the community college programs in the human services, bachelor's degree programs and their graduates cannot be ignored by social workers and other persons concerned with the way various categories of personnel are prepared for and engaged in the provision of social welfare services.

Implications

The prediction by Briggs (1973b: 28) that "professional social workers will find themselves working alongside a wide variety of individuals representing differing backgrounds, levels of achievement, and professional orientations in the provision of services" seems accurate. Many of these new human service colleagues can be expected to possess considerable skill and knowledge that will enable them to make a significant contribution to meeting human needs. This presents both challenge and opportunity to the social work profession which has tended to view itself as a central and integrative force in the social welfare field, historically, philosophically, and functionally. If social work education can develop its organizational, planning, and management components of the graduate curriculum, it could well function as the coordinating and synthesizing force that some critics suggest is currently lacking in the provision of human services in America (Chenault and Burnford 1978).

Graduate-level social workers have typically moved quite quickly into supervisory and other administrative roles in the social services and have had to work with a wide range of persons with diverse educational backgrounds. However, they have lacked specific preparation for these roles. The developments described here tend to confirm earlier conclusions that steps need to be taken by schools of social work to prepare graduate students for administrative, supervisory, and training roles in settings where teams of diverse personnel are likely to be engaged in the provision of social services (Purvine 1973).

Briggs (1973a: 6) has noted that, in the practice field, it is not the absence of adequately tested models of staff differentiation that has delayed their introduction in the social services but the attitudes of social workers that have blocked change. Similarly, within social work education, Sobey (1973: 61) has asserted that faculty resistance to teaching new models of practice has been a major barrier to preparation of students for new practice models. She states that "Irrational fears and resistance to learning and teaching how to work with new colleagues in new service models on shared social goals must be dispelled."

Several years ago CSWE published the findings of a study that concluded that schools of social work should give more attention to the preparation of graduate level students for work with other types of social welfare personnel (Purvine 1973). However, progress in this direction has been slow and there remains a "marked discrepancy between the number of social workers employed in administrative positions (50%) or performing administrative functions (91%) and the number of students enrolled in the administrative specialization in schools of social work (4%)" (Dumpson, Mullen, and First 1978: 35). Clearly professional social work education still has some way to go if it is going to shift its emphasis from direct practice to preparing its graduates to work effectively with the range of paraprofessional colleagues they are likely to find in the human services field.

As well as taking the initiative in developing appropriate models of social service staff differentiation and acquiring the skills needed to plan and manage complex human service operations, social work's leadership role could also be manifested in a willingness to share social work knowledge, skills, and perspectives with its human service colleagues. If, as social workers believe, they have something valuable to offer, this surely is worth sharing with others who are engaged with them in meeting people's needs. Much has been done in this regard in the types of in-service, staff development, continuing education, and other training programs mentioned at the beginning of this section. Social workers can demonstrate their helping philosophy and their commitment to improved services for clients by doing what they can to assist their paraprofessional colleagues (who are not going to go away) to achieve as high a level of proficiency as possible. A positive approach that reflects a professional commitment to make the best use of available human resources would be more appropriate than the current attitude of hostility and resistance that we reported in the last chapter.

DISCUSSION

The pattern of paraprofessional human service worker training and education is quite distinct in the four countries we studied, reflecting the different situations that exist in these countries. In India, for example, very few paraprofessionals receive any formal preparation for their work while in the USA the expectation is that all human service workers will receive some kind of training. In the latter case, an enormous range of types of training have emerged but without much overall planning. Britain, on the other hand, has developed a fairly comprehensive approach to the types of training that should be provided for different categories of paraprofessionals and has promulgated national curriculum models and has developed a framework for provision that reflects, at least in principle, a systematic approach to human resource development. Efforts to develop a comprehensive national approach are also underway in Israel.

In-service or on-the-job training is the predominant model in all four countries. However, the nature and auspices under which this is provided varies tremendously. It can be provided by employers, educational institutions, government bodies, or under a partnership arrangement among these groups. For example, training centers operated or sponsored by government bodies are very important training mechanisms in both India and Israel; employers and educational institutions are the major providers of training in Britain and the USA. In Britain some important training models have been developed at the national level, are jointly operated at the local level by employers and educational institutions, and lead to a nationally issued credential.

There has been a shift of emphasis in national training strategies in some of these countries. For example, in India (as is true in other developing countries), there is recognition that focusing on the training of human service professional personnel at the university level, particularly if the model is Western, is not likely to have much impact on the service needs of people at the grassroots. Greater attention is now being given to the training of front-line paraprofessional personnel in order to have the greatest impact on the country's social development goals. This shift in emphasis is not limited to the less developed countries. In Britain there is recognition that the progress that has been made in the last fifteen years in increasing the pool of professionally trained social workers must be matched by similar efforts to upgrade the skills of the paraprofessional work force if the quality of social service provision is to be adequate. This does not mean that the training of professionals is not considered important, only that it should be placed in proper perspective and that it should be accompanied by the training of the front-line workers who constitute the bulk of the human service work force.

Not only are the priorities between professional and paraprofessional training being reviewed but the nature of professional education is being reassessed. For example, in India, graduate schools of social work are a major training resource for the human services but some observers suggest that their educational approach might not be congruent with local needs and might not be making their best contribution to the nation's social welfare and social development goals. There is a feeling that they need to develop educational approaches that are based on indigenous conceptions of social service rather than Western urban industrial models and that they should be seeking ways of maximizing the contribution of front-line personnel, either through the direct provision of training or by teaching their graduates how to train and make optimum use of front-line workers.

While these observations have special relevance for countries in the less developed regions of the world, they are also applicable to the more developed countries. In Britain, Israel, and the USA there is reason to believe that professional levels of social work education should be placing a higher emphasis on training social workers to function in human service systems that use a broad range of personnel. Rather than concentrating on the training of direct service practitioners, they should probably be devoting more resources to training professional personnel who will function in indirect service roles, directing, coordinating, and supervising the work of paraprofessional personnel and providing appropriate in-service training for them.

There are some distinctive features of paraprofessional training in the four countries studied that we think are worth underlining since we believe that they may have applicability beyond their country of origin or because they are particularly noteworthy. For example, we were impressed by the work of national statutory bodies in Britain, the Local Government Training Board, and the Central Council for Education and Training in Social Work, in developing and promulgating models and standards for paraprofessional training. In particular, CCETSW's efforts to take a comprehensive approach to human service personnel training, to promote partnerships between employers and educational institutions at the local level, and to issue nationally recognized credentials for persons who complete approved training, are impressive. This is the most systematic national approach to human service personnel training that we were able to find. While we do not suggest that it is applicable to or practical in other countries, we believe that it has features that are worthy of consideration elsewhere. Israel's attempts to develop a comprehensive approach to paraprofessional training using a national training curriculum that is offered through a number of training centers in different parts of the country may be more appropriate for those countries or regions that do not have a well-developed system of local educational institutions.

In India the reassessment of the role of graduate schools of social work that we have already discussed cannot be overemphasized. Not only should the less developed countries reconsider whether Western models of social work education are really what they need but, in developing and developed countries alike, there is a strong argument for shifting the emphasis of graduate social work education toward preparation for planning, directing, coordinating, and otherwise maximizing the contribution of front-line human service personnel, who in most cases will be paraprofessionals.

Our study of paraprofessionals in Israel suggests that training and supervisory practices (and frequently the two overlap) that capitalize on group interaction and support are particularly effective with paraprofessional personnel. When learning takes place in a supportive interactive group, problem-solving skills are maximized, helping methods are improved, and the paraprofessional's sense of competence and areas of special expertise are strengthened.

Finally, within the enormously diverse (almost chaotic) array of paraprofessional training programs that exist in the USA, those that are offered by community colleges have special significance. They are accessible to most paraprofessionals (geographically, financially, and academically). They issue a formal academic credential (the two-year associate degree) that represents a half-way point between a high-school diploma and a four-year college or university degree and, therefore, serves as a bridge to full professional status for many paraprofessionals. They prepare people for a wide range of jobs in the human services, provide job mobility and opportunity for career advancement for employed paraprofessionals. Similar programs exist in comparable educational institutions in other countries (for example Australia, Britain, and Canada) where they are equally important training resources for paraprofessional human service personnel. The absence of a system of community or technical colleges in many countries precludes the application of this or similar models of training. However, we would suggest that there is a need in most countries for some type of formal training mechanism in most countries that will bridge the enormous gulf between the completely untrained paraprofessional worker and the university-trained professional.

8

Opportunities for career advancement

The degree to which opportunities for career advancement have been developed for paraprofessional personnel in each country is reviewed in this chapter. Barriers that exist to opportunities for career mobility are identified and analyzed. Innovative approaches to surmounting these barriers that have been developed in certain localities are examined in terms of their wider applicability.

BRITAIN

The opportunity for career advancement for the paraprofessional social service worker is a topic that is receiving increased attention in the British social work literature and, in recent years, a number of specific steps have been taken to remove or at least reduce systemic barriers that exist to paraprofessional career mobility.

Payne (1982) notes that, as greater numbers of paraprofessionals have been employed and the importance of their contribution to the social services has been recognized, there has been growing pressure to address issues related to their career development. He compares this to similar developments in the USA where large numbers of paraprofessionals were brought into human service employment in the 1960s and early 1970s.

"This has led in the USA to planning for career lattices . . . , which has grown from the new careers idea that it is worth finding ways of employing people who have not gained or cannot gain conventional education which alone allows them to take up professional roles. A variety of different paths is devised through patterns of experience and in-service training which will enable staff to achieve promotion in a hierarchical agency and broaden their responsibilities."

(Payne 1982: 99)

Payne sees some evidence that "the developing structure of social services education in the United Kingdom is moving towards providing such a pattern" (99) and he cites the emergence of the Certificate in Social Service (CSS) which we have described as an example of this type of opportunity for career advancement for paraprofessionals.

Of course, CSS training is a potential avenue for career advancement for only one (relatively small) segment of the paraprofessional work force. Cypher (1979: 211), a former officer of the British Association of Social Workers, notes that within the social services there are "many occupational groups, each making a different kind of contribution which requires a variety of training arrangements, although some of these will have common elements in the curricula." Cypher's concern is not only to upgrade the skills of these various groups but to ensure that their contributions are recognized and fairly rewarded. "What seems to be vital for the 1980s is that the contributions of the many staff, with their different types of knowledge and practice skills combined through team work, are not dashed on the rocks of unjust salary and status differentials" (211).

This is a particular concern in residential and day care services which "account for nearly two-thirds of the annual social services budgets of local authorities and employ over half of their social services staff" (Barclay Report 1982: 55). Only a very small percentage of the staff of residential and day services have any kind of recognized qualification (Barclay Report 1982: 26) and, consequently, many of these workers are locked into low-status and low-paying jobs. Most of the persons employed in these positions are women, as is the case with most social work assistants and practically all home helps. Low status, low pay, and limited opportunity for promotion have characterized these types of jobs (Payne 1982: 25).

"Tending remains closely associated in people's minds with a feminine role, and social policies have done little that might change it. For example, we do not staff our caring services in ways which remotely challenge that stereotype. Eighty per cent of the staff in old people's homes are women; the figure is 75 per cent in children's homes; virtually all our home helps are women and so are our nursery school teachers and nursery nurses. . . . Our sex discrimination legislation may have created opportunities for some women to do traditionally male work, but little, if anything, has been achieved in bringing men into the female occupations; that is hardly surprising in the case of tending since it is characterised by low pay and low status."

(Parker 1981: 25)

The Barclay Report (1982: 72) emphasized that the roles, training, and career opportunities available to the wide range of paraprofessional personnel engaged in the social services needed to be systematically and urgently reviewed. If the type of community-based social service system envisaged by the Barclay Committee was to be operationalized effectively, it was recognized by at least some members of the committee that the traditional roles of paraprofessional personnel would have to be expanded and that these expanded roles would have to be supported by appropriate training, compensation, and career opportunities.

"The successful extension of community-oriented services will depend upon the capacity of local authorities to recognize, encourage, and accommodate these developments [expanded staff roles] on a systematic basis. This will have implications for the negotiation of wider job descriptions, for salaries, and for training as well as the construction of career paths for those who have the ability and motivation to move on to more responsible posts."

(P. Brown, Hadley, and White 1982: 229)

Opportunities for career advancement

While the primary purpose of most of the training initiatives that have emerged in Britain in recent years (several of which we described in Chapter 7) has been to upgrade the skills and performance of the social service work force, they have also incorporated, by their very nature, opportunities for career progression for skilled and motivated paraprofessionals.

As we have already noted, the major reorganization and expansion of the social services that occurred in Britain in the early 1970s included a national commitment to the development of a cadre of qualified social workers who would form the core of the new consolidated local authority social services departments. Hadley and McGrath (1980: 3) note that "between 1971 and 1976 the number of local authority social workers more than doubled." Much of this growth in the numbers of qualified social workers was achieved by recruiting untrained personnel, having them work as trainees for a period, and then seconding them to (that is giving them paid educational leave to attend) social work training for two years. During the early 1970s it was not unusual for a young person to be appointed as a trainee, seconded after less than a year of work to full-time social work training on full pay for two years, qualify as a professional social worker, and be promoted to a senior, administrative, or training position, all in a period of four or five years. Clearly for those lucky enough to be involved in these arrangements, the opportunities for career advancement were outstanding.

However, now that the period of expansion has ended and even reversed and as the numbers and proportions of qualified social workers have increased, local authority secondment policies have become much less liberal and, in some instances, have dried up. Furthermore, these policies only benefited social service staff who were specifically recruited for social work positions, leaving out the large numbers of paraprofessional social service workers whose role did not fit into this category or for whom professional social work training was not appropriate. For example Hey refers to the plight of some social work assistants employed by local authority social services departments:

"Many of these are older women with experience of bringing up families and of life generally who would not consider, for psychological and/or practical reasons, undertaking professional training. They may well have the 'right' personal qualities and a general level of ability (comparable to the professional level) irrespective of previous educational experience. In some real sense they are underemployed but cannot get employment at a higher level because they lack qualification."

(Hey 1975: 7)

In order to address the needs of those social service personnel who are not clearly identified with social work functions or for whom social work training is not appropriate, a number of other training approaches, each with some potential for career progression have emerged. For example social service staff who complete the In-Service Course in Social Care (ICSC) described earlier receive a statement of completion from the Central Council for Education and Training in Social Work (CCETSW), the national standard-setting body for social work education in Britain. Possession of this nationally recognized credential provides the opportunity for horizontal and vertical mobility for the holders, at least in principle. While possession of this credential does not confer professional status on the holders, it may qualify them for more responsible or more skilled paraprofessional jobs.

CCETSW (1983b: 8) discourages colleges that offer ICSC training from prescribing formal entry requirements to these programs since it feels that the training provided should be designed to meet the needs of the participants the local authorities are planning to send for ICSC training. This is intended to prevent the creation of unnecessary barriers to training for gifted but academically ill-prepared paraprofessional social service personnel.

ICSC is not intended to replace either agency-based in-service training or professional social work education. It is seen as only one component of a comprehensive system of social service education. CCETSW (1983b) expects social service agencies to provide orientation for new staff and appropriate in-service training to develop workers' job skills, both before and after ICSC training, based on the needs, interests, and readiness of individual workers. ICSC is a more formal college-based form of in-service training for interested staff. It should enable participants to perform more skilled jobs or to take on greater responsibility in the workplace. In some instances, it might reveal the potential and the motivation of some social service personnel to pursue more advanced training or formal education (9–10). In fact, over 40 per cent of the persons entering CSS training have completed the In-Service Course in Social Care (CCETSW 1983a: 13).

The Certificate in Social Service is the credential with perhaps the greatest potential for providing career advancement for the paraprofessional social worker in Britain. As we have noted in the last chapter, CSS training is provided by specially organized programs (called schemes in Britain) that are administered jointly by students' employers and local colleges. The training, which is modular in design and is comprised of formal classroom instruction and guided on-the-job learning, lasts at least two years. Students are released by their employers for one or two days per week to attend classes and to study. All schemes must be approved by CCETSW which has promulgated strict guidelines that ensure national standards and recognition.

Ash *et al.* (1980: 11) note that the urgent need for a training and certifying mechanism for residential workers was the primary impetus behind the development of CSS training but "it was clear from the outset that other occupational groups should be included." These other groups included the staff of day care services, persons who provided specialized services to handicapped people, coordinators of volunteers, home help organizers, social work assistants, community workers, and the like. CSS training was developed quite specifically to address the need to upgrade the skills of the above wide range of paraprofessional personnel who constitute a significant segment of the social service work force in Britain. While the original goals focused on improving job skills rather than career development (Allen 1984: 18), in fact CSS training has been an important means of gaining recognition and the opportunity for career advancement for many of these workers.

Although CSS training was initiated primarily for social service personnel other than social workers, it soon became evident that there was considerable overlap between CSS training and that provided in professional educational programs leading to the Certificate of Qualification in Social Work (CQSW). A major review of social work and social service training carried out by CCETSW in 1982–83 revealed "widespread agreement that the present complete separation of the CQSW and the CSS patterns of training and qualification should not continue" (CCETSW 1983c: 29–30). As we noted in the last chapter, CCETSW proposes having both forms of training lead to a single professional social work qualification, the CSS alternative being the employment-based route. In the mean time, CSS training programs continue to operate throughout the country and provide an excellent vehicle for career advancement for some paraprofessional social service personnel, especially those engaged in residential and day care services for elderly and mentally handicapped people, children, and youth (CCETSW 1980b). Among the major advantages of this model of training and career advancement is that participants continue to earn their full salaries (a vital consideration for many) and they are engaged in an educational experience that is designed to have a strong practical orientation. As Ash and colleagues have noted:

"For some students one of the attractions of CSS training is that they can train without giving up their jobs. Both students and training staff have seen advantages in a pattern where the interaction between learning and practice is continuous. The objectives and content of training are unlikely to deviate far from the needs of practice, and students have less of a re-entry problem when they complete their training."

(Ash *et al.* 1980: 83)

Barriers or limitations to advancement

Although the thirty CSS schemes that have been developed so far represent almost complete geographic coverage of the United Kingdom, not all local authorities participate in these schemes (CCETSW 1983a: 11), meaning that the employees of non-participating local authorities have no opportunity for CSS training. Within those local authorities that do participate, the demand among paraprofessional personnel for CSS training exceeds the number that can be accommodated (CCETSW) 1983a: 50). When CSS training was introduced in the mid-1970s, it was anticipated that this form of training would become the basic qualifying mechanism for the majority of social service personnel needing training and a qualification (Birch Report 1976).

"The Birch Report, in its preferred projection, envisaged an intake to CSS training of 9,000 students per annum by the mid 1980s. Plainly, this figure is now wholly unrealistic and was always highly ambitious, even before the full force of the economic recession was felt. Latterly, the Council has inclined to the view that a figure of the order of 3,000 should be adopted as a target for the 1980s."   (Ash *et al.* 1980: 97)

In fact, only about 1,300 students per year were entering CSS training in the mid-1980s, representing only about one-third of the number admitted annually to professional social work education programs (CCETSW 1985b: 3). There has been considerable fluctuation in the numbers of students entering some local CSS schemes which "may suggest a lack of consistent commitment by some agencies" or "can be a direct consequence of (externally) enforced cuts in training budgets" (CCETSW 1983a: 11). As the number of participants has remained small in relation to potential demand, there has been a natural tendency for employers and CSS program staff to select the most able candidates for training. This has caused some concern that this may have tended to "push up entry requirements perhaps to the disadvantage of would-be applicants without formal educational qualifications or of less ability" (CCETSW 1983a: 50).

The inability of CSS training schemes to accommodate more than a small proportion of those persons who could benefit from this opportunity is true of other types of training also. For example, it is reported that few local authorities provide systematic in-service training for social work assistants (Hallett 1978: 156), home helps (Local Government Training Board undated b: 2) or the staff of residential facilities (Local Government Training Board undated a: 4). Therefore, while the opportunities for training described here and in Chapter 7 are undoubtedly important potential vehicles for career advancement for paraprofessional social service personnel in Britain, as is the case in most countries we have studied, these mechanisms tend to serve a relatively small percentage of the paraprofessional work force.

Discussion

The training policies of the national government and of local authority social services departments in Britain have been heavily oriented to staff at the professional level. This has been advantageous to people occupying professional social work positions in the British social services, many of whom experienced unprecedented career advancement during the 1970s. Corresponding attention, resources, and opportunities have not been accorded to the paraprofessional. In recent years, some steps have been taken to redress this imbalance. A number of innovative training programs with significant potential for enhancing the career mobility of paraprofessional personnel have been introduced and have shown considerable promise. However, as is true in other countries, the percentage of paraprofessionals who have the opportunity to participate in these programs (while significant) remains quite small.

The role of the Central Council for Education and Training in Social Work in promoting appropriate training for all categories of social service personnel in Britain merits special attention. While CCETSW was established by the national government in the early 1970s with the primary purpose of promoting and regulating "social work" education, by the end of the decade it had assumed responsibility for addressing the training needs of a broad range of social service personnel, in addition to professional social workers. As Cypher (1979: 193) has noted, CCETSW "assumed responsibilities for the training needs of staff in field, residential and day-care settings, and . . . promoted courses in training which are explicitly not intended for [professional] social workers." This contrasts with the activities of standard-setting social work education bodies in other countries. For example in the USA the Council on Social Work Education (CSWE) has explicitly limited its concerns to social work education at the professional level. In fact, it has undergone a reverse process to the one pursued by CCETSW. While CCETSW has expanded its role to address the training of virtually all social service personnel (professional and paraprofessional alike), CSWE has abandoned the concern that it showed during the 1960s for paraprofessional training. The fact that CCETSW is a government body while CSWE is a voluntary organization of social work education programs and affiliated groups and individuals may explain, at least in part, the different orientations of these two organizations. Nevertheless, the advantages of having a body that looks at the total system of social service staff training are clear.

INDIA

As is true in other countries, there are barriers to the creation of appropriate career advancement opportunities for paraprofessional human service workers in India. Some of the barriers reflect conditions that are unique to the Indian situation; others are more universal. In this section, we review these problems, as well as some developments that hold promise of addressing more adequately the career aspirations of paraprofessionals.

Indigenous values

The concept of career generally implies upward mobility in an organizational hierarchy or in an occupational field. It usually involves a step-by-step progression, often tied to years of service or the acquisition of additional skills or knowledge. This conception is basically Western and industrial in orientation and may not always be relevant to less developed countries. India is a case in point where opportunities for career advancement for paraprofessionals have not been given much importance by social welfare personnel planning bodies, reflecting the situation that exists in the broader society. A number of factors account for this situation. Among these is the fact that India has had a long tradition of voluntarism. This is still very much a part of the country's ethos; it is expected that people should help each other without material compensation. There are literally thousands of voluntary organizations in India and they serve as models for the rest of the country to reach out to those in need because "it is one's duty".

Equally important are religious considerations. Well over 80 per cent of the country's population are adherents to Hinduism. Hindu doctrine requires that a person's life be regulated by the conception of duties or debts which one has to discharge, including a duty to humanity which has to be discharged by obligation, hospitality, and goodwill. Those who subscribe to this view are not content with merely earning their bread or seeking comfort but believe that they are born not for themselves but for others. Consequently they have difficulty justifying the helping act carried out for monetary benefit.

Another factor is the tradition of mutual help which has been an important aspect of rural community life for centuries. In times of crisis, the community has come to the fore to support and help persons in need. In many respects, the emergence of organized human services, including the paraprofessional worker, was a response to the inability of individuals, families, and communities to cope with a host of problems ranging from infant mortality, malnutrition, poverty, and exploitation – factors beyond the scope of mutual help to rectify. However, faith in mutual aid is still very strong and is manifested in widespread disbelief that the professional helper's intervention can solve a family's problem that they and the community could not have solved by themselves. These and other cultural values tend to block consideration of appropriate career planning for human service personnel, especially when these are indigenous front-line paraprofessionals.

Women and careers

Chauhan (1985) has observed that the majority of persons who enter the human services at the paraprofessional level in India are women. This has implications for careers in general and career mobility in particular. In India a woman's role is still highly circumscribed with clearly specified functions and responsibilities. Her place is in the home caring for her family, raising children, and carrying out domestic responsibilities. While it is quite common for a wife to work outside the home to supplement her family's income, it is much less common for her to put job or career before family or even to seek to balance the two. For example, it is unheard of in India for a husband or family to transfer residence in order to advance a woman's career aspirations. In urban and rural areas alike, home and family are expected to come first, no matter what the woman's job situation is. Two kinds of discontinuous work force participation result – dropping out of the labor force for a period of months or years for childbearing and child care and giving up a specific job when family needs or a husband's relocation require a change in residence. Such intermittent participation in the labor force means that women typically have less training or continuous work experience, and fewer career advancement opportunities than men.

   During the past decade, a greater sensitivity to the economic plight of women, particularly in rural areas, has emerged and some steps have been taken to improve their situation. There has been increased recognition that women face special problems in remote geographic areas. For example, there is higher involuntary unemployment and greater iliteracy compared to men. Specifically, while 47 per cent of rural men are literate, only 25 per cent of rural women can read and write (Ministry of Rural Development 1984).

While boys are usually sent to school, girls are kept at home to help their mothers and look after their younger brothers and sisters. Compounding this problem is the fact that in much of Indian society women are not considered to have the same status as men, resulting in a situation where insufficient attention has been given to their education, development, and economic well-being.

In order to address some of these problems, a program of social development for women has recently been instituted in India, with particular attention to women in rural areas. As we mentioned in Chapter 5, under this program women are being trained in income-generating activities such as basket-weaving, craft, construction, and farming skills. Perhaps more importantly, there are efforts to increase literacy, to find meaningful employment and to limit family size. The goal is, in the main, to provide greater educational and economic opportunities for women, This program, referred to as the Development of Women and Children in Rural Areas (DWCRA) Program, has played an innovative and significant role in integrating women into the mainstream of society. It is too early to assess the outcome of this program but it has been given high priority by the national government and is a step in the right direction if for no other reason than it reflects recognition that a problem exists and some commitment to remedying the situation.

Problems of job definition

Another major barrier to the creation of career opportunities for paraprofessionals is the absence of clear job definitions for the many kinds of human service workers who have been recruited in recent years to tackle India's enormous social and economic problems. Only when jobs are clearly defined is it possible to identify the levels of knowledge and skills that should be addressed by professional and paraprofessional training programs and how these different levels might be arranged in some hierarchical order. For example Gangrade (1985) and others note that a major problem in the social welfare field is the failure to identify those jobs that require social work education and those that require other types of training.

"Many evaluation committees have pointed out that the standards of service are unsatisfactory because of the lack of

SOCIAL CARE AT THE FRONT LINE

professional manpower at different levels. . . . Little has been done to remedy this situation. Unless unions, state public service commissions, and the Department of Personnel in the Central Government . . . make social work education a prerequisite for jobs in social welfare and social development there is little possibility of adequately relating social work education to the existing jobs in the government, semigovernment and the private sector."

(University Grants Commission 1980: 43)

It has also been suggested that "the jobs that exist today are blind alley jobs in subordinate positions and are intended to support the functioning of other personnel. There is no career ladder" (Desai 1985). There appear to be limited opportunities for growth and advancement in the job situation.

This issue is complicated by the fact that paraprofessional personnel function in relation to many professions besides social work. Each helping profession or human service field has its own kind of paraprofessional to assist, support, and facilitate the work that needs to be done (Kulkarni 1980: 143). In other words, it is not enough to assume that paraprofessionals exist only in and for the social work profession. In many instances, paraprofessionals function in an auxiliary role to several professions at the same time.

For example in India there is much emphasis on family health in general and family planning in particular. A project which one of the authors (Schindler) visited in a poor area in Bombay revealed the type of issue likely to emerge when paraprofessionals work for one or more allied professions.

> "The concept was to develop a health service including maternity and child welfare activities. Paraprofessionals were part of a comprehensive interdisciplinary health team dealing with malnutrition, child care, tuberculosis and family planning. Although the program was staffed primarily by social workers, paraprofessionals were guided and supervised by medical personnel."

(Parikah 1985)

This is a common pattern in urban and rural projects alike. Social work rarely has exclusive jurisdiction over the training, deployment, or supervision of paraprofessional human service workers. Paraprofessionals frequently perform multisectoral and interdisciplinary tasks. Consequently training programs probably should include content from a variety of allied professions, such as health, education, home science, and agriculture, as well as content related to urban and rural poverty. This makes it difficult to develop clear career paths for paraprofessional personnel since there is considerable ambiguity about the direction in which these careers should lead. The problem is further compounded in India (as in many developing countries). Because of limited resources and chronic shortages of adequately trained personnel, field-level workers (whether professional or paraprofessional) have necessarily been multipurpose in function. The issue to be resolved is which profession is best suited to undertake the training of these multipurpose workers. At the time of writing, the schools of social work in India are viewing this responsibility as theirs.

The role of schools of social work

There is growing international recognition that paraprofessional training and the relationship between training and career development have to be strengthened. It has been suggested that the working conditions, financial, and other rewards, and opportunities and incentives of front-line personnel have to be improved if they are to make their best contribution to human service activities.

"As front line workers gain in experience and effectiveness, many will want more responsible or financially remunerating work. If they have no advancement opportunities they will probably leave social service work. Professional advancement for front line workers is difficult in present forms of administration. If this can be facilitated, it will stimulate paraprofessionals to advance in the administrative system through extra training and experience."

(United Nations 1979: 26–27)

Despite the barriers noted above, there appears to be some movement in India towards implementation of these suggestions. The University Grants Commission (1980) strongly recommended that leadership in paraprofessional recruitment and training be undertaken by schools of social work. The faculties of three major schools of social work (Tata, Bombay, and Delhi) concur with these recommendations and believe that colleges and universities will have little choice but to design and be actively engaged in paraprofessional education.

Accelerating social change, massive social problems, rapid population growth, and a severely limited supply of professional personnel all dictate the continued use of trained front-line paraprofessionals. To give just one example, in the five-year plans of the government of India, the welfare of backward classes (particularly tribal welfare) has been given special attention. However, the number of professionally trained social workers engaged in this field of service is miniscule. Furthermore, tribal welfare requires persons who have first-hand knowledge of the language, culture, religion, and way of life of specific tribal groups which makes the use of indigenous paraprofessionals particularly appropriate. Among the suggestions made for addressing this type of situation is the establishment of "roving" or mobile campuses to meet the educational needs of indigenous front-line workers in remote geographic areas.

There is general agreement in Indian schools of social work that in the past thirty years the social work profession has failed to participate in and contribute to large-scale country-wide programs of high national priority, such as community development, family-planning, and human settlement, particularly in rural areas. Today, the social work schools are beginning to see that they have a role and responsibility to train tomorrow's social workers, including front-line and indigenous paraprofessionals, for these high priority areas. If they fully accept this responsibility, the training they provide for paraprofessionals will have some impact on the career opportunities of these workers.

Careers in child care services

During the past thirty years both the central and state governments have established their own institutes or centers for training, the most prominent being in the field of child care. As mentioned in Chapter 5, the Integrated Child Development Services (ICDS) program offers the widest and most comprehensive employment and training opportunities for paraprofessionals, as a direct consequence of the dramatic growth that has occurred in child care services in India in recent years. For example under the ICDS

program, in 1984 almost 10 million children were given immuniz-
ations and health checkups, over 6 million received supplementary
nutrition, and more than 3 million participated in pre-school
education. It is estimated that these numbers are likely to double by
1990 (Ministry of Social Welfare 1984).

It would be impossible to carry out this ambitious program
without the recruitment and contribution of paraprofessionals.
Chowdhry has put it in these terms:

"For one thing it is impossible to obtain professional manpower
for the millions of children in this country. Naturally the
situation in the rural areas is critical. Professionals never reach
these areas and even if they did they could not communicate
with the population. Both in education and health we rely
primarily on the person in the field. The medical profession has
now also recognized the importance of the paraprofessional.
How could they possibly reach the vast population and dispense
immunization shots, measles vaccine, diphtheria, tetanus and
typhoid injections without them. At times we hear criticism that
at least these persons should be able to read and write. I tell them
'Let the best not be the enemy of the good.'"

(Chowdhry 1985)

The issue of career development has not been of major concern in
the ICDS, since the majority of workers do not think in these terms.
While the ICDS has incorporated some opportunities for career
mobility in its personnel system, these are primarily lateral in
nature, that is paraprofessionals can be given increased responsibility,
and take on additional tasks as they gain more experience and skill
but there is no concern for vertical mobility. Quite simply, career
mobility is not viewed as a central problem at this time. The
priority issues are the recruitment and training of sufficient
numbers of staff. The present staffing arrangements call for a ratio
of one paraprofessional or *anganwadi* worker to a target population
of 1,000 children. As we mentioned earlier, children in India form a
significant percentage of the population. Of the total national
population of 683 million, 270 million or 40 per cent are below the
age of 15 and 109 million or 16 per cent are below 6 years
(Population Reference Bureau 1983). It is recognized that these
children will largely determine the course of India's social and
economic future. And yet, with all the resources invested by the

ICDS and other government agencies, only 15 per cent of India's children are reached by these services. Without the recruitment of additional numbers of front-line paraprofessionals and a long-term commitment to their retention and development, the possibility of reaching millions of needy children will be jeopardized.

Initiatives by paraprofessionals

We mentioned in Chapter 5 that there are groups of paraprofessionals in India, primarily in urban areas, who are taking a more aggressive role in promoting social change. They seek redress for what they see as society's denial of the rights and failure to support the progress of the disadvantaged groups they represent. The front-line paraprofessionals who lead this also express a need for greater job security and benefits for themselves and their co-workers. At the time of writing, some of these workers are attempting to create their own organization in order to fight for greater work rights. Siddiqui (1985) and other social workers suggest that this initiative will be thwarted unless the social work profession gives a helping hand in providing some structure to their endeavors. However, unlike the schools of social work which are presently resolved to bring paraprofessionals into the mainstream of social work education, the practice arm of the profession is, at best, apathetic towards the paraprofessional.

A number of factors seem to have contributed to this situation. As we noted earlier, the Indian Association of Trained Social Workers has had only limited success in its efforts to develop a viable organization that is widely recognized as an important professional body. Policies and direction have been unclear and diffuse. One of the reasons for this, Gangrade (1985) suggests, is the leadership's preoccupation with global issues, neglecting causes that are closer to home. The organization has, therefore, failed to address a number of issues, including the place of paraprofessionals. It has also been suggested that the profession must achieve clarity in regard to its own goals, purposes, and endeavors before it can relate to the position of paraprofessionals. There is also the reality of job competition, particularly in urban areas, which appears to be an additional reason for failing to address the paraprofessional issue in positive terms. However, unless the profession addresses itself seriously to the paraprofessional movement, there is the possibility that other professions will take on that responsibility.

Summary

A variety of cultural, religious, and other factors influence the way careers are viewed in India, creating barriers to the development of career opportunities for paraprofessionals. However, in spite of the difficulties that exist, there are at least two bodies that can make major contributions to paraprofessional career development. On the one hand, the schools of social work are committed to integrating paraprofessionals into the mainstream of social work education. If they follow through on this commitment by providing appropriate formal training opportunities for paraprofessionals, this would constitute the beginnings of a career structure in the social welfare field. On the other hand, the Integrated Child Development Services are the largest employers and trainers of paraprofessional personnel in India. If the activities of the ICDS continue to expand to meet the needs that have been identified, this will almost inevitably create the need to develop opportunities for career advancement for at least a portion of the enormous numbers of front-line paraprofessionals involved.

Despite the passive role played by the social work profession in relation to the paraprofessional up until now, we believe that this is likely to change in view of the enormous shortages of trained human service personnel that exist in India and as the important role of the paraprofessional is increasingly recognized. Furthermore, there are already some indications that paraprofessionals may take a more active role in the future in determining their own destiny.

ISRAEL

As is true in India, little time and effort has been devoted to the planning of human service personnel systems in Israel. As a consequence, there is no national plan for the career development and advancement of paraprofessionals (Kadmon 1983).

Despite this absence of planning, it is evident that the numbers of persons employed in the human services has been increasing quite dramatically in recent years. It can be seen from *Table 5* that the

TABLE 5 *Employed persons by economic branch and year*

	personal and other services	public and community services	financing and business	transport and communication	commerce, restaurants, and hotels	public works	electricity and water	industry	agriculture	%
1970	7.7	24.0	5.2	7.5	13.0	8.3	1.2	24.3	8.8	100.0
1975	6.1	27.3	6.7	7.3	12.3	8.1	1.0	24.8	6.4	100.0
1977	6.6	28.0	7.2	7.0	12.2	7.4	1.2	24.1	6.3	100.0
1978	6.6	29.2	7.6	6.9	12.0	6.7	1.1	23.8	6.2	100.0
1979	6.2	29.5	7.9	6.9	11.8	6.7	0.9	24.3	5.9	100.0
1980	6.2	29.6	8.2	6.9	11.7	6.4	1.0	23.7	6.4	100.0
1981	5.8	30.0	8.8	6.7	12.0	6.2	1.1	23.4	6.1	100.0
1982	6.1	30.1	9.0	6.8	12.1	6.2	1.1	22.9	5.7	100.0

Source: Statistical Abstract of Israel, 1983. Jerusalem. Central Bureau of Statistics 1983: 357.

percentage of the labor force employed in the public and community services (education, welfare, health, government, and cultural services) grew from 24 per cent to more than 30 per cent between 1970 and 1982. During this same twelve-year period, with the exception of finance and business, employment in all other major segments of the economy (industry, transport, communication, commerce and public works) decreased (Central Bureau of Statistics 1983: 357). Paraprofessionals make up a substantial and growing proportion of the work force in the public and community services, a trend that is likely to continue despite a temporary freeze on hiring caused by the current economic recession.

Almost 50 per cent of the people employed in the public and community services are women. In the social work profession the percentage is much higher (approximately 85 per cent) and among paraprofessional human service workers women constitute over 90 per cent of the work force. Among the issues discussed in this section are the implications of these figures for career planning for paraprofessional human service personnel in Israel.

Career and status aspirations of paraprofessionals

The majority of paraprofessionals entering human service employment in Israel are so-called second career women in their early to mid-forties. A wish for self-fulfillment and the opportunity to be of service to others are among their motives for seeking employment in the human services. However, economic considerations are also important since many are seeking to supplement their family incomes and substantial numbers of them are the primary or even sole income earners in their families. Once they have entered human service employment, they expect opportunities for growth and advancement.

In some of the services we described in earlier chapters, paraprofessionals are relatively well paid, have established job positions and contracts, and are provided with appropriate training opportunities. This is particularly the case in those settings where they provide personal social services to vulnerable or high risk populations. However, this is the exception rather than the rule.

Recognition, improved status, and opportunities for upward mobility are important to many paraprofessionals and, in some instances, these goals are achieved. Many paraprofessionals who were former clients of welfare bureaus or were rehabilitated through participation in self-help groups have made the successful transition to the role of service provider. They associate with and are accepted by their professional colleagues and in many cases, as in Project Renewal, they are bona fide members of interdisciplinary teams.

The recognition and status of the paraprofessional in Israel is likely to be reinforced by those concerns and trends that have led to increased involvement throughout the world of citizens and community members in social policy and planning decisions that affect them. These developments have occurred in response to observations that the public has surrendered too much authority to professional experts in the social planning arena (Illich 1980) and criticisms that the large government bureaucracies have become more unmanageable and more unresponsive to the public as the number of technical experts involved in the decision-making process has increased (Elgin and Bushnell 1977). In the modern complex world, it is difficult for social planners to comprehend, control, and predict all of the contingencies involved in the management of social change (Gilder 1980) and consequently it is deemed advisable to involve people who are at the front line in planning and decision-making. Indeed, as Bell (1973) predicted, in the years ahead, top-level decision-makers can expect to be confronted with increased demands by persons at all levels in organizations and in society for such participation. All of these trends would tend to contribute to increased recognition of the value of front-line paraprofessionals and enhance this status within the human services in Israel.

Barriers to career advancement

Despite these favorable long-term trends, paraprofessional human service workers in Israel still face a number of serious barriers to recognition and career advancement. As is true of their professional colleagues, many of them seek avenues for career advancement but, compared to the situation of the professional, the paraprofessional's opportunities are quite limited. As we found in other countries we studied, a major barrier is the fact that most opportunities for job mobility and advancement are based on the possession of formal educational qualifications. Since the majority of paraprofessionals in Israel are without such qualifications and, indeed, have not completed the twelve years of schooling required for university entrance, they are locked into relatively low level jobs. As yet, the universities have not seen it as their role or function to develop training programs or open up educational opportunities for paraprofessionals who do not meet conventional admission requirements. This differs from the situation in India where steps are being taken to link paraprofessional training to higher education.

While all paraprofessionals in Israel are expected to receive training that will prepare them for practice in the human services, the training that is provided is not of a sequential and cumulative kind that leads to career mobility or progression. In essence, the paraprofessional is recruited and trained for a specific job without much thought for what happens after that. Career mobility can involve opportunities for both horizontal and vertical movement – the concept of a career lattice rather than a simple career ladder. While we did find instances where paraprofessionals were able to move horizontally across different services in a particular human service agency and among agencies, these practices are rare. Similarly, some paraprofessionals are given added job functions and increased responsibilities as their experience and skills grow but this frequently occurs without formal recognition or increased financial reward. Not surprisingly, we encountered much frustration among paraprofessionals and criticism of personnel policies flowing from perceived inequities in income, benefits, and opportunities for career advancement when they compared themselves with their professional colleagues. Many paraprofessionals feel that their job performance compares quite favorably with that of professionally trained workers and some contend that they work harder, for longer hours, and in the provision of more intensive services than professionals typically do. This may be especially true in rural areas.

Job security is another contentious issue and a source of considerable uncertainty in terms of career planning for paraprofessional personnel. This is especially the case in times of economic difficulty and fluctuating national commitments to particular human service programs. While there is generally a high degree of job security for employees in Israel's public services, this is less true for paraprofessionals in most social service agencies. When retrenchments have to occur, it is frequently the paraprofessionals' jobs that are in jeopardy. The fact that they are not protected by any professional association or other occupational organization makes them especially vulnerable. In general, there is no recourse for grievances and no review process for job termination decisions. The security and mobility of the paraprofessional are also limited by the very specific job training that he or she has received which may not be viewed as relevant by a prospective new employer.

A related problem for the paraprofessional is the absence of a clear professional or occupational identity. Membership of a recognized profession is very important for social workers and other helping professionals, not only because it gives meaning and structure to their relationships with clients but because it provides an important sense of identity, security, and belonging. This does not exist for paraprofessionals in Israel yet. The Israeli Association of Social Workers has not sought to bring them under its wing and no other group has emerged that can provide a sense of identity and support for the paraprofessional human service worker.

Women and careers

A recent study of the role and status of women in Israeli society (Peled and Zemach 1983) revealed that a high percentage of the population sees the woman's place as being primarily in the home. An equally high number of respondents offered the opinion that employment of married women outside the home is likely to have a detrimental effect on family functioning. While men were given high approval ratings for success in their careers, women were much more likely to be praised for doing a good job in raising a family. Although dual career couples are quite common in Israel, the husband's career was seen as having priority.

At least four types of relationships appear to exist between two-career couples in regard to the pursuit of their respective careers (Holmstrom 1972). One is the colleague model where marital partners support and influence each other's careers and may engage in joint work. A second type is the independent model where each pursues a separate career with no attempt to share the other's work. A third model is the competitive one in which competition and rivalry may lead to marital discord. The fourth type of relationship has been termed the supportive model. In this case, one career (usually the husband's) is seen as having primary importance and the other partner is expected to play a supportive role in advancing this career. This is the dominant model in Israel.

Consequently for most of the women who constitute the overwhelming majority of the paraprofessional human service work force in Israel, career aspirations are expected to be subordinate not only to their roles as wives and mothers but also to the dictates of their husbands' occupations. They must live where their husbands' work takes them and adopt a life style and a pattern of labor market participation that is greatly influenced by the demands and rewards of their husbands' occupations. In many cases, their participation in the employment market creates strains within the family as a result of the need to modify the traditional roles of family members. The long and irregular hours of many human service jobs (often requiring evening and weekend work) and the new ideas and attitudes acquired in training programs are additional sources of potential strain within the family. In short, there are numerous forces that work against successful participation in the labor force and career advancement of the paraprofessional human service worker in Israel.

Directions for change

While some of these barriers to career advancement are formidable, some change in the present situation of limited opportunity seems inevitable in the decade ahead. This change is likely to occur in response to a number of developments that are already apparent. In the first place, a number of paraprofessional groups (for example, the *matavoti* or home helpers) have become unionized which will enable them to exercise more collective influence over such matters as wages, benefits, job security, and opportunities for career advancement. An interesting related development is the willingness of some of these paraprofessional workers to take employment in the private for-profit sector of the human services, so that the public services are no longer their only option. This proprietary or commercial sector is likely to be an increasingly important source of employment in the human services as it expands to meet the social and health care needs of a variety of vulnerable populations such as the elderly.

This and other developments have implications for the relationship between paraprofessionals and the social work profession in Israel.

It may be that those common interests and allegiances that link the two will weaken and that the paraprofessional group will gain sufficient strength and independence to develop its own identity and organization. On the other hand, the social work profession might contribute to bringing about needed changes in the career structure of the paraprofessional work force. For example, the Israeli Association of Social Workers has recently set up a task force to develop guidelines for different levels of professional jobs, with appropriate training to be specified for each level. A career lattice with specific job descriptions linked to educational qualifications to include the paraprofessional would be extremely beneficial to career planning. However, not much effort or thinking has been devoted to such a design yet and it is unlikely that much progress will be seen in this area in the immediate future.

As we have noted elsewhere, the provision of educational opportunites that lead to a recognized qualification is a key to genuine career advancement for paraprofessional human service workers. The role of the community colleges in the USA is a case in point. The two-year associate degree in the human services that many of these colleges offer provides an important stepping stone to more responsible jobs, higher status, and salaries and (in some instances) to full professional standing for large numbers of US paraprofessionals. An educational resource comparable to the US community college does not yet exist in Israel. However, some alternatives are emerging that may ultimately serve the same purpose. These are the adult vocational training programs that are being developed for a variety of categories of personnel. Particularly significant is the support given to these programs by the Ministries of Labor and Social Welfare. If these programs fulfill their potential, they would constitute a valuable training resource in the human services, enabling paraprofessional career development on a more comprehensive scale in the years ahead.

UNITED STATES OF AMERICA

Opportunities and barriers

In assessing the paraprofessional movement in the USA, Robin and Wagenfeld (1981: 352) note that, if one of the major purposes of the movement was to provide career ladders for the paraprofessional, then the outcome would have to be viewed as questionable. While it is true that "the paraprofessional is now a part of the fabric of the human services" (Gartner 1981: 53), and that "many new careerists were able to . . . escape poverty and establish themselves firmly as successful professionals" (Pearl 1981: 35), opportunities for genuine career advancement for the paraprofessional in the USA are highly variable among individual employers, state civil service systems, fields of practice, and geographic area. Clubok (1980: 6) notes that while the concept of a career ladder in the human services has long been discussed and proposed, in reality it has rarely been translated into practice in most social service organizations (6).

At least on a theoretical level, there are opportunities for paraprofessionals in the USA to become professional social workers. However, this can only be accomplished through formal education, by completing at least a baccalaureate degree (four-year) social work education program accredited by the Council on Social Work Education. Applicants must meet the admission standards of the particular college or university offering the program that they want to enter. These requirements vary among academic institutions, but almost always include at least the possession of a high school diploma.

Community colleges have more flexible admission requirements and some even operate under an "open door" policy that makes them accessible to students with relatively weak academic backgrounds. Therefore, it is possible for an untrained human service worker to attend a two-year community college and, after earning an associate degree, transfer to a four-year college or university and complete a professional social work degree in an additional two years. Some community colleges have formal articulation agreements with neighboring four-year colleges and universities that ensure that the community college graduate can transfer to senior institutions without unnecessary loss of time or credit.

This model of career advancement for the paraprofessional through formal academic channels is likely to be the norm in the USA for the foreseeable future. Despite the fact that it is clear that paraprofessionals without conventional academic credentials can and do provide effective and valuable services to the clients of a wide range of human service programs, current and future trends in the human services suggest that academic training will be critical for all personnel in most fields of service in the years ahead (Anderson, Parente, and Gordon 1981). This presents problems for those paraprofessionals who cannot or perhaps need not undertake college or university education. For example, there are many paraprofessionals who do not have access to formal educational opportunities, either because suitable human service education programs are not available where they live, they cannot meet admission requirements of local institutions, or they cannot afford the expense of pursuing a college or university education. Many rely on full-time employment to support themselves and their families. Other paraprofessionals are older adults who may find the prospect of returning to formal education forbidding, especially if previous educational experiences have been unsatisfactory. Furthermore, large numbers of paraprofessionals have accumulated years of practical experience in human service employment and have undergone substantial amounts of in-service training so that they may be functioning at a very high level of competence. Requiring these individuals to undertake education that is unlikely to add markedly to their knowledge and skills is neither fair to them nor an appropriate use of available resources.

Innovative approaches to worker certification and career advancement

In order to address these problems, two national projects, spearheaded by agencies of the US Government, were initiated in the 1970s with the purpose of providing nationally recognized credentials for paraprofessional human service workers. If these developments fulfill their potential, they will make it possible for significant numbers of paraprofessionals to receive national certification and opportunities for career advancement without necessarily following the traditional academic route.

The Certified Human Service Worker (CHSW) credential
As noted in an earlier chapter, the National Institute of Mental Health (NIMH) played an important supportive role in the development of the paraprofessional movement in the USA by funding training programs for the large numbers of these workers who were needed to staff the rapidly expanding community mental

health services during the 1960s and early 1970s. As the number of community college and baccalaureate-level human service education programs increased dramatically, there was growing pressure to develop mechanisms that would establish standards for these programs and that would ensure that their graduates met appropriate standards of practice competence. It was also recognized that there were large numbers of paraprofessionals employed in the human services who had not graduated from college-based training programs and that some steps needed to be taken to establish a national credential that would attest to the competence of these workers.

In order to address this issue, in the late 1970s, with the support of NIMH, the Southern Regional Education Board (SREB) undertook a standard-setting project that led to the creation of the National Commission for Human Service Workers (NCHSW), an organization that operates a national certification system for paraprofessional human service workers. It has already developed, pilot-tested, and implemented an assessment procedure and issues certificates of competence to paraprofessionals who successfully complete the process (National Commission for Human Service Workers 1983). By the end of 1983 nearly 600 human service workers had successfully completed the procedures required to qualify as Certified Human Service Workers (CHSW). Of those who took the certification examination 58 per cent were either associate degree or bachelor's degree holders; the remaining 42 per cent were agency-trained and/or were currently enrolled in college-level training programs (*NCHSW Worker Forum* 1983: 1).

Although its development was initiated and supported by NIMH, an agency of the US government, the CHSW credential is not yet widely recognized or accepted by employers or academic institutions. If its recognition and acceptance grow, it could be a significant mechanism for career mobility (both horizontally and vertically) for the paraprofessional human service worker in the USA.

The Child Development Associate (CDA) credential

The Child Development Associate (CDA) project is another example of a government-sponsored effort to provide a nationally recognized credential and the opportunity for career advancement for a particular category of human service paraprofessionals – in this case, those working in day care and early childhood education programs.

Particularly in the inner cities, early childhood programs (day care, Head Start, nurseries, and the like) tend to be staffed by persons who have substantial practical child-rearing experience but who lack, in varying degrees, the specialized knowledge and skills necessary for the provision of high-quality developmental experiences for young children. At the same time, many of these staff members are drawn from low-income and minority communities and, despite their innate ability and high potential, they are not able, for a variety of reasons, to follow the traditional academic routes to increased competence and formal credentials.

In 1973 the US Office of Child Development (OCD) selected and funded thirteen pilot projects in different parts of the USA to develop model competency-based training programs that would prepare people to qualify for the new national credential which OCD was calling the Child Development Associate. The level of competency expected of the trainees was derived from a set of competency statements developed under OCD leadership by a national consortium of child development and early childhood education specialists (Office of Child Development 1974). An important aspect of the CDA approach was the provision of the opportunity for experienced paraprofessionals to undergo an assessment process and demonstrate possession of some or all of the required skills and knowledge without necessarily participating in any training activities. It was felt that a competency-based approach such as this could have a significant impact nationally on the quality of service provided for young children in day care and similar programs, as well as providing recognition, a nationally accepted credential, and the opportunity for career advancement for substantial numbers of early childhood education paraprofessionals.

The results achieved by CDA training programs in different parts of the USA in preparing child-care personnel to meet national norms of competent care-giving are encouraging (see, for example, Brawley, Gerstein, and Watkins 1981; Peters and Sutton 1984). While the appropriateness and form of competency-based training for the child-care field are subject to debate and the merits and shortcomings of a particular competency-based program can be argued, the significance of this type of program for the untrained or non-credentialed worker and its potential impact on the quality of child-care service cannot be ignored. As in the case of the Certified Human Service Worker credential, it is not yet clear whether the Child Development Associate credential will receive wide recognition and acceptance in the human services in the USA, despite the support both have received from the US government. If it does become an established qualification, it will provide a signficant mechanism for the recognition and career advancement of paraprofessionals in the field of early childhood education.

The role of the social work profession

Another development that has opened up some opportunities for career advancement for paraprofessionals in the human services is the "declassification" process, referred to in earlier chapters, that has occurrred in certain state civil service systems. A number of states have lowered the educational qualifications for various categories of jobs as a result of court rulings that have found in some instances that educational requirements are unrelated to actual job demands and may be discriminatory in their effects. Another consideration in the "declassification" movement by certain states has undoubtedly been a cost-saving one (Pecora and Austin 1983).

In reality, the major beneficiaries of declassification have tended to be holders of bachelor's degrees in areas other than social work since the four-year college degree seems to be the basic entry qualification for social work positions in state civil service systems (Gilbert 1975). There is little evidence that declassification has opened up significant numbers of professional-level jobs to paraprofessionals who have less than a bachelor's degree.

Unfortunately, the social work profession's reaction to declassification, as we noted earlier, has been to close ranks and to resist perceived encroachment by nonprofessionals by arguing that professionally trained social workers perform at a higher level of competence than persons who have not received professional social work education and that most social service jobs should be filled by professionals (Teare *et al.* 1984; *NASW News* 1978b). This defensive posture has caused it to abandon its formerly constructive efforts to develop comprehensive social service personnel systems, including the promotion of a continuum of education and training for all social service personnel, with corresponding career ladders. This is an unfortunate development and the social work profession needs to reassess its position.

A more constructive approach would be to commit itself to a research program designed to produce a social service personnel model that includes an appropriate and demonstrable matching of worker competence to job requirements. By adopting a total system perspective which recognizes the place of other participants in the human service enterprise, many with valuable contributions to make, the profession could well find itself in partnership with other groups (for example, the public employee unions) that are willing to commit themselves to the same constructive approach to the specification of job requirements and the development of appropriate opportunities for career progression for their members (Karger 1983). The degree to which social workers exercise leadership in the task of conceptualizing and organizing appropriate social service staffing patterns so as to make best use of the present array of available personnel, with the ultimate purpose of providing more efficient and effective services, they will increase their credibility with policy-makers and other interested groups and enhance their ability to influence future developments.

Specifically, the following types of action would appear to be called for:

First, the issue of appropriate roles for the paraprofessional in the provision of social welfare services needs to be addressed. The valuable research that has been done on staff differentiation in the social services (see, for example, Barker and Briggs 1968; Teare and McPheeters 1970; Brieland, Briggs, and Leuenberger 1973; Teare 1981) notwithstanding, there is considerable evidence that the typical approach to paraprofessional job definition in human service agencies is haphazard and expedient rather than systematic (Austin 1978). In the absence of well-thought-out personnel systems, the paraprofessional will continue too often to be used inappropriately to replace professionals or simply not incorporated into social agency personnel systems (Hirayama 1975). Top priority should be given to the specification of appropriate jobs with corresponding career lines for paraprofessional personnel in all social service systems.

Second, while some efforts have been made in the past to address the issues surrounding the development of a continuum in human service/social work education programs (Gore 1969), steps need to be taken to address these issues again on a broader and more systematic basis. For example, a survey of current practices could be undertaken and some broad guiding principles identified.

Third, under present political and economic circumstances in the USA, the human services are no longer an expanding job market. Therefore, human service/social work education programs at all levels should probably redirect a substantial portion of their resources from pre-service training or career preparation (that is the training of new entrants to the human services) to in-service training or career development (training or continuing education for employed but untrained or undereducated human service workers). Clearly it would be unrealistic to expect that jobs in the social services presently occupied by paraprofessionals will be automatically turned over to trained social workers, as more of the latter become available.

"most of the jobs that are filled by underqualified people will not become vacant when educationally qualified persons appear on the scene. The lack of professional education, while decried by the [social work] profession, does not seem to be sufficient to force employers to fire untrained incumbents or to reclassify positions so they will be in the exclusive domain of BSWs and MSWs. (In unionized agencies, these options would not be possible.) Nor do incumbents see it as an adequate reason for voluntarily vacating these positions."

(Hardcastle and Katz 1979: 18)

Providing educational opportunities for underqualified job incumbents is a more realistic and constructive approach, enabling paraprofessionals to upgrade their skills, achieve career advancement, and perhaps eventually join the professional ranks.

DISCUSSION

The knowledge and skills of paraprofessional human service personnel are likely to increase as they gain experience on the job and as a result of their participation in various types of training. As their knowledge and skills grow many will be able to take on greater responsibility or handle more challenging jobs. Opportunities for able workers to take on greater challenges and responsibilities and, along with that, to be accorded higher status and remuneration will be necessary if they are to continue experiencing job satisfaction and make their best contribution to human service provision.

There is fairly widespread recognition in the countries we studied that there is a need to develop appropriate opportunities for career advancement for paraprofessional human service personnel. The degree to which this has been achieved varies considerably among and within countries. Realistically the difficulties faced are much greater in some situations than in others.

For example the obstacles to developing realistic opportunities for career mobility for paraprofessionals in India, especially village-level workers in remote tribal areas, are formidable. Low rates of literacy, geographic isolation from training opportunities and alternative sources of human service employment, and cultural expectations that discourage career advancement for women are some of the factors involved. A significant conceptual, as well as practical problem, is that paraprofessionals are usually multipurpose or cross-sectoral workers who are not identified with any specific profession. Developing career lines is difficult since it is not clear which direction these should take and, at present, none of the established human service professions has taken responsibility for seeing that appropriate training and career advancement opportunities are made available for paraprofessionals.

There is recognition in India that these issues have to be addressed and that barriers have to be overcome where possible. In response to the recommendations of a national advisory group, some schools of social work are planning to implement paraprofessional training programs and, in general, take on a broader role in personnel development in the human services. There is also some consideration being given to experimentation with mobile training programs that would serve paraprofessionals in remote rural areas.

As is the case in most of the countries we studied, the paraprofessional human service work force is predominantly female. The barriers to career advancement for women in India are enormous. However, there is a national commitment to overcome these barriers in order to improve the social and economic status of women, particularly in rural areas. Providing opportunities for training and career advancement for paraprofessional human service workers would contribute to the broader national efforts.

As in India, little attention has been given so far to the development of opportunities for career advancement for paraprofessional human service workers in Israel. The majority are women and many are members of cultural or ethnic minority groups. More often than not they are economically disadvantaged. They are aware of disparities in status and income between their situation and that of their professional colleagues, many of whom are members of the dominant ethnic groups in Israel. Paraprofessionals expect to be given the opportunity to improve their situation and this will require the development of appropriate career ladders. The present avenues are based entirely on the possession of appropriate academic qualifications and, unfortunately, most paraprofessionals in Israel are lacking these qualifications and, therefore, are faced with insurmountable barriers to advancement. Unless some flexibility is built into the system, most will be locked into low-status and low-paying paraprofessional jobs regardless of their capabilities.

In Britain a couple of paraprofessional training programs have been developed that provide useful avenues for career advancement. One of these presently leads to the nationally recognized Certificate of Social Service. If current plans come to fruition, it will constitute an alternative route to a full professional social work qualification for some of the kinds of human service personnel we have referred to as paraprofessionals.

The other training program (the In-Service Course in Social Care) also leads to a nationally recognized certificate. Although this credential does not confer professional standing, it does signify that the holder has undergone a nationally approved training program. At least in principle, this can improve the holder's chances for promotion to a more responsible paraprofessional position that brings higher status and salary. It can also improve the possibility of moving to a more desirable job with another employer or in a different geographic area. The In-Service Course in Social Care can also serve as a stepping stone to professional social work training for some paraprofessionals.

A major advantage of both CSS and ICSC training programs is that they do not require participants to give up their jobs or move away from their homes and families to undertake training. Another advantage is that they have fairly flexible admissions standards.

This means that unnecessary barriers are not created for the typical paraprofessional who must keep working to support one self and one's family and who usually does not have the academic credentials necessary for university entrance.

Not all paraprofessionals in Britain who want and could benefit from CSS and ICSC training are given the opportunity to participate, primarily because of employers' inability or unwillingness to bear the cost of sending more workers. Therefore, opportunities for career advancement are by no means universally available. However, these programs are important avenues to career mobility for those fortunate enough to have the opportunity to participate.

In the USA a model of career mobility and advancement based on the possession of formal academic credentials has been the norm and is likely to remain so for the forseeable future. While some paraprofessionals have been successful in advancing through the formal educational system and achieving professional qualifications, others face formidable barriers to advancement through traditional academic routes. Cost of enrolling in college or university is one barrier. The need to continue working full-time to support themselves and their families is another. Many paraprofessionals are older persons who find the prospect of going to college or university unattractive. Some lack the necessary entry qualifications. Others live in communities where appropriate educational programs are not available. Many experienced paraprofessionals are functioning at a level that is, in all essential respects, quite comparable to their professional colleagues. Subjecting them to the long and expensive process of professional education is neither a good use of their time, talents, and money nor of the country's educational and human resources.

In consideration of these factors, a number of alternative mechanisms for career advancement have been explored in the USA. Two that seem to have some merit, the Certified Human Service Worker assessment procedure and the Child Development Associate training and assessment program have been described. Approaches such as these that assess a worker's competence against nationally established standards and that issue a qualification regardless of a person's formal academic background need to be considered for larger groups of paraprofessionals. These types of programs would appear to be desirable not only in situations where groups of paraprofessionals cannot or should not pursue traditional academic routes to career advancement but also, and perhaps especially, in those situations (for example in remote areas of developing countries) where formal educational opportunities are in short supply or simply do not exist.

In all the countries we studied there is a need to work toward developing more rational personnel systems that recognize that there are many types and levels of jobs in the human services and that clarify the nature of these jobs and the specific skills and knowledge required to perform them. At the same time, there are (or should be) different types and levels of training (formal and informal, traditional and untraditional) that correspond roughly to the jobs that need to be done. The missions of these different educational and training programs and how they relate to each other must be made clear. If these two sides (jobs and training) of the human resource equation can be brought into a reasonably close relationship with each other, the contribution of available personnel resources, including paraprofessional staff, would be maximized and opportunities for career mobility and career advancement would be increased.

The role of Britain's Central Council for Education and Training in Social Work is exemplary in this regard. It has adopted a total systems approach to social service staff training. While it cannot ensure that everyone who needs training will receive it, the council has developed a rational framework within which specific types of professional and paraprofessional training take place. The system is widely understood and generally supported within the social services in Britain. There is a need for comparable bodies in other countries to take a similar system-wide approach to human service personnel development.

9

Paraprofessional human service personnel in international perspective: major findings and implications

This concluding chapter is devoted to a cross-national comparison of paraprofessional personnel in the human services, drawing on the material presented earlier in the book. The most salient issues emerging from our study of the paraprofessional in different countries are discussed in terms of their practical and theoretical implications. Finally, some possible future developments are identified. It is our hope that our findings will increase understanding of current issues and developments in the training and use of paraprofessional human service workers in different countries and in an international context, facilitate more rational and systematic approaches to human service personnel development and use, and perhaps contribute indirectly to the improvement of human service systems in different parts of the world.

CROSS-NATIONAL OVERVIEW

Persons whom we would define as paraprofessionals have always been important front-line personnel in human service systems throughout the world. This continues to be the case today. In all of the countries we studied, they constitute the majority of the human service work force. In some instances they augment the work of professionally trained personnel; in other situations they operate without reference to the functions of social workers or other human service professionals. In many parts of the world they are, for all intents and purposes, the only front-line human service providers available. This is especially (but not exclusively) the case in rural areas of the less developed parts of the world. For example, although 80 per cent of India's population live in rural areas, few professionally trained social workers are found outside the cities (Dave 1985). Even in the USA where there have been significant increases in the numbers of both professional and paraprofessional mental health workers in recent years, "rural areas, small towns and poor urban areas still only have a fraction of the personnel they need" (President's Commission on Mental Health 1978: 35; see also Weber 1976).

A variety of factors have contributed to the widespread use of paraprofessional personnel to perform a broad range of human service functions. Some of these factors have been quantitative or logistical in nature; for example, having insufficient numbers of professionally trained personnel to staff a country's human service or social development efforts, making more efficient use of available resources, and a desire to extend services to remote areas or underserved populations. In addition, qualitative considerations have been important, including recognition that there are many human service functions that are particularly suitable for paraprofessionals and that some communities or client populations can be better served by indigenous front-line personnel.

The widespread use of paraprofessional workers to perform a broad range of human service tasks is explicitly or implicitly supported by government policy in all the countries we studied. However, support of paraprofessionals by professional social work organizations is more equivocal. Social workers in Britain are probably most accepting of the paraprofessional while their counterparts in the USA are more likely to resist the use of this category of personnel.

In all countries most front-line paraprofessional human service workers are women. They are the formal helpers who have the most frequent and regular contact with the clients of human service programs. Although many types of training have been developed for this category of worker (more in some countries than in others) and while some paraprofessionals are highly trained, most have received no or quite limited training for the functions they perform.

Front-line paraprofessionals are more likely than their professional colleagues to share ethnic, cultural, class, religious, language,
and other characteristics with the clients and communities they
serve. This indigenous dimension is widely recognized as an
important element in the paraprofessional's value and effectiveness.
Not only is the social distance between service providers and clients
reduced but service practices are more likely to be adapted to local
needs when paraprofessionals are employed in front-line service roles.

Among the vast range of tasks that paraprofessionals are
performing throughout the world, many are what we have termed
"life-line" functions; that is paraprofessionals are providing health,
nutritional, and personal care services that are vital to the health
and well-being of individuals, families, groups, and communities.
For example, they are engaged in primary health care in rural areas
of India and in aboriginal communities in Australia and they ensure
that frail elderly and disabled people living at home in Britain,
Israel, the USA and many other countries receive nutritious meals
and are properly cared for. Other life-line functions performed by
paraprofessionals in rural India and other less developed countries
include the conservation of water, increasing food supplies,
anticipating and coping with natural disasters like floods and
droughts, and ensuring that proper sanitary conditions are maintained
in villages. Providing personal care for vulnerable populations (the
very young, the very old, sick and disabled people) is an especially
important paraprofessional function and one that is likely to grow
in most countries in the years ahead. Based on our observations of
paraprofessionals in different parts of the world we would stress
that these front-line human service workers cannot be regarded as a
stop-gap or transitional response to shortages of professionally
trained personnel. In some instances, they do function as substitutes
for professionals where these are in short supply but, besides that,
many of them perform distinct and important functions that
professionals do not, should not and (in certain circumstances)
cannot perform.

CLARIFYING THE PARAPROFESSIONAL'S ROLE

Our study confirmed unequivocally that paraprofessional human
service personnel throughout the world are engaged in the provision

of a multiplicity of front-line services to a wide variety of client populations. The tasks and functions that they perform are extremely diverse. In general, they would tend to fall into the three broad categories identified by Katan (1972): finding out about clients and their needs; serving as links between clients and human service organizations; and providing direct assistance to clients. While some of these front-line paraprofessionals function in auxiliary or ancillary roles in relation to social workers or other human service professionals, in many instances they do not, so that the terms paraprofessional, assistant, aide, and the like are not usually appropriate. There is a need to develop a generic title for these front-line workers that reflects the fact that they are performing jobs that have their own meaning and integrity and that are not appendages to other people's jobs.

We have noted in several places in this book that paraprofessionals tend to be the workers who have the most frequent and regular face-to-face contact with the clients of the human services. This makes it especially important that they be carefully selected for the work they do, that their tasks and functions be appropriate and clearly defined, and that they receive whatever training is needed to ensure that they can perform their jobs adequately. While some paraprofessionals perform fairly simple routine tasks that are easy to distinguish from the more complex diagnostic, treatment, administrative, planning, and training functions performed by many professionals, there is a middle range of human service activity in which there is a great deal of overlap between the work of direct service professionals and large groups of paraprofessionals. Making appropriate and useful distinctions between the functions of these front-line professionals and paraprofessionals has been difficult and, so far, not wholly successful. However, it is important that efforts to reach greater clarity in this area continue.

In countries, areas, or settings where there are few professionally trained workers, the question of how best to distinguish between professional and paraprofessional roles and functions is basically irrelevant. In such situations the best that can probably be achieved is for professionals to provide back-up supervision, consultation, or other forms of support to front-line workers. In this regard, it needs to be recognized that there are no absolute standards in human service provision – only what a country or organization can or will provide at a particular point in time. Similarly, there is no natural hierarchy of types of services – only those that are given priority at a given time.

Where both professional and paraprofessional personnel are available, there are ways to identify the roles that are appropriate for each, based on such criteria as the complexity of the tasks that have to be performed, the amount of risk involved for the recipients of service, and the degree of judgment or situational response required of the worker. We believe that greater effort should be made to refine these types of human service staff differentiation criteria and to apply them more widely. Not only will greater clarity about professional and paraprofessional roles and functions tend to reduce conflict between the two groups, it is likely to result in better service to the clients of the social services.

In situations where professionals and paraprofessionals are both engaged in the provision of a human service, relations between the two are likely to be most positive and their work most productive when the roles of each are clearly defined – not in a hierarchical arrangement where the paraprofessional works for the professional but rather works with the professional, contributing his or her particular skills and knowledge to the partnership or team effort. For this type of system to work effectively, the unique value of the paraprofessional's contribution has to be affirmed and supported through the provision of opportunities for recognition, personal development, job enrichment, appropriate training, and career advancement. While we believe strongly that greater clarity is needed in determining what roles and functions are appropriate for paraprofessionals, it is important to avoid overly simplistic or unnecessarily rigid decisions about who can and cannot perform certain tasks. As we discussed in Chapter 5, there are many aspects of expertise or competence that must be considered in allocating tasks and functions between professionals and paraprofessionals. We believe that a high degree of flexibility is desirable in the deployment of human service personnel in order that the parapro-fessional's contribution to the provision of human services is fully utilized and the broadest range of human need is addressed. An organic/adaptive (Bennis 1969) rather than mechanistic approach to personnel deployment would appear to be appropriate.

Based on our study, we see particular merit in team approaches to the organization of human service staff at the local level. In all four countries that we studied in detail, we found evidence that good results could be achieved by community-based teams comprised of professionally trained workers and a variety of paraprofessional personnel who bring their joint resources to bear on a range of client needs. A great deal of promising research on social service teams has been done in the USA over the last twenty years and in Britain the value of the community- or neighborhood-based team approach to social service provision is widely recognized. In Israel's Project Renewal and India's Integrated Child Development Services, the use of mixed teams of professionals and paraprofessionals has proven to be an effective way to reach out to disadvantaged and underserved communities. Related to this, we identified a trend in several countries toward greater decentralization of service provision (Martinez-Brawley 1982), based on relatively small geographic units such as the patch in Britain, the block in India, and the *schuna* in Israel.

THE INDIGENOUS DIMENSION

Our study has confirmed for us the importance of the contribution that indigenous front-line paraprofessionals can make to human service or social development programs. Because of their closeness to the recipients of service, they are able to provide services in a way that is more acceptable and potentially more effective than would be the case with professional workers. We concur with the observation that "paraprofessionals who come from the communities which they serve have been found to be more effective in working with the people as they have close ties and may have insights and information not readily available to the outsider" (International Association of Schools of Social Work 1979: 8). For example, it would be doubtful if the kinds of primary health care, including family planning services, that are being provided in India would be as acceptable or effective without the participation of village-level workers who are familiar with the local language, culture, religion, and way of life. Similar observations could be made about front-line paraprofessionals in all countries who are drawn from local communities or who share common experiences and characteristics with client groups. In developed and developing countries alike (Grosser 1969; Srinivasan 1978; Cooper 1980), indigenous parapro-fessionals are considered to be more effective than professionals in working with certain clients and communities or at the very least they are seen as adding a valuable dimension to human service provision. This would tend to support the idea that there is an important place for the paraprofessional in the human services regardless of the quantity of professional personnel available.

Government officials, human service agencies, and professionally trained workers can (and sometimes do) disregard the importance of the indigenous factor in helping. This may reflect a lack of sensitivity or commitment to reach out to minority or other client populations with special characteristics or needs. To the degree that there is a commitment to make human services responsive to the needs of special (usually disadvantaged) populations, then the use of personnel (who will more often than not be paraprofessionals) who share class, cultural, ethnic, language, religious, and other characteristics with these groups will be important.

Questions have frequently been raised about the effect upon indigenous paraprofessionals of the training that is provided for them.

"The aim of many paraprofessional training programmes is to prepare a person from a particular area or group to carry out development tasks. Does the very process of training create a distinction between the worker, and his former peers? If so, is the worker's effectiveness reduced through a loss of relationship, and, if it is, can this be avoided?"

(Rigby 1978: 15)

These questions have not been answered definitely. However, based on our observation in different countries over two decades, indigenous workers do not have to lose their identity and effectiveness in working with their communities as a result of the training they receive. Much depends on the nature of the training provided, especially the ethos that guides it; that is, whether it is profession-centered or client- and community-oriented and the degree of commitment to recognize and affirm the value of indigenous factors and to capitalize upon them.

Similarly, we gave examples earlier of instances where indigenous workers can be used as buffers rather than bridges between human service organizations and professionals on the one hand and minority groups and deprived communities on the other hand. While this is a very real danger, it is not inevitable. Again, much depends on the sensitivity and commitment of the organizations and professionals involved.

The employment of indigenous paraprofessionals has been viewed as an extension of worldwide efforts to promote local citizen participation in decision-making and action on their own behalf. Although these efforts have taken quite different forms in different parts of the world, most have been based on the broad underlying philosophy that social development goals are likely to be achieved more readily if those groups most directly affected (local communities or recipients of services) participate in the planning and delivery of services.

"Social development has two interrelated dimensions; the first is the development of the capacity of people to work continuously for their own and society's needs. The second is the alteration or development of a society's institutions so that human needs are met at all levels, especially at the lowest, through a process of improving the relationship between people and socioeconomic institutions and recognizing that human and natural forces are constantly intervening between the expression of needs and the means to attain them."

(Paiva 1977: 332–33)

Indigenous paraprofessional personnel were linked conceptually to many of these social development efforts since they could potentially "promote the people's participation in development [and] energize the people's and community's capacities for self reliance" (International Association of Schools of Social Work 1979: 8)

While these efforts to involve local citizens (particularly disadvantaged groups) in decision-making in relation to social planning and development have not always been effective (Alford and Friedland 1975; Boaden *et al.* 1982; International Committee for the Evaluation of Project Renewal 1984; Jain 1986), we believe that they can be and that indigenous paraprofessionals can make a particularly valuable contribution to these efforts because of the unique bridging function they can serve between service providers and service recipients. Once again, whether they are permitted to perform this valuable function will depend on the degree of commitment of public officials, social planners, human service administrators, social workers, and other professionals to genuine citizen participation.

We believe that social workers and other human service professionals can learn a great deal from working alongside paraprofessionals. Not only can they learn to serve a particular group of clients or a specific community better but they can also acquire skills and sensitivities that are applicable in a variety of situations. We concur with Austin's (1978) observation that the introduction of indigenous paraprofessionals into the human services in the USA enriched social work practice in that country. Willingness to learn from creative uses of the paraprofessional in different parts of the world could provide even greater benefits for the human services, their staffs, and the people they seek to serve. Indeed, looking at the paraprofessional movement worldwide, if its potential is fully realized, it could be an important catalyst in the indigenization of the helping services and professions.

DEVELOPING APPROPRIATE SOCIAL TECHNOLOGIES

Just as Schumacher (1973; 1979) challenged the dominant paradigm of economic development that stresses increased industrialization and advocated the use of appropriate technologies that would, in his words, be based on "economics as if people mattered," it has also been suggested that we need to adopt appropriate social technologies in the social development and human service spheres. The essence of Schumacher's (1973: 295) thesis is that "the 'logic of production' is neither the logic of life nor that of society." From an international perspective, not only does development not have to take the form of industrialization, modernization need not be equated with Westernization, and neither industrialization nor Westernization are necessary conditions for economic and social progress (Gunder-Frank 1971; Baran 1973). It has become quite clear that "the most advanced tools of production are not necessarily best in all settings" (Helm 1985: 112). Similarly, in the health, education, and social welfare fields the most sophisticated equipment, practitioners, and procedures may not be applicable or appropriate if the most pressing needs of a country or particular community are to be addressed (Jukanovic and Mach 1975; Banerji 1978; World Health Organisation 1978; United Nations 1979). If it is to be appropriate, a technology must take into acount the values and culture that bind and guide a particular society or community – its "dharmic order" to use a concept derived from the Sanskrit word *dharma* which means "that which holds together" (Muzumdar 1966). Helm (1985: 11) notes that "there is much interest nowadays in the meaning for development of these two entities: culture and values" and she gives examples of social technologies that have been devised in different parts of the world that do not conflict with local culture and values and that are appropriate to a particular society's needs. She cites the example of Botswana's "brigades" (Kukler 1979), unique educational programs combining vocational training with productive work in agriculture that constitute an indigenous educational system geared to the needs of a predominantly rural society.

A recurring theme in international discussions of the training and use of human service personnel has been the need for countries to adopt practices that are congruent with their own particular needs and realities. As participants in an international conference of ministers responsible for social welfare, sponsored by the United Nations (1969: 13), put it: "In developing countries particularly, training for field workers . . . should be economical and practical, and with due attention to indigenous needs and cultural patterns." Many African and Asian respondents to our 1983 international survey noted that the inappropriateness of professional social work methods, based as they are on Western industrialized and urban (primarily North American) concepts and principles, had contributed to the widespread use of paraprofessionals in their countries. They noted that the prevailing models of professional education and practice have not been congruent with the most pressing needs of large parts of the world. Our informants in India were particularly critical of their country's social work profession for failing to adopt practices that would address Indian realities.

Our findings bear out Midgley's (1981: 39) observation that, "as in Europe and other industrial nations, American theories of social work have had a considerable influence on schools of social work in the Third World" and support his contention that "the effectiveness of social work in the Third World and the relevance of its values to other cultures . . . is questionable" (xii). For years, social workers in less developed parts of the world have been pressing their colleagues to address these issues. For example, Paraiso (1966: 20) has criticized Latin American schools of social work for using North American theories and methods without adaptation to local realities and urged them to "develop original conceptual formulations and to identify the mainsprings of a truly Latin American social work philosophy." Drucker (1972) is one of many observers to recommend that social work education in Asian countries incorporate content that would be more relevant to the national development goals of their respective countries and, as Shawkey (1972: 12) pungently put it in relation to the situation in Africa, "With all the major social problems facing Africa, social work cannot continue to fiddle with minor problems."

Yet, despite continuing evidence of the inappropriateness and unworkability of Western social work principles and practices in much of Asia, Africa, and Latin America (Resnick 1980; Midgley 1981; Brigham 1982; Rosenfeld 1985), social work education in these parts of the world continues to be heavily influenced by the dominant North American model.

"Although schools of social work in developing countries differ from each other and from schools of social work in the West, these differences are not substantial. As American standards, theories and methods have been adopted, these differences have become less marked and, as many critics have shown, the content of social work education in the Third World is very similar to that in the United States."

(Midgley 1981: 76)

Compounding the problem is the fact that most schools have a distinctly urban bias despite the fact that an estimated 80 per cent of the population of developing countries live in rural areas (United Nations 1979: 3). Furthermore, the absence or inadequacy of such basic amenities as piped water, sewage disposal, transportation, housing, electricity, and medical care in urban areas of developing countries makes them more like rural areas in the problems encountered (yet greatly aggravated by high population density) than urban areas in more developed Western countries (Brigham 1982: 70).

We strongly believe that greater attention to indigenous training and practice approaches not only is crucial for developing countries but also will enrich social policy formulation, human service systems, and social work practice throughout the world. It is not that there is no place for conventional Western social work methods in developing countries. Undoubtedly, the Westernized segments of those countries (and these will vary in size and other characteristics among countries) will be able to benefit from this type of help. Similarly it would be incorrect to assume that all members of cultural and ethnic minority groups in developed countries can only be helped by persons of similar background. Clearly this is not so. However, there are members of minority groups and communities who, for a variety of reasons, can best be served by human service personnel who share values, experience, culture, language, and other characteristics with them.

THE PROFESSIONAL POSTURE

As we have noted throughout this book, many professional social workers are ambivalent about accepting and supporting the work of paraprofessional human service workers. Because of the embryonic state of the social work profession in most countries, it seems to be vulnerable to the perceived threat that the paraprofessional presents to professional status and recognition and to the job security of its members. Professionals appear to be most accepting of their paraprofessional colleagues when there are shortages of professional personnel or where their respective jobs are well-defined, that is where there is the least ambiguity about who does what and where there is the least threat to the status and security of the professional. It seems to us that accepting and supporting paraprofessionals only when they do not threaten professional interests (while understandable) reflects badly on professionals, calling into question their genuine commitment to human well-being, social justice, and the public good, in the broadest senses of these terms. For example, professionals who are genuinely committed to improving the status of women, the poor, and disadvantaged minority groups place themselves in a strange position when they fail to support paraprofessionals, given the composition of that group in most parts of the world.

Conceptually social workers must move away from a profession-centered approach to human service. Hadley (1981: 38–40) talks about the need for social care in Britain to undergo a "Copernican revolution" whereby the most professionalized services cease to be viewed as the center of the system and natural, informal, community-based care rightly takes center stage, supported and supplemented by formal professional and paraprofessional services. He notes that "the community's capacity to care can be significantly increased by appropriate support, and . . . much of the front line work . . . does not call for highly trained personnel but can be carried out effectively by people currently classified as 'ancillaries', provided that they are adequately backed up by specialists" (39–40).

We are inclined to agree with this reconceptualization of how services should be provided, not only in Britain but also in large segments of the human service systems of most countries. It is especially important in the less developed parts of the world where professionally trained personnel are in short supply or are simply not a very significant factor in the human resource equation. It is interesting that, despite professional misgivings, the contribution of the paraprofessional is supported by government policy or by influential government task forces in most countries. For example, the Barclay Committee in Britain, the University Grants Commission in India, the Ministry of Social Welfare in Israel, and the National Institute of Mental Health in the USA are on record as endorsing the use of paraprofessional personnel or have taken specific steps to strengthen the paraprofessional contribution to their countries' human services.

Based on our findings, we believe that there is some danger that social workers in many parts of the world will be viewed as irrelevant or expendable unless professional education and practice begin to address more diligently the overwhelming problems that large population groups face. Needed modification would include the development of indigenous helping methods or appropriate social technologies addressed to local needs and realities which, in many instances, will involve the support and development of paraprofessional personnel as the primary front-line providers of service and a re-emphasis of the social action component of social work practice.

Despite their dual commitment to remedial intervention with individuals and to actions that will result in improved social conditions, professional social workers are primarily pre-occupied "with the biography of the person rather than the drama of society" (Khinduka 1971: 69). However, social workers who attempt to apply individual counseling or casework theories and principles in deprived communities, especially in the less developed countries, will find that they are inappropriate and ineffective. "Because they were designed to treat the emotional and personal maladjustments of individuals, [they] are irrelevant to the pressing problems of mass poverty and deprivation" (Midgley 1981: 104). In the countries we studied in depth, we found social workers who are beginning to confront this problem and are again raising the question posed by Bisno (1956) three decades ago: "How social will social work be?" For example in India Desai (1985) and others have castigated professional social workers for hiding behind the walls of private industry in managerial positions instead of addressing the problems of the urban and rural poor. In the USA Rubin and Johnson (1984) decry the fact that the majority of students in the graduate social work education programs they studied were intent on becoming psychotherapists and had little commitment to social work's traditional mission or client groups. Rosenfeld (1985) identified a similar situation in Israeli schools of social work which he regarded as indefensible.

In many instances, in developing and developed countries alike, this question of social work's central mission is connected to the issue of how best to provide services to special populations or communities, usually the most needy, in ways that are congruent with the realities of their situation. For example, Ellis (1978) addresses this problem in relation to West African immigrants in Britain. The question is also usually connected to the role of the paraprofessional who is seen as a bridge between the professional and the most needy client populations and, as we have already mentioned, as a potential catalyst in the indigenization of social work.

PROVIDING APPROPRIATE TRAINING

There has long been an imbalance between professional and paraprofessional training in both developed and developing countries. National attention and educational resources have been focused on the education of professional personnel without commensurate investment in the training of paraprofessional personnel, despite the fact that the latter constitute the majority of the human service work force in most countries. In recent years there has been recognition that this is an unsatisfactory state of affairs and in some countries efforts have been made to redress the balance. However, in most instances, the paraprofessional human service worker is more likely than not to be untrained. This appears to be the case even in those countries that have a relatively well-developed range of formal training programs for paraprofessional personnel.

Paraprofessional training appears to have been neglected as a result of a fairly widespread assumption that, in the best of all possible worlds, every client of the human services should have the benefit of professional help – nothing less would do. Not only is this unrealistic, it is unnecessary and may even be undesirable. What is needed in most instances is not either extreme – a totally professionalized or completely untrained human service work force – but some optimum mix of professional personnel and appropriately trained paraprofessionals. Our study indicates that paraprofessional personnel are essential to the proper functioning of large segments of most countries' human services and, if they are to make their best contribution to the well-being of people and communities, they must be provided with appropriate training.

Many different kinds of training have been developed for paraprofessionals in the countries we studied. These include both pre-service and in-service training provided by employers, in government-operated or government-sponsored training centers, in secondary schools, vocational schools, technical institutes, community colleges, colleges of further education, colleges of advanced education, undergraduate colleges, and universities. Much of the training that is provided has been introduced in response to immediate local needs. This is appropriate but it also has disadvantages. The content and quality of the training provided is highly variable and what is learned for one purpose may not be transferable to other situations. With the possible exception of the work done by the Central Council for Education and Training in Social Work (CCETSW) in Britain and the Ministry of Social Welfare in Israel, we saw little effort in most countries to develop a comprehensive approach to the training of human service personnel. While we see nothing intrinsically wrong with developing specific training programs to meet immediate local needs, we believe that ideally these ad hoc responses should take place within an overall framework of human resource development in a particular country. An important step toward more integrated systems of human service training would be the development of closer and more explicit relationships among the different types and levels of training that exist in each country.

For several years the International Association of Schools of Social Work (1979) has been urging professional social work education programs to play a greater role in the training of front-line paraprofessionals. We found some evidence of a trend toward more paraprofessional training occurring within colleges and universities and instances of schools of social work paying greater attention to paraprofessionals either by teaching professional social workers about this important resource or by offering direct training for this category of worker. However, these remain isolated cases and we concur with the assessment that "schools have to be less conservative and more open to new challenges rather than continue to perceive their roles mainly in relation to formal education of professional social workers" (International Association of Schools of Social Work 1979: 15–16). Minimally, in developing and developed countries alike, there is a need for professional social work education programs to take a more comprehensive view of human service personnel training and deployment and to direct their efforts toward maximizing the contribution of all available human resources to their country's or area's human service or social development goals. This would involve for more of them than at present a focus on preparing professional social workers for administrative, planning, and development roles intended (among other things) to make the best use of front-line workers, the majority of whom will continue to be paraprofessionals.

While the initiative taken by some schools of social work in some countries in relation to paraprofessional training is commendable and similar efforts by additional school should be encouraged, a note of caution is in order. If the training curricula of these schools continue to be based on primarily Western industrial, urban models of individual pathology and micro-systems clinical practice, then paraprofessional personnel and the people and communities who need their help will be poorly served, particularly in developing countries. Some social workers are questioning the applicability in their countries of approaches that evolved to meet different needs in other countries and there is some movement toward change. However, it appears that imported models have become entrenched in professional social work education in many parts of the world and are difficult to dislodge (Brigham 1982; Midgley 1981; Resnick

1980). Considerable modification in social work education, including the adoption of indigenous approaches to human service provision, will be needed if schools of social work, particularly in developing countries but also in some situations in the more developed parts of the world, are to help front-line paraprofessionals make their best contribution to human service or social development goals.

PARAPROFESSIONAL CAREERS

Occupational fields are usually organized into distinct levels of work responsibility with jobs requiring different levels of capability and conferring on incumbents increments in prestige and reward. The human services conform to this pattern. Careers in this field involve movement from lower level positions to those of relatively greater responsibility and reward – vertical mobility, career advancement, or the concept of the career ladder. In addition, there are situations in which workers may move laterally between roughly equivalent jobs within the same organization or with different employers – horizontal mobility, with expansion of the career ladder concept into a career lattice.

The degree to which opportunities for either vertical or horizontal career mobility have been developed for the paraprofessional human service worker is highly variable among the countries we studied and between geographic areas within these countries. What is clear is that, with the exception of Japan, the major avenue to career mobility in most countries is through formal post-secondary education. This poses enormous problems for developing countries with severely limited educational resources, especially in the rural areas of those countries. Even in the more developed countries where the structures necessary for educational and career advancement are more widely available and accessible, there are often barriers confronting the individual human service worker. While all the steps and grids of a career lattice may exist in principle, in many instances only a small proportion of the paraprofessional work force can be accommodated in existing formal training programs. While a number of innovative non-traditional approaches have been developed in some countries (for example the Certified Human Service Worker and Child Development Associate movements in the USA) and are being considered in other countries (mobile or roving campuses in India and television courses offered by Britain's Open University), these have not yet had much impact.

We concur with Katzell, Korman, and Levine (1971) that providing appropriate opportunities for career advancement for front-line workers is essential if they are to make their best contribution to the human services since we believe that "workers who are placed in jobs suited to their need for growth and enrichment . . . will be more satisfied and motivated than workers who are mismatched in this regard" (Teare 1981: 97). We recognize that career mobility might be less critical in some countries or in some situations than in others but we believe that the issue cannot be ignored. Similarly the constraints that exist in some countries or situations are formidable but it is important that whatever barriers exist be confronted.

The paraprofessional human service work force worldwide is predominantly a female one. In many instances, these workers are drawn from the poorest segments of the population and are members of disadvantaged racial, ethnic, or other minority groups. While employment in human service jobs or social development programs can be an important step toward greater economic well-being for many of these workers, failure to provide realistic opportunities to progress beyond low-level jobs falls short of a genuine commitment to social justice for the groups involved. In fact the types of jobs provided may simply reinforce the marginal status of many of these workers; that is, maintain them in an essentially peripheral position in society so that their access to economic rewards, dignity and power remain severely limited (Tinker and Bramsen 1976; Mackie and Pattullo 1977; Scott 1984; Larwood, Stromberg, and Gutek 1985).

A number of steps can be taken to increase the opportunities for career mobility of paraprofessional human service workers. For example, at the very least, different levels of paraprofessional jobs can be identified that would allow workers in many situations to progress from one level to the next as their experience, skills, and knowledge increase. These steps can be accompanied by higher pay and changes in job title that confer higher status on those who progress. Ideally, these steps should be developed within a comprehensive human service personnel system that identifies the tasks and functions of various types and levels of workers and that matches these to sets of qualifications that are based on demonstrable worker capabilities. These qualifications might be acquired in a variety of ways, including prior experience and both formal and informal training.

The provision of opportunities for formal training that leads to recognized credentials would contribute most to the horizontal and vertical mobility of the paraprofessional, especially when these credentials correspond to clearly identified steps in well-developed human service personnel systems. The degree to which these training opportunities can be made accessible to people when they want and could benefit from them and in ways that are appropriate (for example without having to stop working or undertake lengthy formal education) would further enhance career advancement possibilities. Related to this need for flexibility is the desirability of developing alternative non-traditional ways (such as those already mentioned) of certifying that certain workers have achieved a level of competence that will qualify them for a recognized credential. Such non-traditional approaches to the achievement of credentials would appear to be appropriate not only in situations where groups of paraprofessionals cannot or should not pursue traditional academic routes to career advancement but also, and perhaps especially, in those situations where formal educational programs are unavailable.

FUTURE TRENDS

Our study of the types of tasks and functions performed by paraprofessional human service personnel in different parts of the world lead us to conclude that this category of front-line worker will continue to be an important part of the human service work force in the years ahead. Indeed, we feel that a number of worldwide demographic trends will make the contribution of paraprofessionals increasingly important – not merely as substitutes for professionally trained workers in countries, areas, or settings where the latter are in short supply but as providers of certain kinds of services for which they are especially suited. For example, in Britain, Israel, the USA, and many other countries the number of people surviving to an advanced age has been increasing quite rapidly at a time when more and more women (the traditional providers of informal care for the frail elderly) have been entering the employment market and are therefore not available to care for their aging relatives. Similarly, medical advances have increased the life expectancy of people with physical disabilities and mental handicaps, adding further to the number of persons needing some kind of social care – in residential settings, within the community, or in their own homes. In addition, higher rates of work-force participation by women and growing numbers of single-parent families have increased the need for day care services for young children. In essence, what we are seeing on a fairly widespread basis is a rapid expansion of the need for a variety of community-based residential, domiciliary, and day care services for a variety of dependent groups and a corresponding increase in the demand for persons to staff these services. In most instances, these people will be paraprofessional personnel – home helps, family aides, care assistants, wardens of sheltered housing, day care workers, staff of senior centers, and the like.

These trends are clearly illustrated in Britain where there is no shortage of professionally trained social workers but where paraprofessionals constitute the majority of the social service work force and are increasingly viewed as an important and integral part of a well-developed system of social service provision. In fact, several British analysts suggest that professional social workers will increasingly be faced with the need to take on indirect or specialized service roles, coordinating and supporting the work of front-line workers, most of whom will be paraprofessionals (Goldberg 1981: 86). Morris (1974) and Morris and Anderson (1975) see similar trends in the USA where professional social workers would become primarily organizers of growing systems of social care for dependent and vulnerable client populations. Indeed, developments such as these are supported by recent research findings that suggest that social workers are more effective in caring for people than in curing them (Rubin 1985). These emerging social care systems that social workers would coordinate would be staffed primarily by para-professional workers, volunteers, and informal caretakers. While the major concern in Britain, Israel, the USA, and other developed countries is the creation of systems of social care for growing numbers of elderly people, a priority in India and probably in other developing countries also is to address the health, nutrition, and developmental needs of young children.

In addition to these expanding caretaking functions that are emerging in different parts of the world – functions that are especially appropriate for paraprofessional personnel – there are a host of social problems that remain to be addressed in all countries, ranging from mass deprivation, hunger, inadequate health care, and unemployment to mental illness, drug abuse, and juvenile delinquency. We noted in our introductory chapter that human service efforts expanded throughout the world during the 1950s, 1960s, and early 1970s in recognition of these pressing problems. While the global recession of the late 1970s and 1980s, accompanied by a more conservative climate in the Western industrialized nations, curtailed the continued expansion of these efforts, the needs to which they were addressed have not diminished. Quite the contrary; in fact, the worldwide human service agenda is full and will need increased attention in the years ahead. While individual countries will set their own policies, priorities, and strategies for promoting the well-being of their people, pressing social problems will have to be addressed more fully throughout the world, creating a greater than ever need for human service personnel, most of whom are likely to be front-line paraprofessionals. We believe that the question of how to identify, develop, amd make best use of available human resources in national human service and social development efforts will become a major policy and planning issue in the coming years. We would like to believe that the current pause in national and worldwide commitments to improved human well-being have given us the opportunity to reflect on and learn from what has been done so far so that we can move ahead in a more rational and organized fashion when the next expansion of human service, social welfare, and social development programs occurs.

Finally, the job creation potential of expanded systems of human service provision should be mentioned. The advanced industrial (or post-industrial) nations are experiencing increasing difficulty in ensuring access to employment for all people available for and desiring work. For example, Britain, the USA, and many other developed countries are undergoing irreversible declines in their industrial sectors, resulting in severe displacement of workers and the exclusion of large segments of their populations from employment opportunities. Economic and demographic trends suggest that this situation is unlikely to improve in the foreseeable future. As was recognized in the USA in the 1960s, the human services have the potential for employing a large proportion of the work force that cannot be absorbed by other sectors of the labor market. It seems inevitable that the employment-creation potential of the human services will have to be rediscovered if human potential is not to be wasted on a massive scale. The human service jobs that can be developed most easily are, of course, those at the paraprofessional level.

References

Albee, G. W. (1959) *Mental Health Manpower Trends*. New York: Basic Books.

Alexander, C. A. (1975) Implications of the NASW Standards for Social Service Manpower. *Journal of Education for Social Work* 11(1): 3–8.

—— (1977) Management of Human Service Organizations. In J. B. Turner (ed.) *Encyclopedia of Social Work*. Washington, DC: National Association of Social Workers.

Alford, R. B. and Friedland, R. (1975) Political Participation and Public Policy. In A. Inkeles, J. Soleman, and N. Smelser (eds) *Annual Review of Sociology*. Palo Alto, Calif.: Annual Reviews.

Algie, J. (1980) Priorities in Personal Social Services. In M. Brown and S. Baldwin (eds) *The Year Book of Social Policy in Britain*. London: Routledge & Kegan Paul.

Allen, D. (1984) The Impact of CSS Training. In H. Barr (ed.) *Certificate in Social Service: The Durham Papers*. London: Central Council for Education and Training in Social Work.

Alley, S., Blanton, J., Feldman, R., Hunte, G., and Rolfson, M. (1978) *Case Studies of Mental Health Paraprofessionals: Twelve Effective Programs*. New York: Human Sciences Press.

Almanzor, A. C. (1979) The Role of Schools of Social Work in Paraprofessional Training: Current and Prospective. In *Paraprofessional Training for Social Development: The Role of Schools of Social Work*. Colombo: International Association of Schools of Social Work, Sri Lanka School of Social Work, and Sri Lanka Foundation Institute.

Anderson, J. K., Parente, F. J., and Gordon, C. (1981) A Forecast of the Future of the Mental Health Professions. *American Psychologist.* 36(8): 848–55.

Arole, R. S. and Arole, M. (1984) *Report* (mimeographed). The Comprehensive Rural Health Project. Jamkhed, India.

Ash, E., Barr, H., Cornwell, A., Ruddick, J., and Skidmore, A. (1980) *The Certificate in Social Service: A Report to the Council from the Staff.* London: Central Council for Education and Training in Social Work.

Association for the Development and Advancement of Manpower in Social Services in Israel (1985) *Report* (mimeographed). Tel Aviv. (In Hebrew.)

Austin M. J. (1978) *Professionals and Paraprofessionals.* New York: Human Sciences Press.

Banerji, D. (1978) Third World Health: A Colonial Legacy. *Earthscan Bulletin* 1(6): 23–37.

Baran, P. (1973) *The Political Economy of Growth.* Harmondsworth: Penguin.

Barclay Report (1982) *Social Workers, Their Role and Tasks.* London: Bedford Square Press.

Barker, R. L. and Briggs, T. L. (1966) *Trends in the Utilization of Social Work Personnel: An Evaluative Research of the Literature.* New York: National Association of Social Workers.

—— (1968) *Differential Use of Social Work Manpower.* New York: National Association of Social Workers.

—— (1969) *Using Teams to Deliver Social Services.* Syracuse, NY: Syracuse University School of Social Work.

Bayley, M., Parker, P., Seyd, R., and Tennant A. (1981) *Neighbourhood Services Project – Dinnington* (Paper no. 1, Origin, Strategy and Proposed Evaluation). Sheffield: University of Sheffield, Department of Sociological Studies.

Bell, D. (1973) *The Coming of Post Industrial Society.* New York: Basic Books.

Ben Gurion University of the Negev (1981) *Project Education and Community Development.* Ber Sheba: Institute for Education and Community Development.

Bennis, W. (1969) Beyond Bureaucracy. In A. Etzioni (ed.) *Readings in Modern Organizations.* Englewood Cliffs, NJ: Prentice-Hall.

Bessell, B. (1982) Equal But Different? *Community Care*. 402 (March 11): 17.
Billis, D., Bromley, G., Hey, A., and Rowbottom, R. (1980) *Organising Social Services Departments*. London: Heinemann Educational.
Birch Report (1976) *Manpower and Training for the Social Services: Report of a Working Party*. London: HMSO
Bishop, J. (1984) Employment Initiatives. In *Annual Report 1984*. London: Councils for Voluntary Service – National Association.
Bisno, H. (1956) How Social Will Social Work Be? *Social Work* 17(2): 12–18.
Black, J., Bowl, R., Burns, D., Critcher, C., Grant, G., and Stockford, D. (1983) *Social Work in Context: A Comparative Study of Three Social Services Teams*. London: Tavistock.
Blayney, K. D., Truelove, J. W., and Hawkins, J. (1976) Institutional Linkage for Training Health Technicians. *Journal of Allied Health* 5(3): 29–34.
Boaden, N., Goldsmith, M., Hampton, W., and Stringer, P. (1982) *Public Participation in Local Services*. London: Longman.
Boehm, W. W. (1978) *Human Well-Being: Challenges for the Eighties – Social, Economic and Political Action*. New York: US Committee of the International Conference on Social Welfare.
Booler, J. C. (undated) Foreword. In *Training of Home Helps*. Luton: Local Government Training Board.
Brawley, E. A. (1975) *The New Human Service Worker: Community College Education for the Social Services*. New York: Praeger.
——(1978) Maximizing the Potential of the Social Work Team: Some Organizational and Professional Considerations. *Journal of Sociology and Social Welfare*. 5(5): 731–43.
——(1980) Social Work's Diminished Commitment to the Paraprofessional. *Journal of Sociology and Social Welfare*. 7(5): 773–88.
——(1981a) Community College Programs for the Human Services: Results of a National Survey. *Journal of Education for Social Work* 17(1): 81–7.
——(1981b) Human Service Education Programs: Their Nature and Significance for Social Work. *Journal of Education for Social Work* 17(3): 90–7.
——(1982) Bachelor's Degree Programs in the Human Services: Results of a National Survey. *Journal of the National Organization of Human Service Educators* 4: 18–23.

Brawley, E. A. and Schindler, R. (1972) *Community and Social Service Education in the Community College: Issues and Characteristics.* New York: Council on Social Work Education.
—— (1985) *Paraprofessional Social Welfare Personnel in Thirteen Countries: Research Report.* University Park, Pa: Pennsylvania State University, Department of Sociology.
—— (1986) Paraprofessional Social Welfare Personnel in International Perspective: Results of a Worldwide Survey. *International Social Work* 29 (2): 165–76.
Brawley, E. A., Gerstein H., and Watkins, K. M. (1981) A Competency-Based Training Program for Day Care Personnel. *Child Care Quarterly* 10(2): 126–36.
Brawley, E. A., Bruno, A. F., Feinstein, R. M., and Lynch, R. S. (1980) College-Based Staff Training Programs for the Human Services. *Urban Affairs Papers* 2(4): 51–63.
Brieland, D., Briggs, T. L., and Leuenberger, P. (1973) *The Team Model of Social Work Practice.* Syracuse, NY: Syracuse University School of Social Work.
Briggs, T. L. (1973a) An Overview of Social Work Teams. In D. Brieland, L. Briggs, and P. Leuenberger (eds) *The Team Model of Social Work Practice.* Syracuse, NY: Syracuse University School of Social Work.
—— (1973b) Social Work Manpower: Developments and Dilemmas of the 1970s. In M. Purvine (ed.) *Educating MSW Students to Work With Other Social Welfare Personnel.* New York: Council on Social Work Education.
Briggs, T. L., Johnson, D. E., and Lebowitz, E. P. (1970) *Research on the Complexity–Responsibility Scale.* Syracuse, NY: Syracuse University School of Social Work.
Brigham, T. M. (1982) Social Work Education Patterns in Five Developing Countries: Relevance of US Microsystems Model. *Journal of Education for Social Work* 18(2): 68–75.
Brill, N. I. (1976) *Teamwork: Working Together in the Human Services.* Philadelphia: J. B. Lippincott.
Broome Regional Aboriginal Medical Service (1985) Broome Regional Aboriginal Medical Service Health Worker Training. *Kimberley Land Council Newsletter* 5(1): 37.
Brown, M. (1982) Bursting Out of the Ragbag. *Social Work Today* 13(39): 8–9.
Brown, P., Hadley, R., and White, K. J. (1982) A Case for

Neighbourhood-Based Social Work and Social Services. In Barclay Report *Social Workers, Their Role and Tasks.* London: Bedford Square Press.

Butterworth, E. and Holman, R. (eds) (1975) *Social Welfare in Modern Britain.* Glasgow: Fontana/Collins.

Carr-Saunders, A. M. (1965) Metropolitan Conditions and Traditional Professional Relationships. In R. Fisher (ed.) *The Metropolis in Modern Life.* New York: Doubleday.

Central Bureau of Statistics (1983) *Statistical Abstract of Israel, 1983.* Jerusalem: Israel Government Printing Office.

——(1984) *The Demographic Characteristics of the Population of Israel.* Jerusalem: Israel Government Printing Office.

Central Council for Education and Training in Social Work (1975) *A New Form of Training: The Certificate in Social Service.* London: CCETSW.

——(1980a) *Regulations and Guidelines for Courses Leading to the Certificate in Social Service (CSS).* London: CCETSW

——(1980b) *A Follow-Up Survey of Students Awarded the CSS in 1977 and 1978.* London: CCETSW.

——(1981) *The In-Service Course in Social Care.* London: CCETSW.

——(1983a) *Certificate in Social Service: Second Progress Report.* London: CCETSW.

——(1983b) *Regulations and Guidelines for the In-Service Course in Social Care (ICSC).* London: CCETSW.

——(1983c) *Review of Qualifying Training Policies: Report on Responses.* London: CCETSW.

——(1985a) *Policies for Qualifying Training in Social Work: The Council's Propositions.* London: CCETSW.

——(1985b) *Data on Training, 1983.* London: CCETSW.

Chenault, J. and Burnford, F. (1978) *Human Services Professional Education: Future Directions.* New York: McGraw-Hill.

Child, J. (1970) More Myths of Management Organization? *Journal of Management Studies* 7(2): 376–90.

Chin, R. (1969) The Utility of System Models and Developmental Models for Practitioners. In W. G. Bennis, D. Benne, and R. Chin (eds) *The Planning of Change.* New York: Holt, Rinehart, & Winston.

Claxton, C. S. and McPheeters, H. L. (1976) Survey Report:

Human Services in the South. *Community and Junior College Journal* 47(1): 26–9.

Cloward, R. and Piven, F. (1969) The Professional Bureaucracies' Benefit Systems As Influence Systems. In R. Kramer and H. Specht (eds) *Readings in Community Organization Practice.* New York: Prentice-Hall.

Clubok, M. (1980) *Issues in the Utilization of the Social Service Technican.* SCAN Document no. 310–01625–980. Washington, DC: National Conference on Social Welfare.

Coggs, P. R. and Robinson, V. R. (1967) Training Indigenous Community Leaders for Employment in Social Work. *Social Casework* 48(5): 278–81.

Cohen, N. E. (1955) An Over-All Look. In J. E. Russell (ed.) *National Policies for Education, Health and Social Services.* New York: Doubleday.

Cohen, S. and Morgenstein, B. (1974) *Life Conditions of the Aged.* Jerusalem: National Insurance Institute. (In Hebrew.)

Committee on Practice and Knowledge (1964) *An Approach to Evaluating Social Work Tasks.* Minneapolis, Minn: National Association of Social Workers, Southern Minnesota Chapter.

Community Care (1980) Unemployed Get the Chance to be Social Workers. 319 (July 17): 8.

Conyers, D. (1982) *An Introduction to Social Planning in the Third World.* New York: John Wiley.

Cooper, M. (1980) Normanton: Interweaving Social Work and the Community. In R. Hadley and M. McGrath (eds) *Going Local: Neighbourhood Social Services.* London: Bedford Square Press.

Councils for Voluntary Service – National Organization (1984) *Employment Project Pack.* London: Councils for Voluntary Service.

Cypher, J. (ed.) (1979) *Seebohm Across Three Decades: Social Services Departments Past, Present and Future.* Birmingham: British Association of Social Workers.

Dalali, I. D., Charuvastra, V., and Schlesinger, J. (1976) Training of Paraprofessionals: Some Caveats. *Journal of Drug Education* 6(2): 105–12.

Danish, S. J. and Brock, G. W. (1974) The Current Status of Paraprofessional Training. *Personnel and Guidance Journal* 53(4): 299–303.

Darvill, G. and Munday, B. (eds) (1984) *Volunteers in the Personal Social Services*. London: Tavistock.

David, H. (1965) *Manpower Policies for a Democratic Society: The Final Statement of the National Manpower Council*. New York: Columbia University Press.

Denham, W. H. and Shatz, E. (1969) Impact of the Indigenous Nonprofessional on the Professional's Role. In W. C. Richan (ed.) *Human Services and Social Work Responsibility*. New York: National Association of Social Workers.

Department of Health and Social Security (1981a) *Care in Action: A Handbook of Policies and Priorities for Health and Personal Social Services in England*. London: HMSO.

—— (1981b) *Care in the Community: A Consultative Document on Moving Resources for Care – England*. London: HMSO.

—— (1983) *Supporting the Informal Carers: Report of the Conference*. London: HMSO.

Department of Social Services (1932) *Social Services of the Vaad Leumi*. Jerusalem.

Desai, A. S. (1975) Social Welfare in India: Present Problems and Suggestions for Reorganization. *Indian Journal of Social Work* 18(2): 13–23.

Dexter, M. and Harbert, W. (1983) *The Home Help Service*. London: Tavistock.

Divre Haknesset (1956) *Report of Parliament*. Jerusalem. (In Hebrew.)

Dolgoff, R. and Feldstein, D. (1980) *Understanding Social Welfare*. New York: Harper & Row.

Doron, A. (1976) *Cross National Studies of Social Service Systems*. Jerusalem: Ministry of Labor and Social Affairs.

Drucker, D. (1972) *An Exploration of Social Work in Some Countries of Asia with Special Reference to the Relevance of Social Work Education to Social Development Goals*. Bangkok: UNICEF.

D'Souza, N. (1982) Training Paraprofessionals in Community Work. Paper presented at the 21st International Congress of Schools of Social Work, Brighton, England.

Dubey, S. N. and Murida, R. (1972) Social Welfare and Panchayadi Raj. *Indian Journal of Social Work* 39(4): 377–87.

Dumpson, J. R., Mullen, E., and First, R. J. (1978) *Toward Education for Effective Social Welfare Administrative Practice*.

New York: Council on Social Work Education.

Elgin, D. S. and Bushnell, R. A. (1977) The Limits to Complexity: Are Bureaucracies Becoming Unmanageable? *The Futurist* 11: 337–51.

Ellis, J. (ed.) (1978) *West African Families in Britain.* London: Routledge & Kegan Paul.

Etgar, T. (1980) *Aides and Paraprofessionals as Support Personnel in Family Development.* Jerusalem: Department of Social Welfare. (In Hebrew.)

Etzioni, A. (1964) *Modern Organizations.* Englewood Cliffs, NJ: Prentice-Hall.

——(1969) *The Semi-Professions and their Organization.* New York: Free Press.

European Centre for Social Welfare Training and Research (1977) *Para-Professionals in Social Welfare.* Vienna: European Centre for Social Welfare Training and Research.

Feldman, E. J. (1978) Comparative Public Policy: Field or Method? *Comparative Politics* 10(2): 287–305.

Feldstein, D. (1968) *Report of Technical Education Project: Community College and Other Associate Degree Programs for Social Welfare Areas.* New York: Council on Social Work Education.

Fine, S. A. and Wiley, W. W. (1971) *An Introduction to Functional Task Analysis: A Scaling of Selected Tasks from the Social Welfare Field.* Kalamazoo, Mich: Upjohn Institute for Employment Research.

Finer Report (1974) *Report of the Committee on One-Parent Families.* London: HMSO.

Flexner, A. (1915) Is Social Work a Profession? In *Proceeding of the National Conference of Charities and Corrections, 1915.* New York: National Conference of Charities and Corrections.

Ford, J. (1972) *A Model for Training New Careerists in Family Therapy.* Philadelphia: University of Pennsylvania, Child Psychiatry Division.

Gangrade, K. D. (1970) Western Social Work and the Indian World. *International Social Work* 13(3): 1–11.

Gartner, A. (1971) *Paraprofessionals and their Performance: A Survey of Education, Health and Social Service Programs.* New York: Praeger.

——(1981) Paraprofessionals: Past, Present and Future. In S. S.

Robin and M. O. Wagenfeld (eds) *Paraprofessionals in the Human Services*. New York: Human Sciences Press.

Gidron, B. and Katan, J. (1985) *Nonprofessional Workers in Human Service Organizations*. Jerusalem: Israeli Schools of Social Work. (In Hebrew.)

Gilbert, B. (1975) *An Analysis of Hiring Requirements for Social Service Classifications in State Merit Systems*. Washington, DC: National Association of Social Workers.

Gilder, G. (1980) *Wealth and Poverty*. New York: Basic Books.

Gleazer, E. J., Jr. (1968) *This is the Community College*. New York: Houghton-Mifflin.

Glennerster, H. (1975) Social Services in Great Britain: Taking Care of People. In D. Thursz and J. L. Vigilante (eds) *Meeting Human Needs: An Overview of Nine Countries*. Beverly Hills, Calif: Sage.

Goldberg, E. M. (1981) So – What About Social Work? A Postscript. In E. M. Goldberg and S. Hatch (eds) *A New Look at the Personal Social Services*. London: Policy Studies Institute.

Goldberg, E. M. and Fruin, D. J. (1976) Towards Accountability in Social Work. *British Journal of Social Work* 6(1): 4–19.

Gordon, A. D. (1960) People and Labor. In A. Hertzberg (ed.) *The Zionist Idea*. New York: Meridian Books.

Gore, M. (1969) Two Goes into Four-Year College Programs in Social Welfare. *Social Work Education Reporter* 17(4): 12.

Government of India (1982) *India: Research and Reference Division*. New Delhi: Publication Division.

Greenwood, E. (1957) Attributes of a Profession. *Social Work* 2(2): 44–5.

Grosser, C. (1966) Local Residents as Mediators between Middle Class Professional Workers and Lower Class Clients. *Social Service Review* 40(1): 56–63.

—— (1969) Manpower Development Programs. In C. Grosser, W. E. Henry, and J. G. Kelly (eds) (1969) *Nonprofessionals in the Human Services*. San Francisco: Jossey-Bass.

Grosser, C., Henry, W. E., and Kelly, J. G. (eds) (1969) *Nonprofessionals in the Human Services*. San Fransisco: Jossey-Bass.

Gunder-Frank, A. (1971) *Capitalism and Underdevelopment in Latin America*. Harmondsworth: Penguin.

Hadley, R. (1981) Social Services Departments and the Community. In E. M. Goldberg and S. Hatch (eds) *A New Look at the*

Personal Social Services. London: Policy Studies Institute.

Hadley, R. and McGrath, M. (eds) (1980) *Going Local: Neighbourhood Social Services*. London: Bedford Square Press.

—— (1984) *When Social Services Are Local: The Normanton Experience*. London: Allen & Unwin.

Hage, J. and Aiken, M. (1970) *Social Change in Complex Organizations*. New York: Random House.

Hallett, C. (1978) Ancillaries. In O. Stevenson and P. Parsloe (eds) *Social Services Teams: The Practitioner's View*. London: HMSO.

Hardcastle, D. A. and Katz, A. J. (1979) *Employment and Unemployment in Social Work: A Study of NASW Members*. Washington, DC: National Association of Social Workers.

Hartnoll, M. C. (1984) The Distinctive Nature of CSS – Its Strengths and Weaknesses. In H. Barr (ed.) *Certificate in Social Service: The Durham Papers*. London: Central Council for Education and Training in Social Work.

Heidenheimer, A., Heclo, H., and Adams, C. T. (1976) *Comparative Public Policy: The Politics of Social Choice in Europe and America*. London: Macmillan.

Helm, B. (1985) Social Development and Nation Building. *Social Development Issues* 9(1): 102–14.

Hesbur, R. K. (1979) Modernization, Mobilization, and Rural Development. *Indian Journal of Social Work* 39(4): 377–87.

Hey, A. M. (1975) *Emerging Professional and Occupational Groups in Local Authority Social Services Departments*. Document no. 2483. Uxbridge: Brunel Institute of Organisation and Social Studies, Social Services Unit.

—— (1978) *Social Work – Practice, Careers and Organisation in Area Teams: A Working Paper*. Uxbridge: Brunel Institute of Organisation and Social Studies, Social Services Unit.

—— (1980) Specialization in Social Work. In J. Cypher (ed.) *Seebohm across Three Decades: Social Services Departments Past, Present and Future*. Birmingham: British Association of Social Workers.

Heyman, M. (1961) Criteria for Allocation of Cases According to Levels of Staff Skill. *Social Casework*. 42(7): 325–31.

Higgins, J. (1981) *States of Welfare: Comparative Analysis in Social Policy*. Oxford: Basil Blackwell and Martin Robertson.

Hirayama, H. (1975) Nonprofessional Workers in Community Mental Health and Neighborhood Health Centers: An Analysis of the Role Functions of the Indigenous Paraprofessional and the Associate Degree Technician. Doctoral dissertation. Philadelphia: University of Pennsylvania.

Hokenstad, M. C. (1977) Higher Education and the Human Service Professions: What Role for Social Work? *Journal of Education for Social Work* 13(2): 52–9.

Holmstrom, L. L. (1972) *The Two-Career Family*. Cambridge, Mass: Schenkman.

Hughes, E. C. (1960) The Professions in Society. *Canadian Journal of Economics and Political Science* 26(1): 54–61.

Illich, I. (1980) *Tools for Conviviality*. New York: Harper & Row.

Indian Council of Social Welfare (1982) *Action for Social Progress: The Responsibility of Government and Voluntary Organizations*. National Committee Report to the 21st International Conference on Social Welfare, Brighton, England.

International Association of Schools of Social Work (1979) *Paraprofessional Training for Social Development: The Role of Schools of Social Work*. Colombo: International Association of Schools of Social Work, Sri Lanka School of Social Work, and Sri Lanka Foundation Institute.

International Committee for the Evaluation of Project Renewal (1983) *Report*. Jerusalem: Government of Israel, Ministry of Housing, Office of the Deputy Minister.

—— (1984) *Report*. Jerusalem: Government of Israel, Ministry of Housing.

Israeli Association of Social Workers (1981) *Directions for Project Renewal*. Tel Aviv: Israeli Association of Social Workers.

Itzhaki, C. (1981) *Utilization of Neighborhood Workers*. (In Hebrew.)

Jaffe, E. (1981) Project Renewal: An Insider's View. *Journal of Jewish Communal Service* 47(3): 181–84.

Jain, L. C. (1986) *Grass Without Roots: Rural Development under Government Auspices*. Beverly Hills, Calif: Sage.

Jenkin, P. (1981) Trumpet Volunteers. *Guardian*. 21 January.

Johnson, D. and Ferryman, Z. C. (1969) Inservice Training for Non-Professional Personnel in a Mental Retardation Center. *Mental Retardation*. 7(5): 10–13.

Joint Commission on Mental Illness and Health (1961) *Action for Mental Health*. New York: John Wiley.

Joshi, D. C., Krishnayya, J. G., and Gupta, C. B. (1978) *Design of Voluntary Health Projects*. Pune, India: Systems Research Institute.

Jukanovic, V. D. and Mach, E. P. (1975) *Alternative Approaches to Meeting Basic Health Needs in Developing Countries*. Geneva: World Health Organization.

Kadmon, I. (1981) *Evaluation and Recommendation of Manpower Needs in Israel*. Tel Aviv: Israeli Association of Social Workers.

—— (1983) *Career Development in Israel*. Jerusalem: Joint Distribution Committee. (In Hebrew.)

Kahn, A. J. (1964) The Next Steps: A Post Conference Commentary. In *Experimentation in Differential Use of Personnel in Social Welfare*. New York: National Association of Social Workers.

—— (1973) *Social Policy and Social Services*. New York: Random House.

Kanev, I. (1951) *Tochnit Lebituach Sozali*. Tel Aviv: Program for Social Insurances.

Karger, H. J. (1983) Reclassification: Is there a Future in Public Welfare for the Trained Social Worker? *Social Work* 28(6): 427–33.

Katan, J. (1972) The Utilization of Indigenous Nonprofessionals in Human Service Organizations and the Factors Affecting it: An Exploratory Study. Doctoral dissertation. Ann Arbor, Mich: University of Michigan.

—— (1974) The Utilization of Indigenous Workers in Human Service Organizations. In Y. Hasenfeld and R. English (eds) *Human Service Organizations*. Ann Arbor, Mich: University of Michigan Press.

Katz, E. and Eisenstadt, S. N. (1960) Some Sociological Observations on the Response of Israeli Organizations to New Immigrants. *Administrative Science Quarterly* 5(1): 113–33.

Katzell, R., Korman, A., and Levine, E. (1971) *Research Report No. 1: Overview Study of the Dynamics of Worker Job Mobility*. Washington, DC: US Department of Health, Education, and Welfare.

Kestenbaum, S. and Bar-On, Y. (1982) Care Aides: An Answer for Israel. *Public Welfare* 40(4): 30–5.

Kestenbaum, S. and Shebar, V. (1984) The Social Work – Paraprofessional Partnership: A Direction for the Eighties. *Social Development Issues* 8(1–2): 136–43.

Khinduka, S. K. (1971) Social Work in the Third World. *Social Service Review* 45(1): 62–73.

Kilbrandon Report (1964) *Report of the Committee on Children*

and Young Persons in Scotland. London: HMSO.
Klein, R. (1982) Weighing Standards Against Elitism. *Social Work Today* 13(44) 7–10.
Knittel, R. E., Child, R. C., and Hobgood, J. (1971) Role and Training of Health Education Aides. *American Journal of Public Health* 61(8): 1,571–580.
Kukler, R. (ed.) (1979) *Botswana's Brigades.* Gabarone: Ministry of Education.
Kulkarni, P. D. (1977) Challenge of Development and Social Work. *Indian Journal of Social Work* 38(3): 285–95.
——(1980) Evaluation Report. In E. Pangalangan and L. de Guzman (eds) *Paraprofessionals in Social Development: Implications for Social Work Education.* Vienna: International Association of Schools of Social Work.
Kupat Holim (1913) Takanot Vehodiot Shel Kupat Holim (By Laws of the Sick Fund) *Hapoel Hatzair* 6(35): 15–16.
Kuperman, D., Terenechofsky, S., and Meire, P. (1980) Mediator: A Professional Role in a Multifunctional Team. *Society and Welfare.* March 89–99. (In Hebrew.)
Lakshamanna, M. (1979) Undergraduate Social Work Education in India: Retrospect and Prospect. *Indian Journal of Social Work* 40(2): 147–52.
Lambert, C. and Lambert, L. (1970) Impact of Poverty Funds on Voluntary Agencies. *Social Work* 15(3): 167–81.
Larwood, L., Stromberg, A. H., and Gutek, B. A. (1985) *Women and Work: An Annual Review.* Beverly Hills, Calif: Sage.
Lauffer, A. (1977) *The Practice of Continuing Education in the Human Services.* New York: McGraw-Hill.
Lauffer, A. and Gorodezky, S. (1980) *Volunteers.* Beverly Hills, Calif: Sage.
Lipset, S. M. and Schwartz, M. (1966) The Politics of Professions. In H. M. Vollmer and D. L. Mills (eds) *Professionalization.* Englewood Cliffs, NJ: Prentice-Hall.
Loavenbruck, G. and Crecca, C. (1980) *Continuing Social Work Education: An Annotated Bibliography.* New York: Council on Social Work Education.
Local Government Training Board (undated a) *Care Assistants in Residential Homes for Elderly People.* Luton: LGTB.
——(undated b) *Training of Home Helps.* Luton: LGTB.
——(undated c) *Wardens of Sheltered Housing.* Luton: LGTB.

Loewenberg, F. M. (1968) Social Workers and Indigenous Para-professionals: Some Structural Dilemmas. *Social Work* 13(3): 65–71.

Mackie, L. and Pattullo, P. (1977) *Women At Work*. London: Tavistock.

MacLennan, W. (1965) Training for New Careers. In *New Careers: Ways Out of Poverty for Disadvantaged Youth*. Washington, DC: Howard University Center for Youth and Community Studies.

Magill, R. S. and Clark, T. N. (1975) Community Power and Decision Making: Recent Research and its Policy Implications. *Social Service Review* 14(1): 33–45.

Mannheim, K. (1968) *Ideology and Utopia*. New York: Harcourt, Brace, & World.

Manshard, C. (1941) Education for Social Work. *Indian Journal of Social Work* 11(1): 9.

Marley, P. and Wulff-Cochrane, E. (1985) *Private and Voluntary Residential Care*. London: Central Council for Education and Training in Social Work.

Marmor, T. and Bridges, A. (1977) *Comparative Policy Analysis and Health Planning Processes Internationally*. Washington, DC: US Department of Health, Education, and Welfare.

Martinez-Brawley, E. E. (1982) *Rural Social and Community Work in the United States and Great Britain: A Cross Cultural Perspective*. New York: Praeger.

Mathieu, M. (1979) The Secretary-General's Statements at the Opening Session. In *Paraprofessional Training for Social Development: The Role of Schools of Social Work*. Colombo: International Association of Schools of Social Work, Sri Lanka School of Social Work, and Sri Lanka Foundation Institute.

——(1980) Foreword. In E. Pangalangan and L. de Guzman (eds) *Paraprofessionals in Social Development: Implications for Social Work Education*. Vienna: International Association of Schools of Social Work.

Mayur, R. and Nadkarni, C. V. (1981) India 2000. *The Illustrated Weekly of India*. January: 8.

Merton, R. K. (1958) Bureaucratic Structure and Personality. In H. D. Stein and R. A. Cloward (eds) *Social Perspectives on Behavior*. New York: Free Press.

Midgley, J. (1981) *Professional Imperialism: Social Work in the*

Third World. London: Heinemann.

Ministry of Rural Development (1984) *Development of Women and Children in Rural Areas*. New Delhi: Government of India, Ministry of Rural Development.

Ministry of Social Welfare (1974–75) *Report of the Advisory Committee on the Preparation of Regulations for the Supervision of Homes Act*. Jerusalem: Ministry of Social Welfare, Services for the Aged. (In Hebrew.)

—— (1975) *Guidelines for Services Needed for the Aged, 1975-80*. Jerusalem: Ministry of Social Welfare. (In Hebrew.)

—— (1977) *Guide to the Social Services*. Tel Aviv: Ministry of Social Welfare. (In Hebrew.)

—— (1982) Social Welfare in India. Report to the 21st International Conference on Social Welfare, Brighton, England. New Delhi: Government of India.

—— (1984) *Integrated Child Development Services Scheme Revised*. New Delhi: Government of India.

Moore, C. D. and Eldridge, D. (1970) *India Yesterday and Today*. New York: Bantam Books.

Morris, R. (1974) The Place of Social Work in the Human Services. *Social Work* 19(5): 519–31.

Morris, R. and Anderson, D. (1975) Personal Care Services: An Identity for Social Work. *Social Service Review* 49(2): 157–74.

Mumford, L. (1970) *The Myth of Machine*. New York: Harcourt, Brace, & Jovanovich.

Muzumdar, H. T. (1966) *The Grammar of Sociology: Man in Society*. London: Asia Publishing House.

Myrdal, G. (1963) *Beyond the Welfare State*. New Haven, Conn: Yale University Press

—— (1969) *Asian Drama: An Inquiry into the Poverty of Nations*. Vol. I. New York: Twentieth Century Publications.

Nagpaul, H. (1971) Conceptions and Strategies of Social Work in India. *International Social Work* 14(2): 14–15.

—— (1972a) The Diffusion of American Social Work Education to India: Problems and Issues. *International Social Work* 15(2): 1–16.

—— (1972b) Social Work as a Profession in India: Sociological Analysis. *Indian Journal of Social Work* 32(4): 387–411.

Nanavatty, M. C. (1981) Rural Development and Social Work. *Indian Journal of Social Work* 42(3): 265–72.

—— (1984) *Training Requirements of Child Development Workers.* New Delhi: National Institute of Public Cooperation and Child Development.

NASW News (1978a) Licensure Forces Erode Resistance. 23(7): 11.

—— (1978b) State Validation Techniques Under Scrutiny. 23(4): 8.

—— (1984) National Tally of State Laws Reaches 34: Push for Practice Regulation is Paying Off. 29(5): 3.

National Association of Social Workers (1971) Memorandum to ELAN Team Leaders, Chapter Presidents, and SPAC Chairmen. New York: NASW.

—— (1974) *Standards for Social Service Manpower.* New York: NASW.

—— (1982) *Standards for the Classification of Social Work Practice.* Washington, DC: NASW.

National Commission for Human Service Workers (1983) *Certification of Human Service Workers.* Atlanta, Ga: NCHSW.

NCHSW Worker Forum (1983) Nearly 600 Workers Now Certified. 1(7): 1.

Nedeljkovic, Y. R. (1977) An Account of Programmes and Policy for the Training of Non-Professionals in Social Work in Yugoslavia. In *Paraprofessionals in Social Welfare.* Vienna: European Centre for Social Welfare Training and Research.

Nouvertne, U. (1977) Roles, Tasks and Training Policies of Paraprofessionals in the Federal Republic of Germany. In *Paraprofessionals in Social Welfare.* Vienna: European Centre for Social Welfare Training and Research.

Office of Child Development (1974) *The Child Development Associate Training Information Series,* no. 1. Washington, DC: US Department of Health, Education, and Welfare.

Pacione, M. (1981) *Problems and Planning in Third World Cities.* New York: St Martins Press.

Paiva, J. F. X. (1977) A Conception of Social Development. *Social Service Review* 15(2) 327–36.

Palmiere, D. (1978) Human Services in Higher Education. In J. Chenault and F. Burnford (eds) *Human Services Professional Education: Future Directions.* New York: McGraw-Hill.

Pangalangan, E. (1979) Opening Remarks of the Regional Project Director. In *Paraprofessional Training for Social Development: The Role of Schools of Social Work.* Colombo: International

Association of Schools of Social Work, Sri Lanka School of Social Work, and Sri Lanka Foundation Institute.

Pangalangan, E. and de Guzman, L. (eds) (1980) *Paraprofessionals in Social Development: Implications for Social Work Education.* Vienna: International Association of Schools of Social Work.

Paraiso, V. (1966) Education for Social Work in Latin America. *International Social Work* 9(2): 17–24.

Parker, R. (1981) Tending and Social Policy. In E. M. Goldberg and S. Hatch (eds) *A New Look at the Personal Social Services.* London: Policy Studies Institute.

Parsloe, P. (1978) Some Educational Implications. In O. Stevenson and P. Parsloe (eds) *Social Services Teams: The Practitioner's View.* London: HMSO.

Pathah, S. (1983) *Social Welfare Manpower.* New Delhi: Government of India.

Pathasarathy, N. R. (1980) Some Aspects of Aging in India. *Indian Journal of Social Work* 40(4): 381–88.

Payne, M. (1982) *Working in Teams.* London: Macmillan.

Pearl, A. (1981) The Paraprofessional in Human Service. In S. S. Robin and M. O. Wagenfeld (eds) *Paraprofessionals in the Human Services.* New York: Human Sciences Press.

Pearl, A. and Riessman, F. (1965) *New Careers for the Poor.* New York: Free Press.

Pecora, P. J. and Austin M. J. (1983) Declassification of Social Service Jobs: Issues and Strategies. *Social Work* 28(6): 421–26.

Peled, D. and Zemach, T. (1983) *The Status of Women in Israeli Society.* Jerusalem: Institute of Applied Research. (In Hebrew.)

Perlman, R. and Gurin, A. (1972) *Community Organization and Social Planning.* New York: John Wiley.

Peters, D. L. and Sutton, R. E. (1984) The Effects of CDA Training on the Beliefs, Attitudes and Behaviors of Head Start Personnel. *Child Care Quarterly* 13(4): 251–61.

Pinker, R. A. (1982) An Alternative View. In Barclay Report *Social Workers: Their Role and Tasks.* London: Bedford Square Press.

Population Reference Bureau (1983) *World Population Data Sheet.* Washington, DC: Population Reference Bureau.

Prakash, B. (1979) Social Services in Rural Development. *Indian Journal of Social Work* 34(4): 391–97.

President's Commission on Mental Health (1978), *Report to the President.* Vol. I – Commission's Report and Recommendations.

Washington, DC: National Institute of Mental Health.

Price, J. L. (1968) *Organizational Effectiveness: An Inventory of Propositions*. Homewood, Ill: Richard D. Irwin.

Project Education and Community Development (1980) *Ofakim Summary Report 1977–78, Stage I*. Ofakim, Israel: Humphrey Center for Social Ecology.

——(1981) *Ofakim Evaluation Report, Stage II*. Ofakim, Israel: Humphrey Center for Social Ecology.

Purvine, M. (ed.) (1973) *Educating MSW Students to Work With Other Social Welfare Personnel*. New York: Council on Social Work Education.

Ranade, S. N. (1979) Panelists' Comments. In *Paraprofessional Training for Social Development: The Role of Schools of Social Work*. Colombo: International Association of Schools of Social Work, Sri Lanka School of Social Work, and Sri Lanka Foundation Institute.

Ranade, S. N. and Chatkrjee, B. (1982) *Action for Social Progress: The Responsibilities of Government and Voluntary Organizations*. New Delhi: Indian Council of Social Welfare.

Resnick, R. P. (1980) Social Work Education in Latin America and the United States: A Look to the Future. *Journal of Education for Social Work* 16(1): 104–11.

Reynolds, B. C. (1951) *Social Work and Social Living*. New York: Citadel Press.

Rigby, B. D. (ed.) (1978) *Short-Term Training for Social Development: The Preparation of Front-Line Workers and Trainers*. New York: International Association of Schools of Social Work.

Robin, S. S. and Wagenfeld, M. O. (eds) (1981) *Paraprofessionals in the Human Services*. New York: Human Sciences Press.

Rodgers, B. N. (1979) *The Study of Social Policy: A Comparative Approach*. London: Allen & Unwin.

Rodgers, B. N., Greve, J., and Morgan, J. (1968) *Comparative Social Administration*. London: Allen & Unwin.

Romanyshyn, J. (1971) *Social Welfare: From Charity to Justice*. New York: Random House.

Rosenfeld, J. M. (1985) The Thread of Life and the Social Fabric. Paper presented on the 60th Anniversary of the Founding of the Hebrew University School of Social Work. Jerusalem: Hebrew University, School of Social Work.

Rowbottom, R. and Billis, D. (1977) The Stratification of Work and Organizational Design. *Human Relations* 30(1) 53–76.

Rowbottom, R., Hey, A., and Billis, D. (1974) *Social Services Departments: Developing Patterns of Work and Organization.* London: Heinemann.

Rowlings, C. (1978) The Allocation of Work. In O. Stevenson and P. Parsloe (eds) *Social Services Teams: The Practitioner's View.* London: HMSO.

Roxborough, I. (1982) *Theories of Underdevelopment.* London: Macmillan.

Rubin, A. (1985) Practice Effectiveness: More Grounds for Optimism. *Social Work* 30(6): 469–76.

Rubin, A. and Johnson, P. J. (1984) Direct Practice Interests of Entering MSW Students. *Journal of Education for Social Work* 20(2): 5–16.

Sadka, N. (1984) *Integrated Child Development Services in India.* New Delhi: UNICEF.

Sali, Y. and Harel, I. (1978) *Survey of Israeli Social Workers.* Jerusalem: Ministry of Social Welfare.

Schindler, R. (1977) Profession of Social Work: Aides. In J. B. Turner (ed.) *Encyclopedia of Social Work.* Washington, DC: National Association of Social Workers.

——(1980) Project Renewal and the Utilization of Indigenous Non-professionals. *Society and Welfare* 3(1): 45–54. (In Hebrew.)

——(1981) Welfare and Work in Israel: A Case Study. *Social Service Review* 55(4): 636–48.

——(1982) *Paraprofessionals in Israel.* Jerusalem: Ministry of Labor and Social Welfare. (In Hebrew.)

——(1985) Paraprofessional Participation, Employment and Career – Myth or Reality: Israel as a Case Study. *International Social Work* 28(2): 7–13.

Schindler, R. and Brawley, E. A. (1986) The Training and Employment of Paraprofessional Social Welfare Personnel in International Perspective. *Indian Journal of Social Work* 46(4): 459–67.

Schumacher, E. F. (1973) *Small is Beautiful: Economics as if People Mattered.* New York: Harper & Row.

——(1979) *Good Work.* New York: Harper & Row.

Schwartz, E. E. and Sample, W. C. (1967) First Findings from Midway. *Social Service Review* 41(2): 113–51.

Scott, H. (1984) *Working your Way to the Bottom: The Feminization of Poverty*. Boston, Mass: Pandora Press.

Seebohm Report (1968) *Report of the Committee on Local Authority and Allied Personal Social Services*. London: HMSO.

Sengupta, S. B. (1976) Planning for the Aging in India. *Indian Journal of Social Work* 36(2): 1–5.

Sethi, G. (1984) Health Personnel: The Case for Auxiliaries. *Indian Journal of Social Work* 45(1): 31–41.

Setleis, L. (1969) Social Work Practice as Political Activity. *Journal of Social Work Process* 17: 141–53.

Shaffer, G. L. (1979) Labor Relations and the Unionization of Professional Social Workers: A Neglected Area in Social Work Education. *Journal of Education for Social Work* 15(1): 80–6.

Shawkey, A. (1972) Social Work Education in Africa. *International Social Work* 15(3): 3–16.

Siddiqui, H. (1984) A Critique of Social Work in South Asia. Paper presented at the 22nd International Congress of Schools of Social Work, Montreal.

Sidel, V. W. (1978) Medical Care in the People's Republic of China: An Example of Rationality. In H. D. Schwartz and C. S. Kart (eds) *Issues in Medical Sociology*. Reading, Mass: Addison-Wesley.

Sinfield, A. (1970) Which Way for Social Work? In P. Townsend (ed.) *The Fifth Social Service: A Critical Analysis of the Seebohm Proposals*. London: Fabian Society.

Singh, N. (1980) Information Base in Block Level Planning. A Case Review Study: India. In B. V. De Silva (ed.) *Information Base for Rural Development Projects*. New York: United Nations.

Sobey, F. (1970) *The Nonprofessional Revolution in Mental Health*. New York: Columbia University Press.

—— (1973) New Educational Content for a Changing Social Work Practice: Focus on Manpower. In M. Purvine (ed.) *Educating MSW Students to Work With Other Social Welfare Personnel*. New York: Council on Social Work Education.

Social Action Research Center (1978) *Paraprofessionals in Mental Health: An Annotated Bibliography from 1966–1977*. Berkeley, Calif: SARC.

Social Services in Knesset Israel (1946) *Knesset Israel* (Temporary Government of the Jewish Community in Palestine). Jerusalem: Vaad Leumi.

Social Work Today (1982) Just People, Just Pain. 13(48): 12–15.

Southern Regional Education Board (1969) *Roles and Functions for Different Levels of Mental Health Workers.* Atlanta, Ga: SREB.

Srinivasan, L. (1978) Paraprofessionals and Nonformal Education – The Social Work Role. In B. D. Rigby (ed.) *Short-Term Training for Social Development: The Preparation of Front-Line Workers and Trainers.* New York: International Association of Schools of Social Work.

Stevenson, O. and Parsloe, P. (eds) (1978) *Social Services Teams: The Practitioner's View.* London: HMSO.

Szold, H. (1931) Letter to her sister in the US from Jerusalem. New York: Haddassah Archives.

Tarmovski, B. (1971) Clubs and Day Centers for the Aged in Israel. *Saad* 15(3): 16–21. (In Hebrew.)

Taylor, C. E. (1972) The Health Team Concept at the Primary Health Level and the Staff Pattern and their Roles. *Indian Journal of Medical Education* 11: 2–3.

Teare, R. J. (1981) *Social Work Practice in a Public Welfare Setting: An Empirical Analysis.* New York: Praeger.

Teare, R. J. and McPheeters, H. L. (1970) *Manpower Utilization in Social Welfare.* Atlanta, Ga: Southern Regional Education Board.

Teare, R. J., Higgs, C., Gauthier, T. P., and Field, H. S. (1984) *Classification Validation Processes for Social Services Positions. Vol. I – Overview.* Washington, DC: National Association of Social Workers.

Thompson, V. A. (1964) Administrative Objectives of Development Administration. *Administrative Science Quarterly* 9(2): 87–96.

Thorson, J. A. (1973) Training Paraprofessionals in the Field of Aging. *Adult Leadership* 22: 9–11.

Tinker, I. and Bramsen, M. B. (eds) (1976) *Women and World Development.* Washington, DC: Overseas Development Council.

Toren, N. (1972) *Social Work: The Case of a Semi-Profession.* Beverly Hills, Calif: Sage.

True, J. E. and Young, C. E. (1974) Associate Degree Programs for Human Service Workers. *Personnel and Guidance Journal* 53(4): 304–07.

Tyndall, N. (1972) *The Work of Marriage Guidance Councils.* Rugby: National Marriage Guidance Council.

United Nations (1969) *Proceedings of the International Conference of Ministers Responsible for Social Welfare.* New York: UN.

—— (1972) *Conference of European Ministers Responsible for Social Welfare.* New York: UN.

—— (1976) *Training for Agriculture and Rural Development.* Rome: UN, Food and Agriculture Organization.

—— (1977) *Improvement of Social Welfare Training: Contributions from Related Fields.* New York: UN, Department of Economic and Social Affairs.

—— (1979) *Social Services in Rural Development: Issues Concerning their Design and Delivery.* New York: UN, Department of International Economic and Social Affairs.

—— (1980) *Development at Grass Roots: Training of Front-Line Personnel in Social Welfare.* New York: UN, Department of International Economic and Social Affairs.

—— (1984) *An Analysis of the Situation of Children in India.* New Delhi: UNICEF.

University Grants Commission (1980) *Review of Social Work Education in India.* New Delhi: Bahadur Shah Zafar Marg.

US Department of Health, Education, and Welfare (1965) *Closing the Gap . . . in Social Work Manpower.* Washington, DC: US Government Printing Office.

US Department of Labor (1967) *Manpower Report of the President and a Report on Manpower Requirements, Resources, Utilization and Training.* Washington, DC: US Government Printing Office.

Vollmer, H. N. and Mills, D. L. (1966) *Professionalization.* Englewood Cliffs, NJ: Prentice-Hall.

Weber, G. K. (1976) Preparing Social Workers for Practice in Rural Social Systems. *Journal of Education for Social Work* 12(3): 108–15.

Wilensky, H. L. (1964) The Professionalization of Everyone? *American Journal of Sociology* 70(2): 137–58.

Working Group on Block Level Planning (1977–78) *Report.* New Delhi: Government of India. Planning Commission.

World Health Organisation (1978) *Primary Health Care: A Joint Report of WHO and UNICEF.* Geneva: WHO.

PERSONS INTERVIEWED BY R. SCHINDLER IN INDIA
AND ISRAEL WHO ARE CITED IN THE TEXT

Apparao, H. (1985) Programme Executive, International Council
of Social Welfare, Regional Office for Asia and Western Pacific.
Interviewed in Bombay.
Apte, J. (1985) Professor and Chairman, Family and Child Welfare
Studies, Tata Institute of Social Studies, Bombay. Interviewed in
Bombay.
Arole, R. S. (1985) Director, Comprehensive Rural Health Project,
Jamkhed, Maharashtra State, India. Interviewed in Jamkhed.
Ben Ahron, Y. (1976) Former General Director, Jewish Labour
Federation (The *Histadrut*). Interviewed in Tel Aviv.
Central Social Welfare Board (1985). Executive Vice President.
Interviewed in Delhi.
Chauhan, V. (1985) Project Officer, UNICEF, West India Office.
Interviewed in Bombay.
Chowdhry, P. (1985) Director, National Institute of Public
Cooperation and Child Development. Interviewed in New Delhi.
Dave, C. (1985) Former Editor in Chief, *International Social Work*.
Interviewed in Bombay and Phalga, India.
Desai, A. S. (1985) Dean, Tata Institute of Social Sciences, Bombay,
and Director, *Review of Social Work Education* (University
Grants Commission, 1980). Interviewed in Bombay.
Gangrade, K. D. (1985) Dean of Faculty, School of Social Work,
University of Delhi. Interviewed in Delhi.
Goldstein, S. (1985) Director of Paraprofessional Services, Ministry
of Labour and Social Welfare. Interviewed in Tel Aviv.
Hoffer, D. (1982) Former Director, School of Paraprofessional
Training, Tel Aviv. Interviewed in Tel Aviv.
Kanev, I. (1975) Former Director of Social Research and Chairman,
Kupat Holim (Workers Health Insurance). Interviewed in Tel
Aviv.
Karandikar, M. (1983, 1985) Program Coordinator, Research and
Social Development, Bombay. Interviewed in Israel and Bombay.
Minasheri, A. (1981, 1982) Director, Social Welfare Bureau,
Ofakim, Israel. Interviewed in Ofakim.
Muzumdar, K. S. (1985) Professor, Bombay College of Social
Work. Interviewed in Bombay.

Panwalkar, P. (1985) Professor of Social Work, Tata Institute of Social Sciences, Bombay. Interviewed in Bombay.

Parikah, I. (1985) Chief Medical Director, Likmanya Nagar Compound, Bombay. Interviewed in Bombay.

Rohatgi, S. (1982) Chairman, Central Social Welfare Board, India. Interviewed in Brighton, England.

Sadan, Y. (1985) Director of Training Institute, Department of Labour and Social Welfare. Interviewed in Jerusalem.

Siddiqui, H. (1985) Vice President, National Association of Indian Social Workers. Interviewed in Bombay.

Silverstein, S. (1985) General Director, Israel Association of Social Workers. Interviewed in Tel Aviv.

Village Committee (1985) Meeting with Village Committee, Jamkhed, India.

Name index

Chin, R. 185
Chowdhry, P. 54, 56, 92, 173, 219
Clark, T.N. 66
Claxton, C.S. 193
Cloward, R. 107
Clubok, M. 229
Coggs, P.R. 192
Cohen, N.E. 149
Cohen, S. 69
Conyers, D. 60
Cooper, M. 47–8, 84, 126, 245
Crecca, C. 192
Cypher, J. 125, 170, 205, 212

Dalali, I.D. 192
Danish, S.J. 192
Darvill, G. 2
Dave, C. 60, 132, 241
David, H. 70
de Guzman, L. 2, 6, 9–10, 13, 16,
    19, 41
Denham, W.H. 152–53
Desai, A.S. 52–4, 99–100, 133,
    137, 171–72, 178, 180, 253
Dexter, M. 50
Dolgoff, R. 108
Doron, A. 680
Drucker, D. 250
D'Souza, N. 58, 97, 134, 179–80
Dubey, S.N. 96
Dumpson, J.R. 199

Eisenstadt, S.N. 144
Eldridge, D. 53
Elgin, D.S. 224
Ellis, J. 253
Etgar, T. 67
Etzioni, A. 132, 146, 149

Feinstein, R.M. 192
Feldstein, D. 70, 73, 108
Ferryman, Z.C. 192
Fine, S.A. 113, 116
First, R. J. 199
Flexner, A. 148
Ford, J. 192
Friedland, R. 247
Fruin, D.J. 85

Gandhi, Mahatma 53
Gangrade, K.D. 54, 59, 171–72,
    176, 178, 180, 215, 220
Gartner, A. 8, 75, 77, 111, 229
Gerstein, H. 192, 232
Gidron, B. 101, 185
Gilbert, B. 233
Gilder, G. 224
Gleazer, E.J. Jr. 73
Glennerster, H. 46
Goldberg, E.M. 49, 85, 90, 259
Goldstein, S. 101
Gordon, A.D. 62
Gordon, C. 230
Gore, M. 235
Gorodezky, S. 2
Greenwood, E. 132, 149
Greve, J. 5
Grosser, C. 8, 73, 111, 145, 245
Gunder-Frank, A. 248
Gupta, C.B. 176
Gurin, A. 105
Gutek, B.A. 257

Hadley, R. 4, 47, 84, 206, 207, 250
Hage, J. 110, 136
Hallett, C. 51, 84, 85, 128–29, 211
Harbert, W. 50
Hardcastle, D.A. 151, 235
Harel, I. 67
Hartnoll, M.C. 130
Hawkins, J. 192
Heclo, H. 42
Heidenheimer, A. 42
Helm, B. 248, 249
Henry, W.E. 73, 111
Herzel, T. 61
Hesbur, R.K. 96
Hey, A.M. 51, 84, 87–90, 128–29,
    207–08
Heyman, M. 112
Higgins, J. 17, 42
Hirayama, H. 75, 76, 111, 153,
    234
Hobgood, J. 192
Hoffer, D. 183
Hokenstad, M.C. 196
Holman, R. 45–6

Subject index

health care (*cont.*):
62–3; *see also* family planning;
mental health
Hinduism 213
hobo (Japan) 26, 30
home helps: Britain 15, 27, 44, 49–
51, 83, 90, 119, 124, 163–64;
Israel 189, 227
housing: Britain (sheltered for
elderly) 49–50, 83–4; India 97–
8; Israel 106, 108
human services: concept 2–5;
expanded 3, 6, 37; *see also*
paraprofessionals

IASSW *see* International
Association of Schools of Social
Work
ICDS *see* Integrated Child
Development Services
ICSC *see* In-Service Course
identity problems 132–33, 136,
226
immigrants (Israel) 61, 109, 143,
147
India 14, 17–20, 33, 35–6, 241–
42, 249; career advancement
opportunities 212–21, 236–37,
257; factors contributing to use
of paraprofessionals 23–4, 52–
61, 78–80; professionals,
relations with 28, 131–39, 156,
159–60, 252–53; role definitions
and utilization patterns 25–7,
90–100, 122, 245; training and
education 30–1, 55, 99–100,
137–39, 170–82, 201, 202, 217,
218, 221
Indian Association of Trained
Social Workers 132, 220
Indian Council of Social Welfare
26, 52, 56–8, 95–6
indigenous values 213–14, 245–48
indigenous workers 7–8, 23, 47,
73, 80, 141, 181
Indonesia 8–9, 17, 19, 23;
professionals in 28; role
definitions 25; training in 30

information gathering role (Israel)
102–05, 108
In-Service Course in Social Care
(Britain) 30, 166, 208, 237–38
in-service training 200; Britain 30,
129–31, 163–70, 205, 208–11,
237–38; United States 192; *see
also* training
Institute of Social Work (Israel) 183
Integrated Child Development
Services (India) 91, 94, 138, 173,
175, 218–21, 245
Integrated Rural Development Plan
(India) 96
International Association of
Schools of Social Work 9, 16,
19–20, 41, 245, 247, 255
international survey of paraprofessionals 1–6, 19–34,
240–61; methods of study 20–1;
see also paraprofessionals
Israel 14, 17–20, 22, 35, 39, 242,
258–59; career advancement
opportunities 221–28, 237;
factors contributing to use of
paraprofessionals 23–4, 61–7,
78–80; professionals, relations
with 28, 139–48, 156, 157, 252–
53; role definitions and
utilization patterns 26, 27, 101–
10, 119, 122, 245; training and
education 15, 30, 64, 140, 182–
92, 202, 225, 228, 254
Israeli Association of Social
Workers 65–6, 140, 228
Ivory Coast 4

Jamkhed Comprehensive Rural
Health Project (India) 93, 98–9,
175–76
Japan 17, 19, 22, 23; careers 31;
professionals 28; role definitions
25–6, 27; training 30–1
job creation *see* unemployment
job definition problem 215–17
job security 225
Joint Commission on Mental Illness
and Health (USA) 71